Adin Ballou

Primitive Christianity and Its Corruptions

Discourses delivered in Hopedale, Mass. Vol. 1

Adin Ballou

Primitive Christianity and Its Corruptions
Discourses delivered in Hopedale, Mass. Vol. 1

ISBN/EAN: 9783337720605

Printed in Europe, USA, Canada, Australia, Japan

Cover: Foto ©Lupo / pixelio.de

More available books at **www.hansebooks.com**

PRIMITIVE CHRISTIANITY

AND ITS CORRUPTIONS.

DEPARTMENT OF THEOLOGICAL DOCTRINES.

DISCOURSES

DELIVERED IN HOPEDALE, MASS.,

A.D. 1869-70.

By ADIN BALLOU.

"*Ye shall know the truth, and the truth shall make you free.*" — John viii. 32.
"*Every plant which my heavenly Father hath not planted shall be rooted up.*"
— Matt. xv. 13.

BOSTON:
UNIVERSALIST PUBLISHING HOUSE.
1870.

Entered according to Act of Congress, in the year 1870, by the
UNIVERSALIST PUBLISHING HOUSE,
In the office of the Librarian of Congress, at Washington.

PREFACE.

I FIRMLY believe that Christianity, as taught and exemplified by Jesus Christ and his apostles, is not only the highest and best religion ever promulgated to mankind, but, in its declared essentials, the one true and absolute religion, indispensable to the perfect holiness and happiness of the human race, and destined to final universal acceptance. I also firmly believe that primitive Christianity began to be corrupted toward the close of the first century; that corruptions gradually increased, in several respects, till they became radical at the union of Church and State, under Constantine the Great, in the fourth century; that thenceforth they became chronic, with various fluctuating aggravations, through the dark ages down to the Protestant Reformation; and that, though partially alleviated by that great agitation and subsequent corrective influences, they still remain in such force as to nullify, to a great extent, the excellence of the pure original. In order, therefore, to its final universal triumph, these corruptions must be thoroughly purged away.

What are they? Some of them are theological, some didactical, and some ecclesiastical. For notwithstanding many are disposed to deny that Christ was a theologian or an ecclesiastic, and to deem him mainly a pietistic and moral teacher, I am obliged to regard him as alike a Master in theology, in personal righteousness, and in church edification. I hold that in all three he was radical, sublime, and harmonic. He declared the true God, his character, will, and purposes, — the true standard of personal righteousness in all relations, — and the constitution of the true church, as aiming at the fraternal unity of all its members. I have earnestly sought to ascertain wherein the prevailing theology of Christendom differs from that of Christ, — wherein its popular standard of piety, morality, and preceptive virtue differs from his, — and wherein its church, priesthood, and ecclesiastical organizations differ from his. Wherein I have found these differences repugnant to primitive Christianity in principle, spirit, and moral tendency, I have set them down as corruptions.

By what means have I endeavored to ascertain these corruptions? By studying the New Testament Scriptures in their proper relation to those of the Old, the Christian Apocryphal Writings, the Works of the Christian Fathers, Ecclesiastical History, and the Treatises of learned men on the general subject. I have not been able to command all the resources of critical learning which I desired for the perfection of my investigations; but on most points have succeeded in satisfying myself, by careful comparison of authorities, as to the substantial facts. I have reached my conclusions in the exercise of an honest, free, and independent judgment. I ask only that my readers should consider my work, and form their conclusions as honestly, freely, and independently as I have mine. They will all find some things worthy of serious reflection, some things to approve, some things which they cannot accept, and, perhaps, some things to shock their prejudices, but nothing which need harm them if they have just confidence in the truth.

This is the first of three intended volumes under the same general title. This deals with the department of theological doctrines, the second will treat of personal righteousness, and the third of ecclesiastical polity. The three will make a unitary whole, — a complete Exposition of Primitive Christianity and its Corruptions. The second and third volumes are planned, but not yet executed. They may not be published during my earthly lifetime, but I shall prepare them at my earliest convenience. I have been advised to submit the present volume to the public at once, and have consented. Its reception may hasten or delay the publication of the others. It was convenient for me to prepare and deliver it as a series of discourses. I might have resolved it into chapters, and the more solid form of a systematic treatise; but I concluded to leave it as originally written, with the addition of some necessary notes. I commend it, as it is, to the candid consideration of all who feel interest enough in its theme to give it a perusal. If the present generation should fail to appreciate it encouragingly, I shall leave the world with a comfortable assurance that future ones will hold it in higher estimation.

ADIN BALLOU.

HOPEDALE, MASS., 1870.

CONTENTS.

DISCOURSE I.

Introductory to the Series 7

ARTICLE I.

THE RELATIONSHIP OF JESUS CHRIST TO GOD THE FATHER, HIS REAL NATURE, DIGNITY, AND AUTHORITY.

DISCOURSE II.

Our Sources of Reliable Historic Information 16

DISCOURSE III.

The Pure Primitive Doctrine concerning Christ's Relationship to the Father. His Real Nature, Dignity, and Authority, as set forth in the New Testament Scriptures . . . 27

DISCOURSE IV.

First Corruptions of the Original Pure Doctrine, and how they arose 37

DISCOURSE V.

More particularly how the First Corruptions of the Original Pure Doctrine arose and proceeded step by step to their Culmination 48

ARTICLE II.

The Nature, Relationship, and Office of the Holy Spirit.

DISCOURSE VI.

The Original and Pure Doctrine concerning the Holy Spirit . 61

DISCOURSE VII.

Corruptions of the Original Pure Doctrine concerning the Holy Spirit. 74

ARTICLE III.

The Nature and Efficacy of the Atonement.

DISCOURSE VIII.

The Pure Primitive Doctrine of the Atonement . . . 83

DISCOURSE IX.

The Pure Primitive Doctrine of the Atonement Verified . . 94

DISCOURSE X.

Wherein, when, and how the Primitive Doctrine was first corrupted. 105

DISCOURSE XI.

Progress and Culmination of the Corruption 116

ARTICLE IV.

Angelology, Demonology, and Resurrection from the Dead; or, The Doctrine of Spiritual and Immortal Existence.

DISCOURSE XII.

The Primitive Christian Doctrine concerning Spiritual Beings . 127

DISCOURSE XIII.

The Primitive Christian Doctrine concerning Spiritual Beings Explained and Defended 137

DISCOURSE XIV.

Corruptions of the Primitive Doctrine 150

DISCOURSE XV.

The Primitive Christian Doctrine of the Resurrection of the Dead 165

DISCOURSE XVI.

The Primitive Christian Doctrine of the Resurrection from the Dead Verified and Illustrated 176

DISCOURSE XVII.

Corruptions of the Primitive Doctrine of the Resurrection from the Dead 189

ARTICLE V.

REGENERATION AND SALVATION.

DISCOURSE XVIII.

The Pure Primitive Doctrine of Regeneration and Salvation, as taught by Christ and his Apostles 199

DISCOURSE XIX.

Is the Doctrine of Christian Regeneration and Salvation, as set forth in the preceding Discourse, true, rational, and worthy of our enlightened support? 210

DISCOURSE XX.

Corruptions of the Pure Primitive Doctrine 223

ARTICLE VI.

Divine Government, Judgment, Retribution, and Discipline.

DISCOURSE XXI.

The Pure Primitive Christian Doctrine 238

DISCOURSE XXII.

The Pure Primitive Doctrine Verified and Explained . . 250

DISCOURSE XXIII.

The Pure Primitive Doctrine further Verified and Explained . 263

DISCOURSE XXIV.

Corruptions of the Pure Primitive Doctrine 278

ARTICLE VII.

The Final Destiny of Mankind.

DISCOURSE XXV.

The Pure Primitive Christian Doctrine of Man's Final Destiny   288

DISCOURSE XXVI.

The Pure Primitive Christian Doctrine of Human Destiny Verified 298

DISCOURSE XXVII.

Corruptions of the Pure Primitive Christian Doctrine . . 309

DISCOURSE XXVIII.

The Evils occasioned by Corrupting the Pure Primitive Doctrine 320

PRIMITIVE CHRISTIANITY AND ITS CORRUPTIONS.

DISCOURSE I.

INTRODUCTORY TO THE SERIES.

"Many false prophets shall arise, and shall deceive many. And because iniquity shall abound, the love of many shall wax cold." — Matt. xxv. 11, 12.

"For I know this, that after my departing shall grievous wolves enter in among you, not sparing the flock. Also, of your own selves shall men arise, speaking perverse things, to draw away disciples after them." — Acts xx. 29, 30.

THE generality of mankind, in all ages, understand the prevailing religion of their country and times substantially as its popular professors and expounders represent it. It is so in respect to Christianity, doctrinal and practical. *That* is Christianity which *passes* for Christianity; and few people suspect that it was ever anything essentially different, in theory or practice, from what it now purports to be. So think most of its friends, and also most of its enemies. But intelligent and thorough investigators know better, and it is time that the common people should be better informed. I propose, therefore, to give you the benefit somewhat of my own researches into this subject, in a series of discourses on the corruptions of Christianity. Therein I will endeavor to show distinctly in what important respects the Christianity of Christ and his apostles was gradually metamorphosed into its subsequent and present predominant forms. In doing this I shall, for the present, confine myself to the department of Theological Doctrines.

Before proceeding directly to my work, it seems proper to inquire briefly, why and how Christianity became grossly corrupted? At first thought, we might assume that a system of divinely ordained truth and righteousness would have been divinely preserved from all human corruption. But this is not according to the nature and course of things in any sphere of human progress. All divine principles, truths, laws, and gifts, communicated to man, are subject, more or less, to his manipulation, use, and abuse. He is allowed to humanize them, — to reduce them in some measure to his own conceptions, ideas, and degree of development for the time being. He is not permitted to annihilate them, and he is held responsible for his use or abuse of them. Still, he is allowed to understand, adapt, and apply them largely according to his own judgment. It must be so in an order of progress. To be anything in the rational and moral world, man must have liberty to choose, judge, and act, somewhat on his own discretion and responsibility. He must assimilate the divine to himself, or himself to the divine, progressively. Hence, temporarily, all misconceptions, perversions, abuses, sufferings, corrections, reformations, and advancements.

We must remember, too, that human progress is not uniformly onward in one channel. It ebbs and flows in numerous collateral channels. There is the channel of mechanical and material progress, by which man becomes master of physical forces and substances. This ebbs and flows as the ages roll on. So is it with strictly intellectual and scientific progress. It cannot be otherwise with social and political progress; nor with religious and moral progress. They all ebb and flow, and seem often to have zigzag movements, yet a gradual spiral ascension. It is also further observable that these numerous currents of progress have some relation to each other. They are not wholly independent, but affect each other sensibly and variously. Thus material, scientific, political, and religious progressions act and react upon one another; and neither kind can get very far ahead of the others in human society. Sometimes one seems to be greatly outstripping the others, yet soon has to halt or retrograde for a season till the others make their advances. We call religious and moral progress the grandest of all these currents, because it is the natural prophet, priest, and king, over all the others. Nevertheless, it must have the modifying influence, sympathy, and co-operation of the others, else it becomes sickly, superstitious, and enervated. Our manhood must be progressive in all the great channels of development, in order to harmony and happiness. And the reason why we see so much progress in some directions and yet so much misery, is that in others, equally or more important, there has been little progress. Just now, material, scientific, political, and literary progressions are far ahead of religious and moral progress. Hence, so much restlessness, discontent, insane fastness, envy, contention, rivalry, dissatisfaction, and misery. Pure religion lurks in the rear, and when it comes up in the hearts, understandings, and lives of the people, their other attainments will become available for nobler uses, and higher happiness.

Now, to come immediately to the why and wherefore of the corruptions of Christianity, let us consider the conditions and circumstances under which it has been operating since its advent into the world.

1. Its founder, Jesus of Nazareth, had no worldly prestige to introduce him to public admiration. His parentage, birth, and early life were humble, obscure, and unknown, except to a few common people. Yet he must have been born under very high spiritual conditions, with a pre-eminently noble moral constitution, and at an early period endowed with the sublimest spiritual gifts. His divine inspirations and illuminations were transcendent. He claimed to be the promised Messiah, or Christ. This was not till after his baptism, by John, at thirty years of age. He commenced his ministry at about that age, and continued it with steady fidelity for three years and a half, attesting his divine mission by the most wonderful works. Many of the com-

mon people heard him gladly, and a few superior moral minds became his devoted disciples. But the leaders of his nation, in church and state, rejected him, persecuted him, and procured his death on vague charges of blasphemy, sedition, and treason, by ignominious crucifixion. On the third day after his death he arose from the state of the dead, manifested himself repeatedly to his disciples during forty days, gave his apostles renewed instructions, and ascended into the heavenly world. Thenceforth they preached his religion, with the utmost zeal and success, and gathered churches, not only in Palestine, but in distant parts of the Roman empire.

Yet to the great mass of Jews and Gentiles their gospel was a stumbling-block or foolishness, and met with both contempt and persecution from nearly all in the influential ranks of society. It was received and cherished only by comparatively a few humble and honest people, in different countries and scattered localities. It was a most unworldly, unpopular, but holy religion. Such was primitive Christianity in the beginning. It had the whole world against it, especially the bigotry of the Jews, the learning of the Gentiles, and the paganism of the Roman empire, then at its zenith, with its proud heathen religions firmly established in all parts of the habitable globe. It must make its converts first from the Jews, and secondly from the pagans, learned or unlearned, in the accessible Roman dominions.

2. We must remember that Jesus left no sacred writings,—no writings at all; that the impressions

he made on mankind were by oral teachings, a holy life, profound love, wonderful spiritual power manifested in miraculous works, and supernal communications to his disciples from the resurrection state after his departure. These were mighty impressions and influences on receptive minds, but weighed little against strong religious prejudices, and the scepticism of haughty philosophies. The Jews insisted on signs from heaven which the devil could not counterfeit, and the Greeks on philosophical literature. Of this last the primitive Christians had none; and though they had plenty of miracles, the Jews offset them all with the assumption that they were wrought by the power of Satan, or some evil spirit, and not of God. Meantime, the great operative influences which first flowed out from Christ himself, and then, after his translation to the immortal state, through his spiritually baptized disciples, grew gradually more traditional, less striking in their demonstrations, and, of course, less powerful on the public mind. The apostles passed away one after another, leaving only the Gospels and Epistles of our New Testament collection, and some of these probably in a partially unfinished state. Thus the new generations were thrown more and more on traditionary and manuscriptural authority, to be interpreted and judged of by themselves under constantly changing circumstances. Such was the state of the church at the close of the first century.

3. We must remember that at this time a wide gulf yawned between the Jewish Christians in Pales-

tine and the Gentile Christians in more favored parts of the Roman empire. Before the destruction of Jerusalem by the Romans, and the breaking up of the nation, the Jewish Christians, heeding Christ's warnings, had fled into the mountainous and more inaccessible parts of the country, where they lived, mostly by themselves, in poverty and obscurity, until ultimately they quite dwindled away. There arose a serious division between these Hebrew Christians and the Gentile churches, before or soon after Paul's ministry. It was on account of the Mosaic law. The Christian Jews adhered tenaciously to that law and most of its observances. The Gentile Christians rejected those observances. Hence, mutual repugnance, denunciation, and disfellowship. Moreover, the Gentile Christians became daily stronger in numbers and wealth; whilst the Ebionites, as the Jewish Christians came to be called, grew fewer, poorer, and of less account. At the same time they were hated and solemnly cursed by the mass of unbelieving Jews. So they entirely lost caste on both sides, and came to be treated as heretics by both. The effect of this was, that while they held to the strict humanity of Christ as the Son of God, the Gentile Christians became all the more disposed to claim for him some kind of original superhuman dignity, and to rid themselves of the odium cast upon him by both Jews and philosophers. This, we shall find, gave rise to the first corruption of Christian doctrine.

4. We must remember that in those times the learning of the civilized world was that of the ancient Eastern sages, or of Plato in the Western countries,

or a mixture of both. The Christians had already begun to court the philosophers, and in order to bring them into the church adopted some of their leading notions in a modified form, especially respecting the *Logos,* so termed. And this became another source of corruption, which slowly went on from bad to worse, as I shall show.

5. Finally, we must remember, that as the Christians, in spite of much persecution, increased and grew influential in the Roman empire, they also grew more worldly and carnally ambitious; till, at the close of the third century, when rivals contested for the throne of the empire, they were strong enough to turn the scale. Hence Constantine the Great bid for their support, obtained it, and so became emperor. The result was, the adoption and establishment of Christianity as the state religion, — the union of church and state. Thenceforth, corruptions and evils perpetually increased until the Protestant Reformation, and have come down to our own times. This great change took place in the early part of the fourth century, and its corruptive consequences were vast. This will fully appear as I proceed.

When all these conditions and circumstances, through which Christianity has passed, are candidly considered, it will not seem so very strange that it became almost radically metamorphosed, so as in many respects to be doctrinally and practically the very contrary of what Christ left it. But if, going back to the earliest records and expositions of it, we find that its inherent excellence transcends that of all other religions, we shall have nothing to do but to slough off its corruptions, embrace it afresh in its purity, work with all our might for its prevalence, hope confidently for its universal triumph, and in the fulness of times enter, with our redeemed race, into the fruition of its promised bliss.

ARTICLE I.

THE RELATIONSHIP OF JESUS CHRIST TO GOD THE FATHER. — HIS REAL NATURE DIGNITY, AND AUTHORITY.

DISCOURSE II.

OUR SOURCES OF RELIABLE HISTORIC INFORMATION.

"God anointed Jesus of Nazareth with the Holy Ghost and with power: who went about doing good, and healing all that were oppressed of the devil; for God was with him. And we are witnesses of all things which he did, both in the land of the Jews, and in Jerusalem; whom they slew and hanged on a tree: Him God raised up the third day, and showed him openly; not to all the people, but unto witnesses chosen before of God, even to us, who did eat and drink with him after he rose from the dead."— Acts x. 38-41.

The relationship of Jesus Christ to God the Father — his real nature, dignity, and authority — presents a theme of theological inquiry and doctrine which lies at the very foundation of Christianity. Unless there is something special, peculiar, distinctive, and pre-eminently authoritative in his relationship to God the Father, Christianity is of no commanding importance to mankind. It would then be simply one among all the other religions of the world; and behind it would lie that absolute religion which contains the essential truth and good of them all without their error and evil. And in that view, our highest duty and privilege would be, never to rest satisfied till we had found the absolute religion.

But the Christian religion claims to be the absolute religion, divinely revealed and attested. It claims that Jesus Christ was the Elect of God the Father, to reveal, declare, teach, exemplify, administer, and establish this religion for the salvation of the human race. If so, he is no ordinary personage, — no casually remarkable teacher and reformer, to be reckoned as one among a thousand somewhat eminent geniuses of various ages and countries, — but is a divinely commissioned, authoritative Master in religion. And such all sects, parties, and classes of Christians have held him to be. Yet what his precise relationship to the Father was, what his real nature, dignity, and authority were, have been questions fruitful of perpetual and often bitter controversy among his professed disciples from the apostolic times to our own.

Now we wish to ascertain and be sure of what was the primitive doctrine on this subject; that is, what Jesus Christ himself declared and taught concerning his peculiar relationship to God the Father, his real nature, dignity, and authority. Then we shall know what other doctrines on the subject are corruptions of the pure original one.

But what are our sources of reliable historic information on this subject? Christ himself has left us no statement or record under his own hand, not a word. We have no Jewish or heathen writers of that age whose works give us light respecting his pretensions or doctrines.* We are dependent wholly on the writings of his disciples, which are comprised in our New Testament collection, — the four Gospels, Epistles, etc. Can these be relied on? Not implicitly on all points and details; for they are not absolutely perfect in all respects. But having acquainted myself tolerably well with the researches of learned critics on all sides of the general subject, I am confident that these can safely be relied on for all really essential facts and statements of doctrine. They have never been invalidated beyond a few exceptional portions and minute incidentals. The main current of their testimony, and especially on the particulars in which they all concur, may be taken as conclusive.

The most important exceptional portions are those in the Gospels of Matthew and Luke, which purport to give accounts of the genealogy, conception, birth, and infancy, of Jesus, down to twelve years of age. The learned Dr. Norton, whose criticisms are very thorough, sets aside the first and second chapters of Matthew in our common version, as no part of the original manuscript. His reasons seem to me unanswerable. He adheres, however, to the first and second chapters of Luke as originally belonging to that Gospel; though he confesses that the style and details are in some respects doubtful. He leaves the matter in a rather unsatisfactory shape. I should be glad to accept his conclusions, but strict truthfulness com-

---

* It seems to Christians in our times astonishing how utterly the learned Jews and Gentiles of the first and second centuries ignored Christ and his religion.

pels me to confess that I doubt the reliability of our common version of Luke, from verse fourth of chapter one, to the end of chapter two. I should prefer to believe in the miraculous conception of Jesus, and in the glorious occurrences narrated in that general connection, if there were not such strong reasons to discredit them. I cannot divest myself of the persuasion that there must have been some extraordinary divine influences operating in close connection with the birth of such a personage as Jesus proved himself to be. But the narrations in question, taken together, or singly, seem to me to be so exceptional and irreconcilable, that I must give them both up as unreliable portions of our present New Testament Scripture. The two principal arguments for their validity are, first, that they are found in all the Greek manuscripts of Matthew's and Luke's Gospels, now extant; and, second, that they have been received by the general Christian Church, both as to authenticity and doctrine, since the middle of the second century, — certainly since the beginning of the third. But these considerations in their support are far outweighed, in my mind, by the following reasons against their validity, namely : —

1. Mark's Gospel, and that of John, entirely omit these narratives, and everything of the kind. They do not make the least allusion to them or one of their remarkable occurrences. How is this to be accounted for on any other supposition than that either they knew nothing of them, or discredited them? Could they possibly have accepted them as genuine and deemed them too unimportant to mention?

2. None of these wonderful events or occurrences

are mentioned or alluded to in any other portions of Matthew's and Luke's Gospels, nor in any other book of the New Testament. How is it possible that such very striking and important facts should be thus ignored by Christ and all his apostles, when they furnished such impressive data of faith and hope? Yet there is no hint that Jesus ever pleaded his miraculous conception, or the wonders that attended his birth, or that Peter, John, or Paul, did so. Could they have deemed them of less importance than orthodox Christians of every age in the Church since they are known to have been first believed true?

3. No expectations appear to have been excited in the public mind, or among family relatives, or in any one's mind, such as would naturally have been the case, by these alleged wonderful divine interpositions and annunciations. Neither Joseph, nor Mary, nor their children, nor their relations, nor their countrymen, are represented, in any part of the New Testament Scriptures, as having remembered and looked for the fulfilment of these things. Even John the Baptist seems to have known nothing of Jesus personally until his baptism. Had the two cousin mothers of John and Jesus suffered all Gabriel's words to pass into oblivion? It is incredible that such miraculous beginnings and foreshowings should have vanished away, leaving so little family and public expectation.

4. The two narratives are incongruous, and in some particulars irreconcilable. That in Matthew makes no mention of Zacharias, Elizabeth, and their son John, or a single remarkable occurrence of their case;

nor of the coming of Joseph and Mary from Nazareth to Bethlehem to be taxed; nor of the manger, the angels, the shepherds, the presentation of Jesus in the temple, etc., etc. But it gives a very different account of remarkable events and occurrences; such as the wise men of the east being guided by a star, first to Jerusalem, and then to Bethlehem after Herod had consulted a council on the subject; then returning to their country by another way; Herod's anger and slaughter of the infants; the flight into Egypt, and return after Herod's death; nothing of which has any mention in Luke. Moreover, the account in Matthew represents the parents as warned of God not to remain in their own former home in Judea, where Archelaus reigned, but to go away to Nazareth in Galilee to dwell, that it might be fulfilled, "He shall be called a Nazarene;" which prediction is not to be found in the prophets. But Luke's account makes Nazareth their original place of residence. These incongruities do not sound to me like probabilities, much less well-founded historical facts.

5. The two genealogies are dissimilar, and irreconcilable with each other. Both purport to trace the pedigree of Jesus through Joseph to David, etc., yet do so by different lines of ancestry. But both of them must be erroneous in the main thing, if Jesus had no human father. How, in that case, was Joseph, David, or Abraham, his paternal progenitor? But if he had a human father, what are we to do with the contrary statement in both narratives that God was strictly his only father?

6. If in the fifteenth year of the reign of Tiberius

Cæsar, Jesus was about thirty years of age, according to the third chapter of Luke's Gospel, ancient history proves that Herod the Great must have been dead a considerable time before he was born; which quite invalidates the whole account as given in Matthew.

7. There is conclusive evidence that Matthew's Gospel was originally written in Hebrew for the use of the Jewish Christians, and that their copies of it never contained this exceptional account of the miraculous conception, birth, and infancy of Jesus. Also, that those most primitive Christians always held the doctrine of his strict humanity exalted only by preeminent divine inspiration and endowment. Mainly on this account succeeding generations of them, called Ebionites and Nazarenes, were denounced and treated by the Gentile Christians as heretics. There is further strong proof that copies of Luke's Gospel early existed among certain eminent men, deemed by the main church heretical, without this exceptional portion of the present received version. These are important facts, which have great weight with me in deciding the question at issue.

8. Finally, it is obvious to all critical students that the style of composition, and the special purpose of these exceptional portions of Matthew's and Luke's Gospels as they now stand, are dissimilar to the main portions. They have strong marks of a different authorship, and a later one. The supernatural is suspiciously excessive in them, and they are strongly mythical in their remarkable aspects. They have the air of exaggerated and uncertain traditions, or of apocryphal stories, designed — piously perhaps — to

make or strengthen converts. The wise men of the east, etc., in Matthew, and Elizabeth's and Mary's reciprocal experiences, poetic soliloquies, etc., in Luke, do not sound like statements of simple historical fact. But I will not amplify; I reiterate, that love of truth for its own sake obliges me to set aside these two exceptional portions of generally received New Testament Scripture as unreliable.* There are many other paragraphs, sentences, phrases, and verbalisms, which sound criticism rejects or corrects as ungenuine; but they are comparatively unimportant, and will need only incidental notice, as I may have occasion to refer to them. The main bulk and current substance of our received New Testament Scripture has been well tested, and its genuineness firmly established. Sceptical minds may deny its authority in matters of religious faith and practice, but they will strive in vain to overthrow its essential genuineness, as to what the solid bulk of it, after the thorough sifting it has received, purports to be. Sound, stringent criticism has only purified, improved, and fortified its intrinsic reliability, as I have no doubt it always will. Blind, traditional, irrational, superstitious faith in it may be shaken, but not sound, intelligent, and salutary faith, which is the only kind worth cherishing.

I have been thus particular in defining what I deem our sources of reliable historic information concerning

---

* If any are disposed to make faith in the alleged facts of these exceptional narratives essential to Christianity itself, let them consider how it happens that neither Christ nor his apostles made them such.

the pure primitive Christian doctrine on the relationship of Jesus Christ to God the Father, — his real nature, dignity, and authority. It will, of course, be of the same use on all other points of faith and practice.

We know what is now believed and insisted on as doctrinal and practical Christianity. We can learn, by diligent reading, what it has been all the way back, from age to age, till we reach the writings of the Apostolic Fathers so called. Of these there were reckoned seven, namely: Clement, Barnabas, Hermas, Ignatius, Papius, Dionysius, and Polycarp; the last of whom suffered martyrdom, A.D. 147.* These fathers are believed to have personally known one or more of the first apostles. The amount of their undoubtedly genuine writings now extant is small, but curious and useful, as showing what Christianity was held to be in their days. There seems to be a period of full half a century, extending from A.D. 70, eventfully marked by the destruction of Jerusalem, to the year 120, extremely barren of reliable information. Perhaps there are a very few apocryphal fragments of that age to be held of partial value. It was a period of commotions and changes in the great world, and in the primitive church. It is probable that all, or nearly all, our New Testament collection of writings, or at least the principal substance of them, were in manuscript before the great event of the destruction of Jerusalem; for, otherwise, it seems to me impossible that they should all be utterly silent concerning that eventful crisis, which took place according to Christ's predictions. We may, therefore, safely con-

* More strictly, the first five.

clude that we have in the genuine Gospels, Acts of the Apostles and Epistles, the most reliable, and indeed the only reliable, source of historic information concerning pure primitive Christianity. There we get, certainly very nearly in substance, what Jesus professed and claimed to be in relation both to God and men, what his first apostles understood and declared him to be, and what leading principles of faith and practice he taught as necessary to human salvation. And this information is just what we want, in order to start fairly in ascertaining the corruptions of Christianity. For, unless we clearly understand the pure, how can we discriminate between it and the impure?

I wish I could impress the importance of this on all your minds. I want to do justice to Christianity. I want *you* to do justice to it. I want intelligent Christian believers, and, if we must have unbelievers, I want them to be intelligent, too. We have had ignorant, presumptuous, and flippant ones enough on both sides. Let all parties learn to understand their whys and wherefores. When it comes to *that*, we shall know where we stand, and what we ought to do.

Meantime, for my own part, I am profoundly persuaded that genuine Christianity, both doctrinal and practical, embodies the sublimest truth and righteousness which the human mind can embrace; that it is what the world needs, and must have, in order to pure and endless happiness; and that none of us can undervalue, contemn, or neglect it, without great temporal and spiritual loss to our souls. All this I hope to make plain and impressive by this series of discourses.

In my next, I shall come directly to the present point in hand; namely, to show what the doctrine of pure primitive Christianity was concerning the relation of Jesus Christ to God the Father, and so his real nature, dignity, and authority.

ARTICLE I.

THE RELATIONSHIP OF JESUS CHRIST TO GOD THE FATHER. — HIS REAL NATURE, DIGNITY, AND AUTHORITY.

DISCOURSE III.

THE PURE PRIMITIVE DOCTRINE CONCERNING CHRIST'S RELATIONSHIP TO THE FATHER, — HIS REAL NATURE, DIGNITY, AND AUTHORITY, AS SET FORTH IN THE NEW TESTAMENT SCRIPTURES.

"Then came the Jews round about him, and said unto him, How long dost thou make us to doubt? If thou be the Christ, tell us plainly. Jesus answered them, I told you, and ye believed not; the works that I do in my Father's name, they bear witness of me." — JOHN x. 24, 25.

IN the last discourse I endeavored to show that, with certain minor exceptions (which I specified), the writings of our New Testament collection are our reliable sources of historical information, and almost our only reliable ones, for ascertaining precisely what pure primitive Christianity was. Now, from their testimony, we would learn the primitive Christian doctrine concerning the relationship of Jesus Christ to God the Father; that is, his real nature, dignity, and authority. Their testimony must consist partly of declarations purporting to have been made by Jesus himself, and partly of those made by John the Baptist, his apostles, and evangelists; each and all fairly construed.

Some have thought there was considerable difference in the ideas expressed concerning Christ's nature, dignity, and authority in the different gospels and books of the New Testament. But I can find no radical or substantial differences of the kind. On the contrary, there seems to me to be a remarkable agreement.

Three inquiries naturally arise; namely, First, What was Jesus Christ declared and held to be as a personal being, an individual entity? Second, What were his office, dignity, and authority declared and held to be? And, third, Whence was it declared and held that his office, dignity, and authority originated? How do the New Testament Scriptures answer these inquiries? Let us see.

1. What was Jesus Christ declared and held to be as a personal being, an individual entity? Properly and strictly a man; entirely reverent, submissive, obedient, dutiful, and righteous toward God; in true unison with God; the lover and friend of all mankind; the moral pattern and model for all his followers. As a man, he assumed nothing and claimed nothing on account of ancestry, or birth, or a high origin, or a superior constitutional nature, in body, soul, or spirit. Whatever superior predispositional advantages he really had over others, he never set up any pretensions to goodness or greatness on account of them, and claimed only the respect justly due for the fruits he brought forth.

2. What were his office, dignity, and authority

declared and held to be? Those of the Messiah or Christ, which means the Anointed of God, the chosen, sanctified Son of God, predestinated, promised and predicted as such, — as such the highest mediator between God and men; their religious Master, Lord, Discipliner, Reconciler, and Saviour, — as such plenarily endowed, authorized, and empowered for the fulfilment of his commission, — and as such to be believed on, acknowledged, reverenced, obeyed, and harmonized with, by mankind, in order to final perfect happiness. Such are his declared office, dignity, and authority.

3. Whence was it declared and held that his office, dignity, and authority originated? Wholly in God the Father — wholly conferred by God the Father — wholly dependent on him — wholly subservient to his will, purpose, and pleasure — and finally deliverable up to him again, in the grand consummation when they should have fulfilled their designed use. As the Christ, Jesus claimed to have originated nothing, to have no sufficiency but of the Father; to possess no authority but what the Father had given, and to do nothing but what the Father willed, commanded, and empowered him to do. In fine, he ascribed all his official excellence, dignity, and authority to God the Father, operating in and through him by his communicable indwelling Spirit.

These three statements of primitive Christian doctrine are very important; but they are easy to be understood by honest common minds. They might not have been fully comprehended, but yet were well understood by the first disciples, and would forever have been understood, had they not been darkened by mystical and metaphysical teachers, who sought to sublimate them into a more marvellous theology, or sacred philosophy; whereof I shall speak in its place.

But how can you know that I have given substantially the correct answers to these three inquiries? Only by carefully studying the New Testament writings. If you do so, you will find every passage that speaks descriptively of Jesus Christ, expressing one or more of these leading ideas concerning him, and no idea to the contrary. I will give you a few specimens. In some of these you will notice his strict personal humanity most prominently declared, in others his official Christhood, in others the reception of his superhuman endowments and authority from God the Father, and in some of them all three of these ideas expressed or implied.

"When he was come into his own country, he taught them in their synagogues, insomuch that they were astonished, and said, Whence hath this man this wisdom, and these mighty works? Is not this the carpenter's son? is not his mother called Mary? and his brethren, James, and Joses, and Simon, and Judas? And his sisters, are they not all with us? Whence, then, hath this man all these things? And they were offended in him. But Jesus said unto them, A prophet is not without honor, save in his own country, and in his own house." Matt. xiii. 54–57. Also Mark vi. 1–4.

"And he came to Nazareth, where he had been brought up; and, as his custom was, he went into the synagogue on the Sabbath-day, and stood up to read.

And there was delivered unto him the book of the prophet Esaias. And when he had opened the book, he found the place where it was written, The Spirit of the Lord is upon me, because he hath anointed me to preach the gospel to the poor, he hath sent me to heal the broken-hearted, to preach deliverance to the captives, and recovering of sight to the blind, to set at liberty them that are bruised, to preach the acceptable year of the Lord. And he closed the book, and he gave it again to the minister, and sat down. And the eyes of all them that were in the synagogue were fastened on him. And he began to say unto them, This day is this Scripture fulfilled in your ears. And all bare him witness, and wondered at the gracious words which proceeded out of his mouth. And they said, Is not this Joseph's son?" "And he said unto them, Verily I say unto you, No prophet is accepted in his own country." Luke iv. 16–24.

"And behold, one came and said unto him, Good Master, what good thing shall I do that I may have eternal life? And he said unto him, Why callest thou me good? There is none good but one, that is God." Matt. xix. 16, 17. "The Son can do nothing of himself, but what he seeth the Father do." John v. 19. "I can of mine own self do nothing; as I hear, I judge: and my judgment is just, because I seek not mine own will but the will of the Father which hath sent me." Ibid. v. 30. "When ye have lifted up the Son of man, then shall ye know that I am he, and that I do nothing of myself; but as my Father hath taught me, I speak those things. And he that sent me is with me: the Father hath not left me alone; for

I do always those things that please him." John viii. 28, 29.

"He asked his disciples, saying, Whom do men say that I the Son of man am? And they said, Some say that thou art John the Baptist; some, Elias, and others, Jeremias, or one of the prophets. He saith unto them, But whom say ye that I am? And Simon Peter answered and said, Thou art the Christ, the Son of the living God. And Jesus answered and said, Blessed art thou, Simon Barjona; for flesh and blood hath not revealed it unto thee, but my Father which is in heaven." Matt. xvi. 13–17. "While the Pharisees were gathered together, Jesus asked them, saying, What think ye of Christ? whose son is he? They say unto him, The son of David. He saith unto them, How then doth David in spirit call him, Lord, saying, The LORD said unto my Lord, sit thou on my right hand, till I make thine enemies thy footstool. If David then call him Lord, how is he his son? And no man was able to answer him a word." Matt. xxii. 41–46.

"I came down from heaven, not to do mine own will, but the will of him that sent me." "The Jews then murmured at him, because he said, I am the bread which came down from heaven. And they said, Is not this Jesus the son of Joseph, whose father and mother we know? How is it then that he saith, I came down from heaven? Jesus answered and said unto them, Murmur not among yourselves. No man can come unto me, except the Father, which hath sent me draw him?" John vi. 38, 41–44. "If ye were Abraham's children, ye would do the works of Abraham. But now ye seek to kill me, a man that hath told you the truth, which I have heard of God: this did not Abraham." John viii. 39, 40. "Many good works have I showed you; for which of those works do ye stone me? The Jews answered him saying, For a good work we stone thee not: but for blasphemy, and because that thou, being a man, makest thyself God. Jesus answered them, Is it not written in your law, I said, Ye are gods? If he called them gods, unto whom the word of God came, and the Scripture cannot be broken, say ye of him, whom the Father hath sanctified, and sent into the world, Thou blasphemest; because I said, I am the Son of God?" Ibid. x. 32–36.

To the foregoing I will add a few testimonies from others concerning Christ. "The next day John [the Baptist] seeth Jesus coming unto him, and saith, Behold the Lamb of God, which taketh away the sin of the world! This is he of whom I said, After me cometh a man which is preferred before me; for he was before me. And I knew him not: but that he should be made manifest to Israel, therefore am I come baptizing with water. And John bare record, saying I saw the Spirit descending from heaven like a dove, and it abode upon him. And I knew him not: but he that sent me to baptize with water, the same said unto me, Upon whom thou shalt see the Spirit descending and remaining on him, the same is he which baptizeth with the Holy Ghost. And I saw and bare record that this is the Son of God." Ibid. i. 29–34. "He whom God hath sent speaketh the words of God: for God giveth not the Spirit by measure unto him." John iii. 34. Thus far John the Baptist. Next what two disciples of John said, who became disciples of Jesus: "Philip findeth Nathanael, and saith unto him, We have found him of whom Moses in the law, and the prophets did write, Jesus of Nazareth, the son of Joseph. And Nathanael said unto him, Can there any good thing come out of Nazareth? Philip saith unto him, Come and see." He saw and conversed with Jesus, and thereupon exclaimed, "Rabbi, thou art the Son of God; thou art the King of Israel." Ibid. i. 45–49.

Next Peter, Paul, and John: "Ye men of Israel, hear these words; Jesus of Nazareth, a man approved of God among you by miracles and wonders and signs, which God did by him in the midst of you, as ye yourselves also know: Him, being delivered by the determinate counsel and foreknowledge of God, ye have taken, and by wicked hands have crucified and slain: whom God hath raised up, having loosed the pains of death." "Therefore let all the house of Israel know assuredly, that God hath made that same Jesus whom ye have crucified both Lord and Christ." Acts ii. 22–24, 36. See chaps. v. 30–32; x. 37–42; xvii. 30, 31. "There is one God, and one Mediator between God and men, the man Christ Jesus." 1 Tim. ii. 5. "We have seen and do testify that the Father sent the Son to be the Saviour of the world." 1 John iv. 14.

I have selected these testimonies from a host of passages substantially similar in their purport, as fair specimens of what we find to have been declared, professed, and held, according to the New Testament

Scriptures, concerning the relationship of Jesus Christ to God the Father, his nature, dignity, and authority. If they do not conclusively prove him to have been held strictly a man in person, the Christ in office, and all his authority conferred on him by the Father, I cannot understand language. The only difficulty in the case lies in conceiving clearly the operation of the Divine Spirit which pre-eminently inspired him, and rendered him competent for his office of Christ; that is, to speak and act in the name of the Father with full authority for the accomplishment of his glorious mission. From the texts I have quoted, and many others, it is evident that the influx and indwelling of the Divine Spirit which gave him his official Christhood often completely overflowed his mere human consciousness, and caused him to speak in the almost unqualified language of absolute divine consciousness. What he said to his apostles on a certain occasion — not to premeditate their defence before human tribunals, — "For it is not ye that speak, but the Spirit of your Father which speaketh in you" (Matt. x. 19, 20) — seems in the highest degree true of himself in his sublimest official moods. He then rises in language and consciousness of divine authority above his mere human selfhood, as one of and from heaven, the very mouth of God himself. This was indeed his function as the Christ of God, and we do not see how he could otherwise have fulfilled the design of that office, which was to express the will, and manifest the spiritual perfection, of God most effectually to mankind. But this high function of his official dignity, and this intensity of divine inspiration which it expressed, soon gave rise, in a certain class of minds, to the idea of two natures in his proper being — human and deific — manhood and Godhead. And thence ultimately grew the doctrine of the Trinity, with all its bitter controversies. How this proceeded from step to step I shall plainly show hereafter. What I now wish to impress particularly on your minds is, the importance of keeping distinctly in view the three before stated cardinal truths : 1st, the strict humanity of his personal being, — body, soul, and spirit; 2d, his divinely appointed and endowed office, as the Christ; and, 3d, that his inspirational power, dignity, and authority were not of himself, but entirely conferred on him by the Father, through the operation of his own communicable Spirit. Such was his doctrine, the apostolic doctrine, the New Testament doctrine, — the pure original doctrine of Christianity, concerning his relationship to God the Father, his real nature, dignity, and authority.

In my next I shall endeavor clearly to show the first corruptions of this pure doctrine, and how they arose.

ARTICLE I.

THE RELATIONSHIP OF JESUS CHRIST TO GOD THE FATHER. — HIS REAL NATURE, DIGNITY, AND AUTHORITY.

DISCOURSE IV.

FIRST CORRUPTIONS OF THE ORIGINAL PURE DOCTRINE, AND HOW THEY AROSE.

"We are not as many which corrupt the word of God; but as of sincerity, but as of God, in the sight of God, speak we in Christ."— 2 Cor. ii. 17.

I HAVE shown you what the original and pure doctrine was concerning the relationship of Jesus Christ to God the Father, his real nature, dignity, and authority; namely, that, in his proper personality as an individual being, he was strictly a man; that, as to his office, dignity, and authority, he was the Christ, the Son of God; and that, as to his divine excellency, it was entirely conferred on him by God the Father. This original and pure doctrine underwent no essential change in the primitive church, till after the apostles and their contemporaries had passed away. John is believed, with good reason, to have outlived all the first disciples, and to have continued in the flesh till near the end of the first century. Meantime a serious division had arisen between the strict Jewish Christians, and the majority of the church, which consisted of Gentile believers mainly, and partly of Jewish believers, — including most of the apostles, evangelists, and Hellenistic Jews so called. All these took the general ground, that the typical and ceremonial laws of Moses were fulfilled by and under Christ; that the new covenant, or Christian dispensation, superseded that of Moses; that the law of Christian righteousness summarized and transcended the old law; and therefore that circumcision, sabbatic observances, and Levitical ordinances were not to be required in the Christian church, and certainly not of Gentile converts. But the strict Jewish Christians took the contrary ground, insisted tenaciously on the continued obligations of Christians to keep the Levitical law entire, and soon broke fellowship with the catholic party. Paul was sorely troubled by these Mosaic Christians, as you will learn by reading the fifteenth and twenty-first chapters of Acts, together with his Epistle to the Galatians, and some strong passages in his other epistles. You will also learn, from these chapters in Acts, that the principal apostles tried hard to compromise the matter and prevent division. And they happily succeeded for a while, but not finally so as to prevent the alienation. After a few years it became irreconcilable, permanent, and bitter.

Those Jewish Christians, in their very honest but mistaken exclusiveness, became a sect, and to the general church a heretical sect, disliked for their bigotry about the Mosaic law at first, then for their views of Christ, and at length set at nought as contemptible. After the destruction of Jerusalem they were few, poor, and uninfluential, in comparison with the general church. Hence they were nicknamed by the latter Ebionites and Nazarenes. But they were honest and faithful to their convictions, in spite of all opposition, contempt, and persecution. For while they lost all favor from the main body of Christians, they got only curses from the mass of their own nation. Their sect continued to make more or less figure in Christian history down to the fifth century, when they seem to have become extinct.

Now the point I have been aiming at is this: That this primitive sect of Christians always, from the beginning to the end, held tenaciously to the strict personal humanity of Jesus, and to his Christhood as divinely conferred on him by the Father. The original Gospel of Matthew, as heretofore stated, without the exceptional portion, was written in the Hebrew language for their use. They made little or no account of the other three Gospels, or the rest of our New Testament collection. The original Matthew sufficed for them, and they held it ever sacred, along with the Old Testament Scriptures.

But the general church, after the apostles and first evangelists had passed away, became subject to powerful influences which gradually developed new theological ideas among them, especially with reference to the personal nature, dignity, and authority of Jesus Christ. What were these powerful influences?

1. They had become numerous and influential enough to attract the attention of various classes of religious philosophers, many of whom were eclectics

of their age, well versed in the doctrines of both Eastern and Western sages, especially the religious philosophy of Plato. Some of these were Jewish thinkers of the school of Philo, who had Platonized Judaism; some were of the Greek school; and others were largely indoctrinated with the Magianism of Persia, which claimed to have received its fundamental tenets from the great Zoroaster. Meantime Egyptian seats of learning were sending forth graduates, and streams of speculative knowledge, chiefly from the grand literary emporium of Alexandria, into all the cities of the Roman empire. Many of these philosophers were struck with admiration by the freshness, vitality, and growing popularity of the new religion. The church was anxious to make converts from all classes, and especially anxious to do so from the ranks of the learned. It greatly needed such for ministers and leaders. At the same time it began to have places of popular distinction and influence, more or less desirable to susceptible, progressive thinkers among the learned. It is true, there was much of persecution and martyrdom to face; but then even martyrdom in such a cause was becoming glorious. The result was, that considerable numbers of these progressive religious philosophers came into the church, and others, who did not fully identify themselves with it, assumed the Christian name, calling themselves Gnostics (from the Greek *gnosis*, knowledge), signifying persons of eminently enlightened minds. And important further results were, controversies, heresies, and corruptions of the primitive doctrine, especially concerning the nature and dignity of Christ. I will show wherein as I proceed.

2. Another influence, of a corrupting tendency, had been operating almost from the beginning, and now, with increase of respectability and the ambition for more, became powerful. This was the reproach cast upon Christianity on account of the mean nativity and ignominious death of its acknowledged founder. He was a Galilean, and had been put to death by crucifixion, — a mode of execution in all those ages deemed proper only for slaves and contemptible malefactors. This was a great stumbling-block to the more respectable Gentiles, and especially to the learned. It was hard for Christians to bear; but it had been borne with great moral heroism by the apostles, evangelists, and first believers, most of whom belonged to the humbler classes. Yet, even then, some shrunk from and winced under it. But now, when numbers of learned and influential persons had joined the church, and hosts more were almost persuaded to do so, the feeling became predominant that this reproach must be neutralized, offset, and overcome. The most natural and feasible way was, to claim something superhuman for the nature and person of Christ; in fine, to assert his divine pre-existence. The motive for this was at once a strong and seemingly laudable one. Moreover, the proposition itself was plausible, and agreeable to the prevailing philosophical ideas of the age. For it seemed incongruous that God should make such a glorious Christ, Lord, and Saviour, out of a poor Galilean, brought up in Nazareth, and crucified between two thieves. He must be a nobler,

Church, of all countries, about one hundred and eighty-six millions.

Over three hundred years ago the Romish section, having become too corrupt to endure the light of education and the printing-press, was rent asunder by the Reformation, so called. Luther, Calvin, and their coadjutors, originated the Protestant Church. This has split up into a host of mutually dissenting sects, which number altogther about ninety-six millions, — nearly one-fourth of all nominal Christians. But their intellectual and moral power is greater than that of the other three-fourths, and in the probable progress of human affairs will gradually work out a complete revolution of the whole Christian Church, — restoring the authority of its primitive principles under circumstances incomparably more favorable to their final universal triumph than those of the apostolic age. This better era is not yet at hand, but the way for it is preparing. The first Protestant reformers were not perfect. They saw some things clearly, others through a glass darkly, and many not at all. A few gross corruptions they saw, abhorred, and assailed with invincible force; such as the Pope's groundless assumptions of ecclesiastical authority, the tyrannical overriding of private judgment and conscience in the name of the church, the despotic denial of the rights of free speech and discussion, the scandalous sale of indulgences, and some other notorious errors and abuses. But the dogma of the Trinity, with other great corruptions, theoretical and practical, they cherished as the apples of their eyes. Moreover, they tried to shut down the very gates of religious diviner being in disguise. And the reigning philosophy, whether Oriental or Platonic, positively affirmed that the very eternal God, the supreme First Cause, created and governed the universe, not directly, but intermediately, by and through secondary gods, who originally emanated in a mysterious manner from himself. This made it easy to slide from the God-exalted humanity of Christ to the notion of his pre-existent, natural divinity, which somehow became incarnated in the body of the Galilean.

3. Natural veneration for the person of Christ became intensified by his departure out of the world, and this was only increased and confirmed by lapse of time, till it reached the highest degree of exaltation. We know how death sanctifies the worth and excellence of those we love. We know how, in all ages, great and remarkable personages have been deified, or sainted, or superhumanized, when time has sanctified their fame. We know that nothing is more natural, or more universal, than this working of veneration on the human mind. It is good in itself; but, like other goods of human nature, liable to excesses and abuses. With Christians this veneration for their Lord and Master steadily increased, from his resurrection and ascension, onward through the last half of the first century into the middle of the second, till it was at length felt to be almost impossible that, as to his nature and personal being, he should have been simply and strictly a man. Indeed, the extraordinary divine gifts which raised him to his Christly dignity and authority seemed to them far more suitable to an

incarnate God than to the noblest mere man, though one of the very highest type.

These strong influences sufficiently predisposed Christians of the second century, and especially the leading minds of the general church, to corrupt the pure primitive doctrine concerning the relationship of Jesus Christ to God the Father. And this they gradually did, by deifying his natural person, as really a pre-existent divine being somehow mysteriously incarnated in humanity. They did not begin by claiming anything like co-equality for him with God the Father, nor co-eternity. This was not achieved till the Council of Nice, A.D. 325, and even then scarcely prevailed. What the first corruptors did, was to assert and contend that Christ emanated, just before the creation of our universe, from the substance of the Father, and by his will was constituted his mediatorial Son, — a kind of secondary God, whose office it was, under and in the name of the Supreme God, to create, govern, and dispose, of all lower natures. Who led off in these new teachings? The converted religious philosophers before mentioned, who had come into the church, and become leading teachers therein. The two most ancient and prominent of them, whose writings have reached our times with much fulness, were Justin Martyr and Theophilus. Justin suffered death at Rome, A.D. 165, for his religion. Theophilus became bishop of Antioch, and died A.D. 182. Both had been eminent heathen philosophers before their conversion, and both brought with them into the church many of their old philosophical ideas, which they variously modified and compounded with Christianity. Theophilus was the first Christian writer who used the term trinity to designate the divine distinction and relationship of Father, Son, and Holy Ghost, — not as ultimately understood, but as he then understood the matter. This was about the year 150. Justin Martyr wrote two elaborate apologies in behalf of Christianity, addressed to Roman emperors, and also a work in dialogue, designed to support Christianity against Judaism. These three valuable works have come down to us. Some, or all of them, must have been written during the first half of the second century. Those two eminent fathers probably had a considerable number of kindred co-workers, and a multitude of successors.

But these innovators had no easy task of it, to change the primitive orthodoxy. They had the Jews, both the anti-Christian body of the nation, and the forementioned sect of Ebionites, to contend with; who constantly accused them of setting up a plurality of Gods. They also had the Gnostics to silence, who, with their Oriental philosophy, were metamorphosing Christianity into a monstrous system of absurdities. Most of these taught that a long succession of gods, whom they called æons, had emanated in a genealogical line from one most ancient æon, who, some time in past eternity, emanated from the one Supreme God. Each generation of these æons grew less and less pure, and from the lowest of them sprang the Demiurge, a powerful but jealous and vindictive being. He created the world, assuming to be the only true God, as set forth in the Old Testament Scriptures, instituted the Jewish religion, and had caused the principal evils that afflicted the human race. Christ, the oldest and best of the æons, had descended from the heavens to subdue the Old Testament God, and rescue mankind from all his manifold mischiefs. Some of them contended that Christ entered into the man Jesus at baptism, and remained in him till just before his final suffering on the cross, but himself never suffered. Others asserted that the man Jesus, so called, appeared at full age in Galilee, without any natural birth and infancy, having Christ in him, and being only a sort of apparition, — really no man at all, though seeming to be one for the great redeeming æon's convenience. All of them agreed that the material world was inherently malignant; that the Old Testament God and religion were evil; and that Christ, the most ancient and holy æon, had come from heaven to purify all souls, or at least to abolish all the perversions which the Mosaic God had caused.

The new doctors of the church could not endure such doctrines. They held fast to the Old Testament Scriptures, to the one living and true God therein set forth, to the promises and prophecies concerning the Messiah, to the essential harmony between the God of Israel and Christ, and to the fact that Jesus was really a man, though a pre-existent divine person became incarnated in him. But the Gnostics made them a vast deal of trouble, and they had to put them down by stern denunciation and excommunication.

Another serious obstacle in their way was, the aversion of many plain common Christians in the general church, to their Platonic philosophy, so ingeniously worked into Christianity. These were not learned, but devoted Christians of the primitive type. They were afraid of the new doctrinal subtilties concerning the nature of Christ, and clung to the original simplicity of the gospel. It seemed to them that the Platonic doctors were undermining the grand fundamental doctrine, that there was but *one* God, properly so called, the absolute monarch of the universe. Hence they cried out that the "*Divine Monarchy*," as they termed it, was being denied. Tertullian, so late as the beginning of the third century, thus complains of this opposition: "The simple, the ignorant, and the unlearned, who are always a great part of the body of Christians, since the rule of faith itself transfers their worship of many gods to the one true God, not understanding that the unity of God is to be maintained but with the economy (meaning the distribution of the Godhead into three persons), dread this economy, imagining that this number and disposition of a trinity is a division of the unity. They therefore will have it, that we are worshippers of two, and even of three, gods; but that they are worshippers of one God only. We, they say, hold the *monarchy*. Even the Latins have learned to bawl out for monarchy, and the Greeks will not understand the economy" (that is, the trinitarian term of explanation).

But, in spite of all external and internal opposition, the new Platonic Christology and Theology gradually prevailed. After long, rancorous, and complicated, controversy, it became the orthodoxy of the general church, by decree of the Council of Nice, A.D. 325. It is, however, so instructive to trace the growth of these corruptions, from their commencement in the first century to their culmination in the fourth, that I shall make them the subject of another discourse. Meantime, my friends, while learning to discriminate accurately between the genuine Christian doctrine, and its adulterations, let us admire the sublime simplicity of the primitive faith in Jesus Christ, as properly and strictly a human being, — a model man, — anointed pre-eminently by the Father with the Holy Spirit for his Christly office, and thus sanctified to be the religious head of our race, under God, our Master, Lord, and Deliverer, from all evil, by bringing us into his own spirit and moral likeness. For this glorious consummation let us strive as we never yet have striven, to be his true disciples, through the power of that faith in him which works by love unto eternal life.

ARTICLE I.

THE RELATIONSHIP OF JESUS CHRIST TO GOD THE FATHER.—HIS REAL NATURE, DIGNITY, AND AUTHORITY.

DISCOURSE V.

MORE PARTICULARLY HOW THE FIRST CORRUPTIONS OF THE ORIGINAL PURE DOCTRINE AROSE, AND PROCEEDED STEP BY STEP TO THEIR CULMINATION.

"And the Word [Logos] was made flesh [literally fleshed with a human body] and dwelt among us, and we beheld his glory, as of the only begotten of the Father, full of grace and truth." — John i. 14.

I partly showed, in my last, the first corruptions of the original pure doctrine concerning the relationship of Jesus Christ to God the Father, and how they arose. In this I am to pursue and complete the theme. I propose now to trace the growth of those corruptions from their commencement to their culmination.

They originated in the prevailing religious philosophy of the age when Christianity began to command the attention of progressive minds among the educated classes in the Roman empire. This religious philosophy, as I have stated, was either decidedly Platonic, or a variously eclectic one, compounded of the Platonic and Magian. It undertook to account for the creation, government, and final disposal of the world;

also the origin, prevalence, and final suppression of the evil in the universe. In doing this, it assumed that the infinite, all perfect First Cause, God, must necessarily be so latent and abstract in his nature as always to act mediately, through lower intelligent agencies, on matter and mind, — himself continuing, from and to all eternity, invisible, incomprehensible, and knowable to finite beings only by his secondary mediatorial representatives, that is, partially and imperfectly in various degrees of manifestation. These important ideas had undoubtedly a basis of more or less generic truth. For it seems absolutely impossible that an infinite, all perfect nature should be comprehended by a finite one, except in *degree*, and that an infinite nature in its measureless wholenesss should act upon or through a finite one. So, if the infinite, absolute, all-perfect God acts upon matter or mind limited by time and space, it must be by accommodating himself in some manner to their finiteness; in other words, putting forth limited spiritual manifestations of his attributes. How this could be done was the most profound of philosophical inquiries among ancient thinkers. It must be deemed so among us. There seemed to be but three conceivable modes whereby the infinite, absolute, all-perfect God could act upon and communicate with matter or mind existing as a finite nature. First, by causing secondary gods to emanate from his own essence, at once high enough and low enough to serve as mediators between himself and whatever might be produced still lower; second, by creating out of some essence inferior to his own such mediatorial gods; or, third, by evolving directly out of himself finite portions of his divine spirit, competent to produce the desired effect upon, in, or through a finite nature; in which last mode, such finite portion of his spirit would exercise, in suitable degree, all the attributes and capabilities of his own deific nature.

We find that the sages of India, Egypt, Chaldea, Persia, and Greece generally held that the highest of their mediatorial gods sprang from the infinite God by direct emanation, or by direct creation; and then countless inferior gods, angels, and spirits, either emanated from, or were created by, those principal mediatorial gods. Hence they readily embraced the doctrine of the pre-existence, transmigration, and final reabsorption of all souls into deity. But Moses and the prophets, with Jesus and his apostles, appear to have held the third specified mode of divine action, namely: God's evolving sufficient and suitable portions of his own spirit for the accomplishment of any and every desired result, whether in creating, regenerating, or governing, finite natures; and that in using angels, spirits, or men, as his ministers, he does so by inspiring them with a greater or less measure of his spirit. Hence both Testaments ascribe so much to "the Spirit of God," "the Holy Spirit," "the Spirit," etc., sometimes making it the angel of God or of his divine presence, sometimes his word or voice, sometimes his hand or finger, and sometimes an efflux from him poured out on his inspirees. All forms of expression are used, in either a general or a particular sense, to signify that God does everything directly by his communicable spirit, evolved in suitably adapted portions; and that he himself is to be deemed present and active, to all practical intents and purposes, wherever his spirit operates. The idea is repudiated and denounced in both Testaments, that the infinite, all-perfect God dwells in distant, uncommunicable abstraction, and that some secondary god or gods carry on the affairs of the universe. No prophet, or Christ, however high his mediatorial functions, is set up as anything authoritative further than the indwelling, or inspiring spirit of God makes him so. This shows a radical difference between the theology of the Bible, and the religious philosophies which corrupted primitive Christianity.

Now, when the learned heathen philosophers embraced Christianity, it was quite natural that they should think it might be advantageously modified, or at least favorably explained, by the help of their philosophy; and especially in respect to the peculiar nature, dignity, and authority of Jesus Christ. Of course, they were inhibited from teaching or holding a plurality of gods. This was an abomination to the whole Christian church. But could they not hold and teach that Jesus Christ was the Son of God in some higher sense than that of a divinely inspired, God-anointed man? Might he not be in some sense a pre-existent divine person, or soul, like Plato's first-born of God, the *Logos*, mind or reason of God, — whereby divine creation and government were executed? Yes, he might be, — he probably was, — he must be. How could a mere human being, however excellent, be invested with such an office, such gifts, such power, such authority, such a godlike responsibility? It could not be. He must have some sort of divinity in his very nature as a personal being.

What next was necessary? Texts and declarations of Scripture that seemed to teach his pre-existence and divinity, or at least to favor these ideas. These were plenty enough, if they might take such as related particularly to his office as the Christ. For his official Christhood had been foreordained from the foundation of the human world; and as to the Spirit which anointed him, which made him Christ, which spoke through him, and clothed him with all his authority, *that* was from the beginning, before Abraham, before the world was; so that virtually, as to his office, he was from heaven, and from the most ancient times, and a manifestation of the Father fresh from his bosom. Yet he was none the less strictly a man as to his proper individual personality. His personality was human, but his office and official endowments were divine, — just as divine as the Father by his Holy Spirit could make them. But it was easy to confound his Christly office with his personal nature, and to interpret those passages of Scripture which refer to the Spirit of the Father that anointed and spoke through him, as declaring what was inherent in his strict individual being. This they did, and cited most of the texts now generally used to support the doctrine of his natural deity, as the second person in the Godhead. This was all the easier done, because, about the same time, the learned, both Christians and Jews, adopted the allegorical and mystical method of interpreting Scripture. By this method they could deduce from almost any text the most wonderful internal meaning, not indicated to ordinary understandings by the literal expression. This allegorizing and mysticising of Scripture was carried to great excess during the second and third centuries. It was, indeed, a legitimate outgrowth of the modified Platonic philosophy then prevalent, and, though subsequently severely denounced by many eminent doctors in the church, served admirably the purpose of the transitional theologians. Besides this, the strongly figurative language of Scripture in numerous passages favored their assumptions.

Still there were serious difficulties in the way of deifying Jesus Christ. There were so many plain declarations of his simple humanity in the gospels and epistles, that even the famous Trinitarian, Athanasius, in the fourth century, accounted for the lack of plain declarations on his own side by saying: "All the Jews were so firmly persuaded that their Messiah was to be nothing more than a man like themselves, that the apostles were obliged to use great caution in divulging the doctrine of the proper divinity of Christ." A very significant confession. Then there was the puzzling problem, how to avoid the charge of holding a plurality of Gods. If Christ was very God, in any proper sense, the common people were prone to insist that there must be more than one God. At the same time there was a necessity for maintaining that Christ was both man and God. But how this was to be made out seemed, for a long time, problematical. Some thought he had a human body without a human soul, and that his pre-existent divine nature acted as soul to his body. This was soon found untenable, and the mystery of two whole natures united in one person, without confusion of substance, was ultimately invented. To save the doctrine of one God, nearly all the Christian fathers, previous to the Council of Nice, A.D. 325, pleaded the *subordinate* divinity of Christ, as emanating from, or begotten, at a certain time before the creation of our universe, out of the substance of the Father; thus deriving a begotten subordinate divine person from the supreme unbegotten God. They had not then the assurance of their successors to assert that Christ was "co-equal with the Father in substance, power, and eternity." I will briefly quote some of the explanatory pleadings of these early fathers.

Justin Martyr, about the middle of the second century, was the first who asserted the divinity of Christ; but he did it in a very carefully qualified manner. He was a philosopher, and, when writing to the philosophical emperor of Rome in defence of Christianity, apologized for giving Christ the title, *Son of God*, thus: "This cannot be new to them who speak of Jupiter as having sons, and especially of Mercury as his interpreter, and the instructor of all men." "If Christ be a mere man, yet he deserves to be called the Son of God, on account of his wisdom, and the heathens called God (that is, Jupiter) the father of gods and men; and if, in an extraordinary manner, he be the *Logos* of God, this is common with those who call Mercury the Logos that declares the will of God." On another occasion he said: "Jesus may still be the Christ of God, though I should not be able to prove his pre-existence, as the Son of God who made all things. For though I should not prove that he had pre-existed, it will be right to say that, in this respect only, I have been deceived, and not to deny that he is the Christ, if he appears to be a man born of men, and to have become Christ by election." What he really contended for is thus set forth: "In the beginning, before all the creatures, God begat from himself a certain reasonable power, who by the Spirit is sometimes called *the glory of God*, sometimes *God*, sometimes the *Lord* and *Logos*, because he is subservient to his Father's will, and was begotten at his Father's pleasure."

Theophilus, bishop of Antioch, another of the same school, and cotemporary with Justin Martyr, wrote a little later, saying: "Before anything was made, God had the Logos for his council, being his reason or understanding; but when he proceeded to produce what he had determined upon, he then emitted the *Logos*, the first-born of every creature, not emptying himself of *Logos*, but begetting *Logos*, and always conversing with his own *Logos*."

Tatian, in the same second century only a little latter, explained the subject as follows: "When God pleased, the *Logos* flowed from his simple essence, and this Word (Logos) not being produced in vain, became the first begotten work of his spirit. This we know to be the origin of the Word. But it was produced by *division*, and not by *separation*; for that which is divided does not diminish that from which it derives its power. For, as many torches may be lighted from one, and yet the light of the first torch is not diminished, so the Word (Logos), proceeding from the power of the Father, does not leave the Father void of *Logos*."

Origen, in the third century, makes defence of the new doctrine thus: "To them who charge us that we believe in two Gods, we must reply, that he who is God of himself (meaning God the Father) is *the* God, for which reason our Saviour says, in his prayer to the Father, *that they may know thee, the only true God*. But whatever is God besides him who is so of himself, being God only by a communication of his divinity, cannot so properly be called *the God*, but rather God."

In this way matters went on from bad to worse, with much confusion of opinions, and perpetual metaphysical controversy, down to the beginning of the fourth century, when the famous presbyter Arius arose, and excited one of the most momentous controversies that ever agitated the church. The primitive Unitarianism, and various modifications of it, had been advocated by a few distinguished defenders all through the second and third centuries, and was held by large numbers of the laity. But it had been greatly suppressed and cowered by the influential Platonic doctors. Arius boldly attacked the prevailing doctrine of Christ's deity, denied that he emanated or was begotten out of the substance of the Father, and contended that he was the first of God's creation, — created out of nothing, in absolute subordination to the Father. He held him to be super-angelic, pre-existent before our world was formed, and in due time incarnated in the body of Jesus. All the smothered elements of Unitarianism in the church were now aroused. Hosts of the laity, many of the inferior clergy, and a considerable number of bishops rallied to his support. But a majority of the more influential clergy, with numerous lay adherents, stood up fiercely against him. A violent and almost bloody contest ensued. Meantime Constantine the Great, so called, ascended the imperial throne, by the military aid of the degenerate Christians, and proclaimed the establishment of their religion. He found the church rent by this mighty controversy, and deemed it one of his first duties to pacify the raging parties. The point at issue stood thus: Was Christ begotten before the ages, out of the very substance of the Father, and so absolutely DIVINE? Or was he the first creature of God, higher than any other, but still a mere creature, not consubstantial with the Father? Athanasius was the leading advocate against the Arians, and he had powerful coadjutors. The conflict was greatly intensified by the church having just become united with the state. Power, place, and wealth awaited the party that should be pronounced orthodox. Deposition, banishment, poverty, and perhaps death, awaited the vanquished. Constantine could not quiet the angry combatants by suasion. He therefore called a General Council at Nice, in Bithynia, A.D. 325. It was almost a mob of bishops, or rather two mobs struggling for the ascendency. Victory trembled in the balance, and the emperor threw his sceptre into the scale on the side of the *Divinitarians*. The Arians were crushed, and deposed, or suffered banishment. The deity of Christ became the sword-sustained orthodoxy of church and state, and has ever since, with transitory exceptions, maintained its ascendency. The Nicene Council established its doxy on the point at issue, in these words: —

"I believe in one God, the Father Almighty, maker of heaven and earth, of all things visible and invisible. And in one Lord Jesus Christ, the only begotten Son of God; and born of the Father before all ages: God of God, light of light, true God of true God, begotten, not made; consubstantial to the Father, by whom all things were made. Who for us men, and for our salvation, came down from heaven, and was incarnated by the Holy Ghost of the Virgin Mary; AND HE WAS MADE MAN: was crucified also under Pontius Pilate; he suffered, and was buried. And the third day he rose again, according to the Scriptures. And he ascended into heaven. Sits at the right of the Father. And he is to come again with glory to judge the living and the dead; of whose kingdom there shall be no end."— *Nicene Creed.*

But the work of metaphysical and theological corruption remained to be completed, some centuries later, by what is called the *Athanasian Creed;* from which I present you the following extracts: —

"The Godhead of the Father, and of the Son, and of the Holy Ghost, is all one, the glory equal, the majesty co-eternal. Such as the Father is, such is the Son, and such is the Holy Ghost. The Father is uncreated, the Son is uncreated, and the Holy Ghost uncreated. The Father incomprehensible, the Son incomprehensible, and the Holy Ghost incomprehensible. The Father eternal, the Son eternal, and the

THE RELATIONSHIP OF JESUS CHRIST. 59

Holy Ghost eternal. And yet they are not three Eternals, but one Eternal. As also they are not three Uncreated, nor three Incomprehensibles; but one Uncreated, and one Incomprehensible. In like manner, the Father is Almighty, the Son Almighty, and the Holy Ghost Almighty. And yet they are not three Almighties, but one Almighty. So the Father is God, the Son is God, and the Holy Ghost is God. And yet they are not three Gods, but one God."

"We believe and confess that our Lord Jesus Christ, the Son of God, is both God and Man. He is God of the substance of the Father, begotten before the world; and he is Man of the substance of his mother born in the world. Perfect God and perfect Man; of a rational soul, and human flesh subsisting. Equal to the Father according to his Godhead, and less than the Father according to his Manhood. Who, although he be both God and Man, yet he is not two, but one Christ. One, not by the conversion of the Godhead into flesh, but by the taking of the Manhood unto God. One altogether, not by confusion of substance, but by unity of person. For as the rational soul and the flesh is one man, so God and Man is one Christ."

We have now reached the climax. Thus, insidiously at first, and by a gradual process, did the pure original doctrine of Christ's strict personal humanity, and divinely endowed official Christhood, become metamorphosed, by corrupting patchwork, into one of the most mysterious, inexplicable, incongruous dogmas ever imposed on the human mind. Who, by simply reading the Scriptures, could have imagined such a metamorphosis possible? What would the Jewish people of Christ's times have said if he had set up such pretensions, and demanded such a faith in himself? And what would the first apostles and evangelists have thought, if presented with such an artificial, complex, incomprehensible summary of their teachings? It passes imagination to conceive. And what has Christianity gained by this elaborate tissue of metaphysical mystification, professedly aiming to magnify the natural personality of its founder into absolute co-equality with God the Father? Nothing. Whatever he was, or said, or did, more than a man, sprang from God the Father, and was, of course, divinely authoritative, according to the primitive doctrine. Has this triple personalization of the Godhead, and duplication of Christ's personal nature, made his authority one iota greater? No. But, on the other hand, there has been an incalculable loss to Christianity, by reason of this foolish, man-invented wisdom, working out such a dogma. Vain speculation, division, wrath, persecution, beyond all computation, have been the hateful fruits. Christianity has been distorted in theory, and debased in practice. Now we must undo what has been so perversely done, purge away the corruption wrought, and return as fast as we can to the pure, rational, evangelical, primitive doctrine.

ARTICLE II.

THE NATURE, RELATIONSHIP, AND OFFICE OF THE HOLY SPIRIT.

DISCOURSE VI.

THE ORIGINAL AND PURE DOCTRINE CONCERNING THE HOLY SPIRIT.

"If ye then, being evil, know how to give good gifts unto your children; how much more shall your heavenly Father give the Holy Spirit to them that ask him?"—LUKE xi. 13.

WHAT was the original and pure doctrine of Christianity concerning the Holy Spirit, and what corruptions has it undergone? I will endeavor to answer the first of these inquiries in the present discourse, and the second in my next. In answering the first, I must depend mainly for reliable historic information, as in the former case, on the Scriptures. There is little else to depend on. On this point the primitive Christians seem not to have differed much from the Jews, except perhaps in claiming for their Master, the apostles, and themselves larger gifts of the Holy Spirit than the unbelieving Jews were willing to allow. Their doctrine seems to have been this,— that the Holy Spirit is a potent spiritual element evolved by God at pleasure out of his inherent essence, in order thereby more effectually to execute his will upon, in, and through finite natures — especially moral natures; and that it is communicable in various portions and degrees to human beings, so as to render them conscious of the divine presence, and mediums of superhuman excellence. This is certainly a very rational as well as sublime doctrine.

Why?

1. Because the infinite God, the absolute First Cause, must operate in a finite manner to produce finite effects; that is, by portions of his infinite spiritual nature adapted to limited space, time, and creation. Nor otherwise could he manifest his attributes and will to the comprehension of finite minds, so as to bring them into moral communion and unison with himself. Finite minds can know vast wholes only by such portions, specimens, and samples of them as truly represent their entire nature. How much less the infinite God! No man, nor even the highest conceivable angel, can know God to infinity, but only his essential attributes and will, by a representative portion of his Spirit. Thus by littles which we can analyze, we rise to just conceptions of the grandest wholes. This is alike true in physics and metaphysics.

2. Because God is a Spirit, everywhere present, whose essence is transcendently fine and subtile, the very inmost of all substances, ordinarily invisible, impalpable, and imperceptible to us, — as much finer than the essence of our own spirits as they are finer than our bodies. God's essence is therefore so abstract and latent to our uninspired powers of recognition, that unless he willed to manifest his presence to our consciousness in some finite, accommodated,

adapted mode, we should never know anything of him. This room is now full of latent electricity, probably sufficient to kill one of us if concentrated and exploded. The snow and ice around us in winter contain latent heat enough to swelter us, if it were evolved and conditioned to that end. There is latent light and heat enough in a few pounds of coal, even when in the most frosty state, to dazzle us into blindness, and burn us to death. It only needs to be evolved and applied. So there is probably enough of God's latent spiritual essence now in this house to throw us all into ecstatic visions, or produce any other astonishing phenomenon, if he willed to evolve and set in motion its operative energy. This explains the nature, relationship, and office of that spiritual element called the Holy Spirit.

3. Because human nature, and all moral natures, are constituted in their higher stories, to crave knowledge of and communion with the supreme Parent Spirit. We were created religious beings, to "feel after God, if haply we may find him," as Paul expresses it. Such are the aspirations, susceptibilities, aptitudes, and capabilities whose seeds he planted in all moral natures. It was his will, purpose, and pleasure to bring us all, sooner or later, into a state of moral unison and communion with himself. Therefore, as our Father, he adapts himself to our finite comprehension, by causing suitable portions of his Spirit, evolved with just the proper modifications, to render us spiritually conscious of his divine presence. Thus his Spirit becomes communicable to, in, and through us, when we are in the proper and receptive

state of mind. Hence Jesus and others were said to be "filled with the Holy Spirit." And hence, also, Paul said, "Know ye not that ye are the temple of God, and that the Spirit of God dwelleth in you?" 1 Cor. iii. 16. And again: "Know ye not that your body is the temple of the Holy Ghost, which ye have of God?" Ibid. vi. 19.

For these and many other reasons I most heartily accept and embrace this original pure doctrine of Christianity concerning the divine nature, relationship, and office of the Holy Spirit. And I do not recollect a single passage of Scripture between the lids of the Bible, which, with a fair natural construction, does not accord with it. Different terms are used to express the generic idea of this divine element. Sometimes the term is *Spirit of God*, or *of the Lord;* sometimes simply *the Spirit*, or *thy Spirit*, or *his Spirit;* sometimes the *Word of God*, or *of the Lord;* sometimes the *Hand of God* or *of the Lord*, or *Finger of God*, or *Glory of God;* sometimes the *Comforter*, or *Spirit of truth;* sometimes the *True Light*, or *Light of Life;* and sometimes, in our common translation of the New Testament, the *Holy Ghost*. This last term I regret; because it confuses the unlearned, who do not know that king James' translators took the liberty to render precisely the same *Greek original*, in one passage, Holy Spirit, and in another, Holy Ghost. But, if we bear this fact in mind, the different sound of the two terms need not confuse us. Remember, whenever you read the term Holy Ghost, that in the original it is identical with Holy Spirit.

I do not deem it necessary to quote extensively the

passages in which the Holy Spirit is spoken of in the Old Testament and New, nor even a formal sample of them, to verify my statement of the original pure doctrine. This any one of you so disposed can do at leisure. But perhaps I ought to notice and answer several incidental inquiries which may arise.

1. It will be observed that the Holy Spirit, by whatever term designated, is sometimes spoken of in the neuter gender as an impersonal divine element, and sometimes in the masculine gender as a person, or as possessing personality. It may be asked, Why is this so? I reply: Because as an evolved element, a portion of the infinite divine essence made communicable to the finite soul, it may properly be spoken of as impersonal, thus in the neuter gender. But it must be considered that every conceivable portion of the infinite divine essence contains the attributes, properties, and qualities of the whole, and is a limited representation of the whole. Therefore, if God himself possesses personality, so must every communicable representative portion of his Spirit, in some demonstrative degree. Now God's personality is not a corporeal one, nor an organic one, like that of a creature, but strictly a spiritual, mental, and moral personality. He is not a being of organic structure, — seeing, hearing, feeling, sensing, thinking, and acting, through organized eyes, ears, nervous tissue, brain, and particular functional members; but is an infinite, omnipresent Spirit, with perfect sensation, consciousness, knowledge, wisdom, and goodness in every conceivable part and atom of his nature. It **must be so**; and if so, then the Holy Spirit carries

mental and moral personality with it, in due degree, wherever it becomes a cognizable representative of the Infinite Divine. It is *per se* of and from the divine fountain, evolved and communicated adaptively to finite souls. It is virtually God within them, inspiring, enlightening, teaching, guiding, and sanctifying them; dwelling in, and working out the divine purposes through them. In this view, the Holy Spirit is practically a mental and moral person, unto whomsoever manifested, as really in degree as God is in his infinity. Hence, Jesus said: "When he the Spirit of truth is come, he will guide you into all truth; for he shall not speak of himself, but whatsoever he shall hear he shall speak." John xvi. 13. Again: "When the Comforter is come, whom I will send unto you from the Father, even the Spirit of truth, which proceedeth from the Father, he shall testify of me." Ibid. xv. 26. So Paul: "Now there are diversities of gifts, but the same Spirit." "And there are diversities of operations, but it is the same God which worketh all in all. But the manifestation of the Spirit is given to every man to profit withal;" . . . "dividing to every man severally as he will." 1 Cor. xii. 4, 6, 7, 11. Also: "The Holy Ghost said, Separate Barnabas and Saul, for the work whereunto I have called them." Acts xiii. 2. Thus we may clearly understand why the Holy Spirit is sometimes spoken of in the neuter gender as an impersonal element, and sometimes in the masculine as exercising the attributes of mental personality. But the notion, afterwards corruptively brought into vogue, that the Holy Spirit is a distinct co-equal third person in the Godhead, derives no countenance from such passages of Scripture.

2. It may be questioned whether the term *Logos*, translated *Word*, as used by the Apostle John, and other New Testament writers, and especially as used in the fourth gospel, really means the Holy Spirit. I must answer, that I am sure it does. Why? Because the same nature, relationship, and office, elsewhere ascribed to the Holy Spirit, are ascribed to the *Logos* in this gospel, and in other passages of the New Testament. Let us see. Jesus said to the unbelieving, cavilling Jews: "The Father himself which hath sent me hath borne witness of me. Ye have neither heard his voice at any time, nor seen his shape. And ye have not his word (*ton logon*) abiding in you; for whom he hath sent, him ye believe not." John v. 37, 38. That is, ye have not his Spirit of truth abiding in you. Again: "If he called them gods unto whom the word (logos) of God came, . . . say ye of him whom the Father hath sanctified and sent into the world, Thou blasphemest, because I said I am the Son of God?" What else do I claim, than that God's *Logos* has come to me, and speaks through me, even his Holy Spirit of truth and love? John x. 35, 36. Now turn to that notable passage at the commencement of the same gospel: "In the beginning was the Word (Logos), and the Word (Logos) was with God, and the Word (Logos) was God." Also the same is called "the True Light which lighteth every man that cometh into the world." Then it is declared that "the Word (Logos) was made flesh" (caused to flow into and inhabit the man Jesus), so that he was

rendered the most eminent "Son of God, full of grace and truth;" concerning whom Philip, near the end of the chapter, testified, saying, "We have found him of whom Moses in the law, and the prophets, did write, Jesus of Nazareth, the son of Joseph." And in the third chapter, it is declared of him: "He whom God hath sent speaketh the words of God; for God giveth not the Spirit by measure unto him." Compare with these passages the following: "The Spirit of the Lord is upon me, because he hath anointed me to preach the gospel." Luke iv. 18. "The Father that dwelleth in me, he doeth the works." John xiv. 10. "Jesus of Nazareth, a man approved of God among you by miracles and wonders and signs, which God did by him in the midst of you." Acts iii. 22. "God anointed Jesus of Nazareth with the Holy Ghost and with power; . . . for God was with him." Ibid. x. 38. "As many as are led by the Spirit of God, they are the sons of God;" "heirs of God, and joint-heirs with Christ." Rom. viii. 15, 17. "The Spirit also helpeth our infirmities; for we know not what we should pray for as we ought; but the Spirit itself maketh intercession for us with groanings that cannot be uttered." Ibid. verse 26. "For the word (logos) of God is quick and powerful, and sharper than any two-edged sword, piercing even to the dividing asunder of soul and spirit, and of the joints and marrow, and is a discerner of the thoughts and intents of the heart. Neither is there any creature that is not manifest in his sight." Heb. iv. 12, 13. These passages all teach the same general doctrine, and they mutually explain each other, — showing that the terms

Logos (Word) and Holy Spirit were used to denote the same evolved, communicable Spirit of God, through whose diversified agency he administers his divine moral government.

3. It may be further asked whether something like tri-personal co-equality, between the Father, Son, and Holy Spirit, is not taught in the following texts: "Go ye therefore and teach all nations, baptizing them in the name of the Father, and of the Son, and of the Holy Ghost." Matt. xxviii. 19. "The grace of the Lord Jesus Christ, and the love of God, and the communion of the Holy Ghost, be with you all. Amen." 2 Cor. xiii. 14. Answer. Certainly no such thing as tri-personal co-equality is expressed in these passages. It can only be *inferred*. But what right have we to infer it? Is it because the three names are put in close relation to each other, as expressive of divine excellency and authority in the Father, Son, and Holy Spirit, which Christians are solemnly bound to reverence and obey? No doubt of that. But what authority has the Father, and what authority the Son, and what authority the Holy Spirit? Where shall we go to ascertain? To those Scriptures which explicitly declare what the excellency and authority of each is. There we are taught, with the utmost plainness, that the Father is absolutely supreme; the Son his official Christ, claiming only conferred divine authority; and the Holy Spirit the evolved, adaptable, communicable Spirit of the Father, by means whereof he operates in a manner comprehensible to finite moral agents. Each of the three possesses such high divine excellency and authority, either supreme or subordinate, that

Christianity justly makes it indispensable for its disciples reverentially to acknowledge and conform to it. But this must be done truthfully and understandingly, recognizing the Father for what he is, the Son for what he is, and the Holy Spirit for what *it* or *he* is. In so doing the intelligent Christian will have nothing to do with their tri-personal co-equality, but will worship the Father as infinite and supreme, follow the teachings and example of the Son as the Father's highest anointed human representative, and earnestly endeavor to become the temple of the Holy Spirit, so as to be the Christ-like child of God. This, and no more, is signified by the baptismal formula and the apostolic benediction.

4. It may be asked, why Christ is represented as sending, breathing, imparting, and baptizing with, the Holy Spirit, and the apostles as communicating it by imposition of hands? Answer. Because they themselves were in unison with God, filled with this communicable Spirit, and empowered to impart it to others in various portions and degrees. Such seems to be the law of divine order relative to the communicability of all spiritual magnetisms.

I will close this discourse with a few words of appeal to your understandings and moral affections. Do you not now clearly apprehend the original pure doctrine of Christianity concerning the nature, relationship, and office of the Holy Spirit? How sublimely simple, profoundly rational, and divinely beautiful! Alas, that it should ever have been corrupted by theological mystification! I will show you in what respects, and how, in my next. Meantime I wish I could incite you to make a worthy practical use of the pure doctrine. It is as salutary to just appreciators as it is theoretically excellent. It shows us that though God, the Great First Cause and Controller of all things, is infinite and invisible, yet he is omnipresent, and a condescending Father to his lowest, weakest offspring. His majesty is not that of a cold, distant, inaccessible Sovereign, but of a loving, faithful, beneficent parent, who adapts himself to his children's capacities, provides abundantly for all their wants, and constantly seeks to bring them into bosom communion with himself. Reiterate to yourselves the precious words of Jesus in our prefatory text: "If ye then, being evil, know how to give good gifts unto your children, how much more shall your heavenly Father give the Holy Spirit to them that ask him?" Have any of us ever earnestly asked him for this blessed gift? Has truth, or reason, or conscience, or sorrow, ever excited us to long for this gift? to hunger and thirst after it? to seek after it as the richest of all possessions? Some of us, let me trust. God knows who. How many can at this moment say within the soul, It is I? I have felt the divine discipline chastening my heart. I have realized my frailties, my sinfulness, and those deep spiritual wants which no created thing or being can supply. I have yearned after my heavenly Father by day and by night. I have fervently sought for his Spirit to reveal his presence in my soul, — my mote of conscious being. Blessed man, woman, or child, whoever thou art! For thou has found his freely given Spirit in the humble temple of thy bosom. The great Father has communed with thee, his little child. Is there any such bliss, any such purifying, elevating, sanctifying influence, as this indwelling Holy Spirit imparts? Let me hope that I, too, have known it in some small degree, and that we shall all, sooner or later, realize that divine presence within us which gives fulness of joy and heavenly pleasure for evermore.

ARTICLE II.

THE NATURE, RELATIONSHIP, AND OFFICE OF THE HOLY SPIRIT.

DISCOURSE VII.

CORRUPTIONS OF THE ORIGINAL PURE DOCTRINE CONCERNING THE HOLY SPIRIT.

"I fear, lest by any means, as the serpent beguiled Eve through his subtilty, so your minds should be corrupted from the simplicity that is in Christ." — 2 Cor. xi. 3.

In my last I endeavored to state and explain the original pure doctrine of Christianity concerning the Holy Spirit; namely, That the Holy Spirit is a potent spiritual element, evolved by God at pleasure out of his inherent essence, in order thereby more effectually to execute his will upon, in, and through finite natures — especially moral natures; and that it is communicable in various portions and degrees to human beings, so as to render them conscious of the divine presence. I promised next to show wherein, and how, the original pure doctrine became corrupted. Philosophizing theologians gradually resolved the Holy Spirit into a distinct, co-equal third person of the Godhead: as saith the Athanasian Creed, "One is the person of the Father, another of the Son, another of the Holy Ghost, . . . the glory equal, the majesty co-eternal." "The Father is God, the Son is God, and the Holy Ghost is God. And yet they are not three Gods, but one God." Do you perceive the difference between the original and the corrupted doctrine? They agree in two respects; namely, that the essence of the Holy Spirit is *divine*, — of the very nature of God; and that it possesses mental personality, as God in his wholeness does. But they radically differ in three respects; namely, 1. The original doctrine makes the Holy Spirit to be any portion of God's elementary spiritual essence, evolved at his pleasure, for the purpose of executing his will, manifesting his presence to finite moral natures, and affording them conscious communion with himself. The corrupted doctrine makes the Holy Spirit, in some inexplicable sense, one third of God's absolute deific infinity coordinate with the Father and the Son, the two other personal thirds. 2. The original doctrine makes the Holy Spirit always a subservient agency, or instrumentality, of God, operating as his representative in a finite manner. The corrupted doctrine makes the Holy Spirit as independent and as infinite as the Father himself; operating always as much on his own account as God the Father does on his own, only in harmony with him. 3. The original doctrine makes the Holy Spirit a variegated, multiform outpouring of God's own essential Spirit, carrying with it, in degree, the divine mental and moral personality, so as to be the presence, voice, and inspiration of God to any number of conscious moral beings, in suitable adaptation, at the same time. The corrupted doctrine makes the Holy Spirit one single infinite deific person, co-ordinate and co-equal with two other infinite deific persons; and yet neither of the three must be thought of as a distinct being, or God.

Well, says one, you call this a corruption of the pure primitive doctrine; but what is the harm of it? Answer. It puzzles, confounds, and stultifies the understanding, and thus, to a great extent, rules it out of religious faith and worship. The result is, mental confusion, unmeaning profession, and dwarfing superstition, to a corresponding extent. I am baptized in the name of the Father, the Son, and the Holy Ghost, as a believer in them. According to the original pure doctrine, I can act understandingly in this; because I believe sincerely in the one infinite Father, as the Son, Jesus Christ, has manifested his character to mankind by means of the Holy communicable Spirit, which, with pre-eminent fulness, dwelt in and spoke through him; and whereby, also, all holy prophets, apostles, and people are in some measure inspired. But I cannot understand how there are three almighty, infinite, co-equal divine persons to be believed in, worshipped, and served; who yet are not three Gods, but only one God. I must think of, believe in, and worship the Holy Spirit, and at the same time the other two, yet neither of them as in any respect greater or less than the others. How can I bring this doctrine within reach of my understanding? I hear the three names solemnly pronounced, and the doctrine dogmatically reiterated. I pronounce the names and profess to believe in and worship the ineffable Trinity — the Father, Son, and Spirit — co-equally. All I can understand by it, or explain about it, is, that somehow, quite incomprehensibly to myself, I believe in and worship the Divine Nature. I have a blind faith, a blind devotional sentiment, — in fine, a blind religion, which forbids me to reason and to understand. It is true, I am sincere, and perhaps very religious, but no more so than millions of pagans are. Is this proper and becoming for a rational and accountable being? What is my lack? I am not a whole man; only a part of one, — a religious cripple, or dwarf. Why? My understanding is palsied; it is but a cipher on the left hand of a digit, and in my religion it counts nothing; whereas I am required to love God with all my "understanding" and "mind" as well as all my "heart;" to worship in spirit and in truth, — not with unmeaning external expressions, and vain repetitions; to sing and pray with the "spirit" and "understanding," — not in unintelligible, inexplicable utterances. Our heavenly Father wants us to be both rational and religious. So does Christ. So does the Holy Spirit. Therefore hath the Father manifested his real moral perfections, through his anointed Son, and by means of his communicable Holy Spirit. Thus may we know the only true God, his will and law, and thus lay hold on eternal life. All this is plain enough in primitive Christianity; but it has been darkened, mystified, and superstitionized by these corruptions which I am trying to expose. The nominal church has been too long filled up with mental cripples, tottering along on the crutches and in the leading-strings of blind guides, whose official profession and teachings have often sadly enhanced the necessity for a radical reformation. Such a reformation will yet come; and when it comes, none of our faculties will be left out of religious exercise.

But I promised to show how the original pure doctrine concerning the Holy Spirit became corrupted. I need not be prolix in doing so. The original doctrine was so simple, and so strikingly demonstrated in their experience, that the first and second generations of Christians accepted it, as they did the other primitive doctrines, without any disposition to philosophize on their metaphysical merits. They understood them well enough for practical use, and felt no need of scholastic subtilties to mysterize their faith in them. Not so a little later. After the philosophical metamorphosers had begun their work of deifying Christ, it was very natural that they should discuss the nature, rank, and office of the Holy Spirit. But here neither the Oriental nor Greek philosophy afforded them the helpful suggestions they had respecting Christ, considered as the pre-existent *Logos*, or as the first begotten *Æon*. They did not know, for a considerable time, what, philosophically, to make of the Holy Ghost. Some thought he was nearly akin to the *Logos;* others that he was an exalted angelic creature ; and others, that he was somehow a God or a mysterious power of God, acting a distinguished part in human redemption.

Justin Martyr, the first who supposed the *Logos* to be personally Christ pre-existent, about the middle of the second century, used such language as this: "God, and the Son that came from him, and the host of other good angels who accompany and resemble him, together with the prophetic Spirit, we adore and venerate; in word and truth honoring them." Again: "We place the Son in the second place, and the prophetic Spirit in the third." Again: "The *Logos* in the second place, and the Spirit which moved on the water in the third." Tertullian, later, said: "It is that Spirit which we call the *Word* [*Logos*]. For the Spirit is the substance of the Word, and the Word the operation of the Spirit, and those two are one." But in another place he said: "The Spirit is a third after God and the Son; as the fruit, proceeding from the branch, is the third from the root." Origen, in the third century, suspected the Holy Spirit might be a creature of Christ, since all things were said to have been made by him. Other fathers of those times asserted that the Comforter [The Paraclete], the Spirit, was made by Christ, and less than Christ.

So speculations went on, with various definitions, till the Councils of Nice and of Constantinople, in the fourth century, the last of which nearly completed the dogma of the Trinity, with reference to the third person, as well as to the first and second. But the final finish was put on by the Athanasian Creed, in the fifth or sixth century, as I have already quoted it. Still, there was one important hair left to split, namely, whether the Holy Ghost proceeds from the Father alone or from both the Father and Son. The creedists made a nice distinction between the terms *unbegotten*, *begotten*, and *proceeding*. They said the Father is *unbegotten*, the Son *begotten* from eternity of the Father, and the Holy Ghost eternally *proceeding*. At first the creed stood, that this *proceeding* was from the Father alone. But in the year 447 a Synod in Spain altered the creed in that country, so as to make it say, "From the Father and the Son." Other sections of the church followed, till nearly all in Western Europe read the creed thus: "I believe in the Holy Spirit, which from all eternity proceeded from the Father and the Son." At this the Greek Church, so called, whose metropolis was Constantinople, as that of the Western was Rome, took fatal offence. For they held fast to the old doctrine that the third person in the Trinity *proceeds* eternally from the *unbegotten* first person, the Father. There was much bitter and unyielding controversy between the parties on this theological crotchet. At length, in the year 1054, the two churches separated, and mutually excommunicated each other as heretics, chiefly on account of this petty metaphysical disagreement. Thus the world was presented with the astonishing spectacle of the great Christian Church splitting asunder on the difference between *tweedledee* and *tweedledum*. After spending nine hundred years in inventing and figmenting an inexplicable dogma, never fit to be imposed on the common body of believers, the theological managers fell into this quarrel about mere terms, and are likely to spend nine hundred more in exhibiting the fruits of their anti-Christian wisdom. They have already continued their hostile rivalry for over eight hundred years. About one third of the church, as it then was, took the Greek side, and two thirds the Romish side. At this time the Greek Church, which is the established one of the Russian empire, numbers about seventy-eight millions, and the Romish liberty, free discussion, and conscientious dissent, which themselves had hoisted, and became persecutors of the few noble minds that outran them, and opposed these still cherished corruptions. But the wheels of progress and reform could only be hindered, they could not be stopped. Science, general knowledge, and civilization advanced. Civil and religious liberty advanced. Moral and social reform advanced. Theology and ecclesiasticism improved, by means of research, free discussion, and sectarian divisions, slowly indeed, circuitously, zigzagly, and sometimes almost absurdly, but improved. Constantly the momentum and velocity of progress have increased. Pulling down and building up anew, or leaving the ruins of the old unreplaced with anything as a substitute, have marked the onward march of mind. Scepticism and iconoclasm have played a vigorous part against conservatism, and we have now reached a transitional epoch, which will probably last for several centuries, but which, I believe, will result in a better social organization, both in church and state, than has ever yet been known on earth. This will not come from new fundamental principles of faith and practice, but from clearly understanding, rescuing from corruption, and faithfully applying in every department of human activity, the pure and sublime principles taught and exemplified by Jesus Christ. Whoever dreams of any essentially higher religion than his, will dream in vain; and still vainer will be the dreams of those who imagine that any kind of mere science or philosophy is to be the substitute for positive religious principles. But we must have the *genuine* Christian religion, doctrinally and practically, no corrupt adulteration of it. For this I study and work. In this endeavor, may God enable all in heartily to concur! Then his shall be the glory, and man's the bliss.

ARTICLE III.

THE NATURE AND EFFICACY OF THE ATONEMENT.

DISCOURSE VIII.

THE PURE PRIMITIVE DOCTRINE OF THE ATONEMENT.

"For if when we were enemies, we were reconciled to God by the death of his Son; much more, being reconciled, we shall be saved by his life. And not only so, but we also joy in God through our Lord Jesus Christ, by whom we have now received the atonement."
— Rom. v. 10, 11.

Any solemn act or process which is made an indispensable basis, consideration, or condition of reconciliation between two parties at variance with each other is called atonement, literally *at-one-ment;* because it brings them to be *at one*, or in unison. The original Greek word (katallagē) rendered *atonement* in our text is elsewhere, throughout the New Testament, rendered *reconciliation*. The Christian atonement is that grand process of self-sacrifice whereby Christ insured the reconciliation of mankind to God. It was consummated by his death on the cross. What, then, is the pure primitive Christian doctrine of atonement? Our chief reliance, for a correct answer to this inquiry, must be on the New Testament Scriptures. I will endeavor to state and explain the doctrine as taught in these Scriptures, according to my own best understanding.

The simple doctrine itself seems to me to be this: That God in his love and wisdom foreordained the self-sacrifice of Christ as the indispensable process in virtue of which, that is, through the moral influence of which, he would reconcile the world of mankind unto himself, and render all human beings spiritually Christ-like. Therefore he guarantees a full remission or forgiveness of past sins, and acceptance into his communion, unto every human soul who confidingly, penitently, and obediently, embraces and follows Christ. This was substantially the great central and vital doctrine preached by Jesus, his apostles, and evangelists, in gathering the primitive Christian church. It was a very potent, comprehensive, and effectual doctrine, as they expounded and applied it. Let us try to understand it, in itself, and in its most important bearings.

1. What was the self-sacrifice of Christ? It included all that he voluntarily suffered for the benefit of mankind, — all his temptations, anxieties, and sorrows in their behalf; all his poverty, humiliations, privations, and painstakings to do them good; all his efforts and endeavors, amid contradiction, perverseness, reproach, and opposition, to teach them fundamental religious truth and righteousness; all that it cost him of solicitude, struggle, and perseverance to exemplify the perfect holiness he preached; all that he suffered from the false accusation, persecution, and cruelty, which culminated in his crucifixion, — in fine, all that he endured of care, grief, and pain, in the

execution of his official mission as the Christ. All this he and his apostles declared that he *voluntarily* suffered on the principle of self-sacrificing love to God, man, and the divine laws of order; not from any external necessity, or accidental misfortune, much less from any sinful desert, or folly of his own. This is a very important point in the doctrine of Christian atonement; for the pre-eminent excellency of Christ's self-sacrifice lies in its voluntariness, foresight, and choice, on his part, when, if he had been selfish and lower principled in his motives, he might have avoided it.

2. How came there to be such a Son of man and Son of God, morally disposed to execute such a sublime process of self-sacrifice? Did it happen by some wonderful chance or accident? No. It was foreordained and amply provided for by God the Father, as part of his original purpose in behalf of the human race. For what did he create them? A destiny of immortality, holiness, and happiness; and there was a wisest and best method for carrying them up out of rudimental ignorance, folly, and sinfulness, through ages of discipline, to that glorious destiny. Our Christ was their foreordained prophet, priest, and king, — just the one to execute this process of all-redeeming self-sacrifice.

3. Yet why and how was such a process of self-sacrifice necessary, yea indispensably necessary, to the grand result? Not to placate an angry God, not to appease his holy wrath, not to satisfy his penal justice, not to render him more loving, merciful, or forgiving, towards mankind, — not to reconcile *him* to them, but

them to him. How? By making an unequivocal and most demonstrative manifestation of God's moral character, love, wisdom, and holiness, in word and deed. God spoke through him by his indwelling Holy Spirit; he thereby lived in his life, loved in his loves, worked in his deeds, and manifested his own moral perfections through him. Remember that the Son claimed nothing as merely of himself; it was all of the Father. How else could he have showed us the Father? How else could we have seen, and understood, and learned to appreciate the Father's pure holiness, profound love, and tender compassion toward his sinful creatures? How else could we have been drawn to the Father, and become reconciled to him, as his obedient children? Beautiful and blessed doctrine! In the holy sympathy of the Son, we feel assured of the infinite Father's sympathy for all his erring and suffering offspring. Through him we are drawn into the divine bosom, weeping for our sins, and, freely accepted, bidden to "go and sin no more." Was not such a process of self-sacrifice indispensably necessary to bring us home to our Father's house?

But it was equally necessary for another great purpose: To show us how we must come to feel and act, in order to be truly wise, holy, and happy. Christ was the true moral representative of the regenerate man, — the living sample of what he suffered so much to render man in spirit, conduct, and character. He was our model, and forerunner. We must come into the same receptive, submissive, and dutiful relations; we must put on the same humility, meekness, truthfulness, purity, forbearance, patience, and self-sacrificing charity; we must come into the fellowship of his sufferings; we must be baptized with the same Holy Spirit, and become its living soul-temples; we must suffer and die, if need be, for others, even our enemies, as he did; we must learn to be obedient sons and daughters of God, as he was; in fine, we must put on Christ, and grow into true Christ-likeness. He is "the way, the truth, and the life" for us. And in striving with all our heart, mind, and strength, for this, the same Father who helped him on to victory will see that his strength is made perfect in our weakness, and that his grace is sufficient for us. It was indispensably necessary that the Captain of our salvation should leave us the perfect example he did, in executing that transcendent process of self-sacrifice. Else we should not have known our own highest duty as his disciples, nor understood that, without the same spirit and its fruits, we are none of his, and can never enter into his glory until ransomed from the bondage of selfishness. Alas, for those deluded souls who vainly imagine that his merits will be imputed to them without profoundly reverencing and habitually cherishing his spirit of self-sacrifice!

4. How is it that God guarantees a full remission or forgiveness of past sins, and acceptance into his communion, unto every human soul who confidingly, penitently, and obediently embraces and follows his Son? This is all that any sinner can do; it is the best he can do, even with divine aid. What more should such a heavenly Father as Jesus revealed require of sinners? The gospel of Christ is preached to them; it touches

their hearts; it convicts them of their sinfulness and alienation from God; it shows them that nothing but just condemnation, darkness, and unhappiness were before them in their downward course; it promises them peace and joy in the new life offered them under Christ; and it says, "Go and sin no more." They half believe in the Father and Son, — in the gospel; but, alas, what a load of guilt and shame and despondence weighs them down, in view of their past sins and follies! How can they hold up their heads? How can such a soul hope to be received, even as the humblest servant, into his heavenly Father's household? He is repentant; he is ready to make restitution and reparation for wrongs done to fellow-man so far as he can; but it is almost nothing that he can do, at best, to undo what he has done amiss; he longs to enter on a new and reformed life; and he is willing to follow and obey the blessed Christ in the future, if only this dreadful load of conscious guilt can be lifted from his shoulders, and he can be helped into newness of life. So he bows down under his burden, weeps, prays, and knows not what to do. The self-righteousness of men has no sympathy with him. Human respectability turns its back upon him, and says, "Thou hast made thy bed; lie down in thy shame and sorrow." Bold philosophy bids him bear his burden with stoical firmness, and drink the dregs of his ill-mingled cup without complaint till it be emptied. It frigidly tells him "there is no such thing in this universe as the forgiveness of sins, nothing but unmitigated penalties, which must in all cases be paid to the uttermost farthing." And the godless scoffer cries out at him, "O fool, cease to trouble thyself for the past; it is water spilled on the ground that cannot be gathered up; away with this superstition; put on a bold face; lay hold on pleasure where thou canst find it; eat, drink, be merry, and drown thy sorrow in the exhilarating stream of sensual gratification." Not so the sympathetic Christ; not so the loving, compassionate all-Father; not so the holy angels of heaven; not so the true Christian soul. A voice comes in gentle strains from the divine sanctuary: "Poor child, thou hast done what thou couldst; thy sins are forgiven thee; thou art welcome to thy Father's house and service; I will never cast thee out; I will never reproach or condemn thee for thy past; go and sin no more; I will never leave nor forsake thee; only learn to love, pity, and forgive others, as I have loved, pitied, and forgiven thee." And all heaven reverberates with melodious pæans of "Amen." The forgiven one is not released from the mere natural consequences of transgressed laws. Some of these may last long, and but slowly lose their bitterness; yet he can now bear them hopefully; for the heavenly Father and all his family have spoken peace to his soul, and sanctified his remaining troubles for his everlasting good.

5. Finally, what is the end and aim of all this? — this grand process of self-sacrificing atonement; this Christly manifestation of the infinite Father in his true moral perfections; this sampling of regenerate humanity; this modelhood of Jesus as our moral exemplar; this forgiveness of sins upon faith, repentance, and fidelity to the holy Master. What is it? Recon-

ciliation of sinners to God, as fast as they can be convicted and converted. Then willing, confirmed, habitual obedience of the regenerate, till at length no temptation in the universe shall have the least charm to draw them into sin again while God exists. And this convicting, converting, and regenerating work is to go on, and on, and on, till Christ shall have impressed his moral likeness on every soul for whom he suffered and died, yea, till all things shall be subdued unto him, and God "be all in all."

Is it any wonder that such a gospel, and such a doctrine of reconciliation, preached by such a Christ, and his inspired apostles, stirred the human souls to whom it was proclaimed as none were ever stirred before? Too many Pharisees, in their self-righteousness, rejected the counsel of God, and spurned a salvation that welcomed publicans and harlots, through faith and repentance, into the kingdom of heaven. Too many Sadducees turned away with contempt and unbelief. Too many philosophers disputed and cavilled. But some of all these classes responded gratefully to the appeals of truth and love. The common people heard gladly, and penitent magdalens, prodigals, publicans, and sinners, with tears of joy, entered by faith into the great Reconciler's church, — the fold of the good Shepherd, so willing to lay down his life for the sheep. Behold the woman washing his feet with her tears of contrition and wiping them with her dishevelled hair! Hear Zaccheus, the rich publican, exclaim, "The half of my goods I give to the poor, and if I have wronged any man, I restore unto him fourfold!" See the throngs of publicans and sinners that reverently draw near to him while phylacteried scribes murmur at him, saying, "This man receiveth sinners, and eateth with them!" Mark, then, his significant answer: "I am not come to call the righteous, but sinners, to repentance." Hear what the officers said, when asked by the rulers why they had not arrested him: "Never man spake like this man!" Note the message he sent back to the great Baptist in prison, when he had inquired through two of his disciples: "Art thou he that should come, or do we look for another?" "Go and show John those things which ye do hear and see. The blind receive their sight, the lame walk, the lepers are cleansed, the deaf hear, the dead are raised up, and the poor have the gospel preached unto them." Matt. xi. 3–5. Finally, behold him in his agony on the cross, his precious blood trickling down to the ground from those spiked hands and feet, speaking words of pardon and comfort to the penitent thief, commending his broken-hearted mother to the care of the beloved John, and praying for his murderers, saying, "Father, forgive them, for they know not what they do!" Do we wonder that the centurion exclaimed, "Truly this man was the Son of God!" Do we wonder that such an impersonation of self-sacrificing love should command the highest veneration and love of his disciples, and of the purest souls in all after ages? Do we wonder that his death, and blood, and cross should be regarded as the most sacred symbols of human redemption, the grandest and most acceptable offering ever made to God in behalf of sinful and suffering humanity; the one conclusive and perfect atonement, efficacious for the regeneration of the whole world; the unblemished self-sacrifice of the Lamb of God, the Prince of martyrs, Prince of love, and Prince of peace? Not the infinitely punished substitute of a guilty race, quenching the wrath of an offended God in his own vital blood; but the model Son of man, and peerless Son of God, illustrating the highest human and divine loves by the sacrifice of himself as a ransom for all human kind from the bondage of selfishness, sin, and corruption. Such is the pure primitive Christian doctrine of atonement. I will demonstrate it by adequate proofs in my next discourse, and afterwards proceed to show wherein and how it became most grossly corrupted.

And now let me close by suggesting to you, how completely the excellency and glory of Christ would be blotted out by reversing the character he acquired in this grand process of voluntary self-sacrifice. Just suppose him to have been a poor, overtasked, cruelized, and finally crucified slave, with little knowledge or foresight, with no sublime moral motives in respect to God or man, compelled to toil and suffer most grievously unto death by tyrannical brute force. Then, oh, how much to be pitied, but how little to be venerated and glorified! On the other hand, suppose him to have been a worldly monarch, prince, or courtier, surrounded by regal splendor and luxury, exercising the power of life and death over millions of subjects; or a prince of wealth, like Crœsus, and worshipping mammon; or a great military hero and conqueror, like Alexander or Cæsar; or a famous philosopher, like Plato, of masterly intellect in abstract ideas, but with little practical love to God or man; or a world-admired poet, artist, or scientist, yet a selfish, sensual voluptuary; or a Rt. Rev. Pontiff on a spiritual and temporal throne, his feet kissed by superstitious slaves, and his authority supported by mercenary soldiers and inquisitors! Then we should have had no Christ, and no redeeming self-sacrifice of the cross; no "Lamb of God that taketh away the sin of the world!"

ARTICLE III.

THE NATURE AND EFFICACY OF THE ATONEMENT.

DISCOURSE IX.

THE PURE PRIMITIVE DOCTRINE OF THE ATONEMENT VERIFIED.

"In this was manifested the love of God toward us, because that God sent his only begotten Son into the world, that we might live through him." — 1 John iv. 9.

In my last discourse I stated and illustrated what I understand to be the pure primitive Christian doctrine of atonement. I promised, in this, to verify my statement of the doctrine by proofs from the New Testament Scriptures. Let me repeat my doctrinal statement: God in his love and wisdom foreordained the self-sacrifice of Christ as the indispensable process in virtue of which, that is, through the moral influence of which, he would reconcile the world of mankind unto himself, and render all human beings spiritually Christ-like. Therefore he guarantees a full remission, or forgiveness, of past sins, and acceptance into his communion, unto every human soul who confidingly, penitently, and obediently embraces and follows Christ.

Here are several prominent ideas to be kept distinctly in view: 1. That God in his love and wisdom foreordained this atonement; 2. That it consists in the voluntary self-sacrifice of Christ; 3. That it was indispensable as a process of moral power; 4. That its design was to reconcile mankind to God by rendering them spiritually Christ-like; 5. That it was intended to effect the reconciliation of all mankind; 6. That God guarantees the remission, or forgiveness, of past sins and acceptance into his communion, to believers in it; and, 7. That those only are regarded as true believers who confidingly, penitently, and obediently embrace and follow Christ. In the preceding discourse I explained and amplified these points. What I am now to attempt is, verification of the doctrine stated, as the pure primitive one taught by Christ and his apostles. Each of the texts cited will present one or more of the above seven distinctive ideas. I will follow the general order of those ideas, as nearly as the nature of the case allows.

1. God in his love and wisdom foreordained this atonement. In the twenty-fourth chapter of Luke's Gospel, we have an interesting account of Christ's appearing, after his death, to two of his disciples on their way from Jerusalem to the village of Emmaus. They did not recognize him; for "their eyes were holden that they should not know him." So he entered into conversation with them. They were in a disconsolate state of mind, and dwelt very naturally on the subject of his recent, to them calamitous, death. After allowing them full opportunity to unbosom themselves, he said unto them, "O fools, and slow of heart to believe all that the prophets have spoken! Ought not Christ to have suffered these things,

and to enter into his glory?" Verses 25, 26. See the whole context. In the same chapter, at his interview with the eleven apostles, he said unto them, "These are the words which I spake unto you, while I was yet with you, that all things must be fulfilled which were written in the law of Moses and in the prophets, and in the psalms, concerning me." "Thus it is written, and thus it behooved Christ to suffer, and to rise from the dead the third day." Verses 44, 46.

In his prayer, just before arrest, as recorded in the seventeenth chapter of John's Gospel, he said, "I have glorified thee on the earth: I have finished the work which thou gavest me to do. And now, O Father, glorify thou me with thine own self, with the glory which I had with thee [that is, in design, or purpose] before the world was." Again: "For thou lovedst me before the foundation of the world." Verses 4, 5, 24.

The Apostle Peter thus testified: "Him, being delivered by the determinate counsel and foreknowledge of God, ye have taken, and by wicked hands have crucified and slain." Acts ii. 24. Again: "Ye were not redeemed with corruptible things, as silver and gold, from your vain conversation received by tradition from your fathers: but with the precious blood of Christ, as of a lamb without blemish and without spot: Who verily was foreordained before the foundation of the world, but was manifested in these last times for you." 1 Pet. i. 18–20. Paul said, "Unto me, who am less than the least of all saints, is this grace given, that I should preach among the Gentiles the unsearchable riches of Christ; and to make all men see what is the fellowship of the mystery, which from the beginning of the world hath been hid in God, . . . according to the eternal purpose which he purposed in Christ Jesus our Lord." Ephes. iii. 8, 9, 11. Also: "For when we were yet without strength, in due time Christ died for the ungodly. For scarcely for a righteous man will one die: yet peradventure for a good man some would even dare to die. But God commendeth his love toward us in that while we were yet sinners Christ died for us." Rom. v. 6–8. Again: "God who is rich in mercy, for his great love wherewith he loved us, even when we were dead in sins, hath quickened us together with Christ." Ephes. ii. 4, 5. John said: "Herein is love, not that we loved God, but that he loved us, and sent his Son *to be* the propitiation for our sins." 1 John iv. 10.

2. Our next grand idea of the Christian atonement is, that it consists in the voluntary self-sacrifice of Christ. This is declared in such passages as the following: "Whosoever will be chief among you, let him be your servant: even as the Son of man came not to be ministered unto, but to minister, and to give his life a ransom for many." Matt. xx. 27, 28. "As the Father knoweth me, even so I know the Father: and I lay down my life for the sheep." "Therefore doth my Father love me, because I lay down my life, that I might take it again. No man taketh it from me, but I lay it down of myself. I have power to lay it down, and I have power to take it again. This commandment have I received of my Father." John x. 15, 17, 18. "For ye know the grace of our Lord Jesus Christ, that though he was rich, yet for your

sakes he became poor, that ye through his poverty might be rich." 2 Cor. viii. 9. "Who being in the form of God [as to the dignity of his Christly office] thought it not robbery to be equal with God [more correctly *like God*, as to personal authority]. But made himself of no reputation, and took upon him the form of a servant, and was made in the likeness of men: and being found in fashion as a man became obedient unto death, even the death of the cross." Philip. ii. 6, 8. "If the blood of bulls and of goats, and the ashes of an heifer sprinkling the unclean sanctifieth to the purifying of the flesh, how much more shall the blood of Christ, who through the eternal Spirit offered himself without spot to God, purge your conscience from dead works to serve the living God?" Heb. ix. 13, 14. "For Christ is not entered into the holy places made with hands, the figures of the true; but into heaven itself, now to appear in the presence of God for us. Nor yet that he should offer himself often, as the high priest entereth into the holy place every year with blood of others: for then must he often have suffered since the foundation of the world: but now once in the end of the world [the consummation of the age] hath he appeared to put away sin by the sacrifice of himself." Ibid. verses 24–26.

3. The next prominent idea of the Christian atonement is, that it was indispensable as a process of moral power. There was an indispensable moral necessity for it, in order to reconcile mankind to God, through its influence on human nature, in bringing them to repentance and holiness of life. This is set forth in the

following and similar passages: "I am the living bread which came down from heaven: if any man eat of this bread, he shall live forever: and the bread that I will give is my flesh, which I will give for the life of the world." "Verily I say unto you, except ye eat the flesh of the Son of man, and drink his blood, ye have no life in you." "He that eateth my flesh, and drinketh my blood, dwelleth in me, and I in him." John vi. 51, 53, 56. As some murmured at the literal sense of this language, Jesus explained his meaning: "It is the Spirit that quickeneth; the flesh profiteth nothing; the words that I speak unto you are spirit, and are life." Verse 63. "I, if I be lifted up (that is, by my self-sacrificing death on the cross), will draw all men unto me." Ibid. xii. 32. Peter said: "This is the stone which is set at nought of you builders, which is become the head of the corner. Neither is there salvation in any other: for there is none other name under heaven given among men whereby we must be saved." Acts iv. 11, 12. Paul said: "Who gave himself for our sins, that he might deliver us from this present evil world, according to the will of God." Gal. i. 4. Again: "Be ye therefore followers of God as dear children; and walk in love, as Christ also hath loved us, and hath given himself for us, an offering and a sacrifice to God for a sweet-smelling savor." Ephes. v. 1, 2. Again: "Who gave himself for us, that he might redeem us from all iniquity, and purify unto himself a peculiar people zealous of good works." Titus ii. 14. Peter said: "If when ye do well, and suffer, ye take it patiently, this is acceptable to God. For even hereunto were ye called; because Christ also suffered for us, leaving us an example, that ye should follow his steps; who did no sin, neither was guile found in his mouth: who, when he was reviled, reviled not again: when he suffered he threatened not; but committed himself to him that judgeth righteously: who his own self bare our sins in his own body on the tree, that we, being dead to sins, should live unto righteousness: by whose stripes ye were healed." 1 Pet. ii. 20–24. Again: "It is better, if the will of God be so, that ye suffer for well-doing, than for evil-doing. For Christ also hath suffered for sins, the just for the unjust, that he might bring us to God." Ibid. iii. 17, 18.

4. Next comes the great, comprehensive idea, that the Christian atonement was designed to reconcile mankind to God by rendering them spiritually Christlike. Several of the testimonies just cited plainly involve this idea. But I will present a few others, perhaps more explicit: "The disciple is not above his master; but every one that is perfect shall be as his master." Luke vi. 40. "I have given you an example, that ye should do as I have done unto you." John xii. 15. "I pray, that they all may be one; as thou, Father, art in me, and I in thee, that they also may be one in us," "even as we are one: I in them, and thou in me, that they may be made perfect." Ib. xvii. 20, 23. Paul said: "For whom he did foreknow, he also did predestinate to be conformed to the image of his Son, that he might be the first-born among many brethren." Rom. viii. 29. Again: "Till we all come in the unity of the faith, and of the knowledge of the Son of God, unto a perfect man,

unto the measure of the stature of the fulness of Christ." Ephes. iv. 13.

5. The fifth cardinal idea in the Christian atonement was its universality. It was for the benefit of all mankind. "Behold the Lamb of God, that taketh away the sin of the world!" John i. 29. "For God sent not his Son into the world to condemn the world, but that the world through him might be saved." Ibid. iii. 17. "I, if I be lifted up from the earth [that is, by death on the cross], will draw all men unto me." Ibid. xii. 32. "For it pleased the Father that in him should all fulness dwell; and having made peace through the blood of his cross, by him to reconcile all things unto himself; by him, whether things in earth, or things in heaven." Col. i. 19, 20. "For there is one God, and one mediator between God and men, the man Christ Jesus; who gave himself a ransom for all to be testified in due time." 1 Tim. ii. 5, 6. "We see Jesus, who was made a little lower than the angels for the suffering of death, crowned with glory and honor, that he by the grace of God should taste death for every man." Heb. ii. 9. "And he is the propitiation for our sins: and not for ours only, but for the sins of the whole world." 1 John ii. 2.

6. God guarantees the remission, or forgiveness, of past sins, and acceptance into his communion, to sincere believers in this atonement, that is, in Christ its great offerer. Here be careful not to infer that God never did or can forgive the sins of his penitent creatures without their having knowledge and faith in Christ. This is not the idea; because many true

souls, before and since Christ's atonement, were ignorant of it, yet found acceptance with God. Be careful, furthermore, not to infer that this atonement rendered God any more merciful than before. It was only his highest and most orderly method of inducting the masses of mankind into acceptance and communion with himself. Nor yet must we imagine this atonement to be a price paid to God, or a debt due him from sinful man, which, being paid, past sins are cancelled thereby, and Christ's merits imputed to believers. But we must understand that the process was a powerful moral one for bringing believers into that highest and best state of mind in which past sins can be forgiven, and they accepted into free spiritual communion with their heavenly Father. Thus is it taught in such passages as the following: "It behooved Christ to suffer, and to rise from the dead the third day. And that repentance and remission of sins should be preached in his name among all nations, beginning at Jerusalem." Luke xxiv. 46, 47. "Those things which God before had showed by the mouth of all his prophets, that Christ should suffer, he hath so fulfilled. Repent ye therefore and be converted, that your sins may be blotted out, when the times of refreshing shall come from the presence of the Lord." Peter, Acts iii. 18, 19. "To him give all the prophets witness, that through his name whosoever believeth in him shall receive remission of sins." Peter, Acts x. 43. "Be it known unto you therefore, men and brethren, that through this man is preached unto you the forgiveness of sins; and by him all that believe are justified from all things, from which ye could not be justified by the law of Moses." Paul, Acts xiii. 38, 39. See also Rom. iii. 23–26. "Having predestinated us unto the adoption of children by Jesus Christ to himself, according to the good pleasure of his will, to the praise of the glory of his grace, wherein he hath made us accepted in the Beloved: in whom we have redemption through his blood, the forgiveness of sins, according to the riches of his grace." Ephes. i. 5, 7.

7. Finally, comes the important idea, that those only are regarded as true believers who confidingly, penitently, and obediently embrace and follow Christ. If mere profession were enough, Christianity would be worthless; for it would leave mankind just where it found them, — dead in sin, unreconciled to God, and aliens from him by wicked works. Its object is to render them morally Christ-like, holy, and happy. Therefore any professed faith in him and his atonement which does not work by love and purify the heart, is not only useless and vain, but a mockery. Hence the following testimonies:—

"If any man will come after me, let him deny himself, and take up his cross, and follow me." Matt. xvi. 24; Luke ix. 23. "By their fruits ye shall know them. Not every one that saith unto me, Lord, Lord, shall enter into the kingdom of heaven; but he that doeth the will of my Father who is in heaven." Matt. vii. 20, 21. Read also verses 22, 23, etc. "And why call ye me Lord, Lord, and do not the things which I say?" Luke vi. 46. "Now, if any man have not the Spirit of Christ, he is none of his. And if Christ be in you the body is dead because of sin; but the spirit is life because of righteousness." Rom. viii. 9, 10. "What doth it profit, my brethren, though a man say he hath faith, and have not works? Can faith save him? If a brother or sister be naked, and destitute of daily food, and one of you say unto them: Depart in peace, be ye warmed and filled; notwithstanding ye give them not those things which are needful to the body, what doth it profit? Even so faith, if it have not works, is dead, being alone. James ii. 14–17. "If we say that we have fellowship with him, and walk in darkness, we lie and do not the truth. But if we walk in the light, as he is in the light, we have fellowship one with another, and the blood of Jesus Christ his Son cleanseth us from all sin." 1 John i. 6, 7. "Hereby perceive we the love of God, because he laid down his life for us: and we ought to lay down our lives for the brethren. But whoso hath this world's good, and seeth his brother have need, and shutteth up his bowels of compassion from him, how dwelleth the love of God in him?" 1 John iii. 16, 18.

Here I close. I think I have not only stated correctly the pure primitive doctrine of Christian atonement, but proved my correct understanding of it by the extracts made from the New Testament Scriptures. The samples given are fair and just. They pertinently, consistently, conclusively, and beautifully illustrate the seven cardinal ideas of the true atonement. In my next I will commence to show how and when this primitive doctrine became corrupted.

ARTICLE III.

THE NATURE AND EFFICACY OF THE ATONEMENT.

DISCOURSE X.

WHEREIN, WHEN, AND HOW THE PRIMITIVE DOCTRINE WAS FIRST CORRUPTED.

"Beware lest any man spoil you through philosophy and vain deceit, after the tradition of men, after the rudiments of the world, and not after Christ." — COL. ii. 8.

The first corruption of the pure primitive Christian doctrine of atonement supposed that the sufferings and death of Jesus were a price paid to Satan for the ransom of mankind out of his power. Such a notion seems to us of these days incredibly absurd. Yet it was the prevailing orthodoxy of the church, in respect to the atonement, for at least three centuries, commencing in the latter half of the second century. It originated, like most other theological corruptions, with the converted philosophers and metaphysicians who took the lead of the church after the apostolic age. They had deified Christ, and they must needs give corresponding explanations of the nature and efficacy of his atonement. They did not change the original distinctive character of it, as a voluntary self-sacrifice, the purest and sublimest martyrdom; but reiterated and magnified this view of it for a long period. Yet they felt bound to show that its grand design was to ransom mankind from the captivity of sin, death, and hell, in which Satan held the whole human race.

To understand correctly their doctrine on this point we must understand their antecedent and correlative notions concerning Satan, human sinfulness, the penalty for sin, and the dominion of the underworld, or Hades. All the primitive Christians, and their successors for a long time, were established in the belief that there was a vast underworld, having various apartments for different classes, into which human souls, both righteous and wicked, from the beginning of the race, had descended at death. It was believed to be an immense cavernous region in the bowels of the earth, — a subterranean world, of more or less imperfect existence even to the best souls, and a gloomy prison to all the more sinful classes. Indeed, they held it to be a kind of prison to the whole human race; though the patriarchs, prophets, and saints enjoyed there comparative quietude and the comfortable hope of an ultimate resurrection to heavenly realms. Physical death was only a necessary preliminary to the descent of souls into the underworld, and the grave, or sepulchre, the external doorway thither. Satan was held to be the Lord of that underworld, holding all departed spirits and demons there as his prisoners and subjects. He allowed none to come out thence, except such demons as he could employ in works of mischief and destruction in the upper world and its atmosphere — to delude, harass, and afflict mortal humanity. Satan, having first seduced mankind into alienation from God and thus got possession of them, became their accuser, punisher, and supreme jailor. And all this was so in accordance with God's penal law, which gave them over to the dreadful control of the evil master they had chosen to serve. Thus, by reason of original and consequent sin, the whole human race became legitimate captives of Satan, and so his prisoners in the underworld.

Now the grand desideratum was how to recover mankind from this captivity to Satan. A ransom must be paid to the great jailor, who legitimately held them, body and soul, under his power of death. Our philosophical theologians had seized on several strong figurative phrases of Christ and the apostles, such as "ransom," "redemption," "death tasted," "bought with a price," "purchased with his own blood," etc. etc.; all which they interpreted to signify, more or less clearly, that the chief object of Christ's atonement was to ransom mankind from Satan, and to get the keys of the underworld into his strong hand, so as to insure the resurrection of all the dead at his own pleasure. Their notions were not very clear, much less coherent, on the subject; nor did they entirely agree among themselves just how the ransom was paid to Satan. But the result was, that Christ, by means of his self-sacrificing toils, sufferings, and death, got lawful possession of all Satan's captives, went down himself into the underworld, took the keys of death and hell, preached his gospel there to the long confined prisoners, and actually ascended thence in triumph, leading up into resurrection glory a host of ancient patriarchs, prophets, and saints.

But say you, with astonishment, Were these really the predominant beliefs of the Christians for several centuries? Certainly they were. Ecclesiastical history, and the writings of the fathers that have reached our times, leave not a shadow of doubt of it. I will now give you a few extracts from those Christian fathers, that you may judge for yourselves.

Hear what Origen taught. He was born A.D. 185, and died 254. He was the most illustrious among the Christian doctors of his time. Commenting on the passage in 1 Peter i. 18, 19, he wrote thus: "If, therefore, we were bought with a price, we were bought, doubtless, from some one whose slaves we were, and who demanded such a price as he pleased for the release of those whom he held. It was the devil, however, who held us, to whom we had been allotted (or into whose power we had been dragged), by our sins. He therefore demanded as our price the blood of Christ." Again: "Here I would admonish of their error those who, from a conceit of glorifying Christ, confound what pertains to the First-born of the whole creation with what refers to the soul and body of Jesus, or perhaps to his spirit; regarding what was seen and dwelt in this life as wholly one and unconfounded. For they inquire of us, Was the Divinity which inhered in the image of the invisible God, . . . was he given as a ransom? and to whom was he given? To an enemy who held us captives until the ransom was paid? And was that enemy competent to exact such a ransom? I do not say these things as despising the SOUL of Jesus, or making it of small account. I only contend that it was the ransom given by the whole Saviour." Again: "It is requisite, for some secret and incomprehensible reasons in nature, that the voluntary death of a righteous man should disarm the power of evil demons, who do mischief by means of plagues, dearths, tempests, etc. Is it not probable, therefore, that Christ died to break the power of the great demon, the prince of the other demons, who has in his power the souls of all the men that ever lived in the world?"

Irenæus, a cotemporary with Origen, said: "Christ would not have had real flesh and blood wherewith to buy us out, unless he had been recapitulating in himself the old formation in Adam." "And since the Apostate acquired his mastery over us unjustly, the Word behaved justly even to the Apostate, redeeming from him his own, not by force, as he [Satan] originally mastered us when he seized rapaciously what was not his, but by persuasion, and as became a divine being, persuading him without violence to accept what he wished."

St. Augustine, who lived later, and died A.D. 430, differed widely from Origen on several points of doctrine, but not in respect to the point before us. His language was: "What is the power of that blood, in which, if we believe, we shall be saved, and what is the meaning of being reconciled by the death of his Son? Was God the Father so angry with us that he could not be pacified without the death of his Son? By the justice of God, the race of man was delivered to the devil; the sin of the first man being transferred to all his posterity, the debt of their first parents binding them: not that God did it, or desired it, but he permitted them to be so delivered. But the goodness of God did not forsake them, though in the devil's power, nor even the devil himself, for he lives by him. If, therefore, the commission of sin, through the just anger of God, subjects man to the power of the devil, the remission of sins, by the gracious forgiveness of God, delivers man from the devil. But the devil was not to be overcome by the power, but by the justice, of God; and it pleased God, that in order to deliver man from the power of the devil, the devil should be overcome, not by power, but by justice. What, then, is the justice by which the devil was conquered? What but the righteousness of Jesus Christ? And how is he conquered? Because, though there was nothing in him worthy of death, he [the devil] killed him. Was not then the devil to have been fairly conquered, though Christ had acted by power, and not by righteousness? But he postponed what he *could* do, in order to do what *ought to be done*. Wherefore it was necessary to be both God and man: man that he might be capable of being killed; and God to show that it was voluntary in him. What could show more power than to rise again, with the very flesh in which he had been killed? He therefore conquered the devil twice; first by righteousness, and then by power." Again: "The blood of Christ is given as a price, and yet the devil, having received it, is not enriched, but bound by it, that we might be delivered from his bonds."

Proclus of Constantinople, a writer of the same age,

but a little later, said: "The devil held us in a state of servitude, boasting that he had bought us. It was necessary, therefore, that, all being condemned, either they should be dragged to death, or a sufficient price be paid; and because no angel had wherewithal to pay it, it remained that God should die for us."

I find but one of the fathers of that age dissenting from the general doctrine that the ransom was paid to the devil. This was Gregory Nazianzen, in the fourth century. He seems to have been shocked at the notion of a price paid to Satan for the liberation of mankind, and rather inclined to think that God himself received the price in some mystical sense. He was quite in doubt how to understand the matter. Here are his words: "To whom and for what was the blood of Christ shed? We were in the possession of the devil, being sold to him for sin, we having received the pleasures of sin in return. But if the price of redemption could only be received by him who had possession of us, I ask *to whom* was this blood paid, and for what cause? For if it was paid to that wicked one, it was shameful indeed; and if he not only received a price from God, but God himself was that price, for such a price it was certainly just that he should spare us. Was the price paid to the Father? But how, for we were not held by him, and how could the Father be delighted with the blood of his only begotten Son, when he would not receive Isaac, who was offered to him by Abraham? Or rather did the Father receive the price, not because he desired or wanted it, but because it was convenient that man should be sanctified by what was human in God, that, by conquering the tyrant, he might deliver us, and bring us to him." Having artificialized and mystified the nature and office of Christ, it is no wonder that those metaphysical doctors were thus muddled on the atonement.

However, they generally concurred in the notion that the ransom was paid to Satan. But when they came to consider just how the matter was carried through, they found themselves involved in almost inextricable difficulties. One of these difficulties was, to understand how the devil could be induced to make such a bargain, or compromise, as, in consideration of one man's sufferings and death, to him of no real value, to give up his whole kingdom, and become himself virtually an outcast and a vagabond in the universe, or, worse still, an abject prisoner! This was to make him a greater simpleton, if possible, than he was a fiend. They concluded, on the whole, that he must have been deceived, partly by himself, and partly by God, and that, after all, there was a mighty struggle in the underworld between him and Christ before the latter mastered the situation.

Hear how Origen explained the case: "To whom did he [Christ] give his soul a ransom for many? Not, of course, to God. Was it then to the Evil One? [Certainly] for he held us in his power until the soul of Jesus should be given him as our ransom. He being deceived by the supposition that he could hold it in subjection, and not perceiving that it must be retained at the cost of torture which he could not endure. Wherefore Death [Satan's principal angel] thinking to have become already his master, is his master no longer; he being rendered "free among the dead," stronger than the power of Death; and so much stronger, that of those whom Death had overcome, all who wished could follow him, Death no longer availing anything against them."

Again: "The adverse powers, when they delivered the Saviour into the hands of men, did not perceive that he was delivered up for the salvation of any; but since none of them knew the "*wisdom of God concealed in a mystery*," they, so far as in their power, delivered him to be killed, that his enemy, Death, might seize him for a subject, as he had seized those who died in Adam." Again: "The Saviour had arranged that the devil should be ignorant of his dispensation, and assumption of a body. Therefore he concealed it at his birth, and afterwards commanded his disciples that they should not make him known, etc." It was the general opinion of the church, in those times, that Satan was in some way deceived, or blinded, respecting Christ's hidden invincibility, and that he did not give up his captives in the underworld till Christ overwhelmed him with a personal victory there. Let me quote again from Origen: "Christ voluntarily 'emptied himself, and took the form of a servant,' and suffered the rule of the tyrant, 'being made obedient unto Death;' by which death he destroyed him who had the dominion of Death, that is, the devil, that he might liberate those who were held by Death. For, having bound the strong one, he went into his house, into the house of Death, into the underworld, and thence plundered his goods, that is, carried off the souls which he held — and thence *ascending on high led captive* the captives."

Irenæus said: "The enemy being in turn conquered, Adam received life; his salvation is the abolition of death. Therefore when the Lord vivified man, that is, when he vivified Adam, death was abolished." "The Word steadfastly bound him [Satan] as his fugitive, and plundered his goods, that is, the men who were detained by him, and whom he used unjustly. And with justice was *he* led captive who had led man captive unjustly; but man was drawn out from the power of his possessor." Ignatius said: "Christ was crucified and died, whilst the inhabitants of heaven, earth, and the underworld looked on. Inhabitants of the underworld, that is, the multitude of those who ascended with the Lord. And he descended into the underworld alone, but ascended with a multitude, and rent the eternal inclosure, and destroyed its middle wall."

The foregoing quotations are sufficiently indicative of the theological views held by the leading doctors of the church in the latter part of the second and the whole of the third and fourth centuries respecting the atonement. They show conclusively enough that the first corruption of this doctrine consisted in supposing it to have been a ransom paid to Satan for the recovery of mankind out of the captivity in which he held them, not merely in this world, but more especially in the underworld of spirits. This did not continue many ages to be the popular notion of Christian atonement. The seeds of a corruption still more subversive of the primitive doctrine had been sown, and in due time brought forth a rank harvest of tares. In my next I will show how the work of adulteration proceeded, and what was its culmination. Meantime how profitable will it be for us to keep in memory the pure primitive doctrine of atonement, cherish it in our hearts, bring forth its fruits in our lives, and learn to discriminate truthfully between it and every phase of its corruptions.

ARTICLE III.

THE NATURE AND EFFICACY OF THE ATONEMENT.

DISCOURSE XI.

PROGRESS AND CULMINATION OF THE CORRUPTION.

"Know ye not that a little leaven leaveneth the whole lump." — 1 Cor. v. 6.

I showed in my last how the pure primitive Christian doctrine of atonement began to be corrupted, toward the end of the second century, by the supposition that it was a ransom paid to Satan for the redemption of mankind held by him as his captives. I stated that this hypothesis prevailed among the theologians of the church for at least three centuries. But the seeds of a much worse corruption were sown in process of time. Indeed, during the latter part of those centuries this evil seed was sown. For you may have observed in my quotation from St. Augustine, in the fifth century, that he represented mankind as having been subjected "*through the just anger of God* to the power of the devil." This idea was a seminal one, and soon germinated into an odious form. For if *the just anger of God at human sin* required that the whole race should be delivered over to the great jailer and tormenter, then that anger lay at the bottom of the matter, and the theological mind had not far to travel to reach the conclusion that God himself must be appeased, rather than Satan. Hence, very naturally and logically, the schoolmen of the church evolved the important idea, that the atonement was necessary to make penal satisfaction for sin to divine justice, and thus to render it consistent for a just God to show mercy to believing penitents. This prominent idea gradually superseded the former one. Satan's claims were ignored, and the present dominant hypothesis of Christian atonement became orthodox. But this development required many centuries. It hardly reached maturity till the Protestant Reformation. I will now trace its progress step by step.

St. Augustine, alias Austin, who died in the fifth century, and from whom I have quoted, seems to have remained the standard expounder of Christianity, at least in the western division of the church, for a long period. Indeed, there were few authors of note who followed him for several centuries, certainly none that superseded or rivalled him as authority in theology. Gregory the Great, who became Pope A.D. 590, is the next eminent writer from whom I am able to quote on this subject. He said: —

"The rust of sin could not be purged without the fire of torment. Christ therefore came without fault, that he might subject himself to voluntary torment, and that he might bear the punishment due to our sins." Yet "Christ might have assisted us without suffering, since he who made us could deliver us from suffering without his own death. But he chose this method, because by it he showed more love to us."

This language indicates the mixture of truth and error in Gregory's views of the atonement, and how difficult it was for him to put his new wine into the primitive bottles.

Theodore Abucara, a Greek Christian writer of the ninth century, taught thus: "God, by his just judgments, demanded of us all the things that are written in the Law; which, when we could not pay, the Lord paid for us, taking upon himself the curse and condemnation to which we were obnoxious." The celebrated Anselm, in the eleventh century, a writer long in high repute, wavered somewhat, yet approximated the unfolding hypothesis. His language was: "Of innumerable other methods by which God, being omnipotent, might have saved men, he chose the death of Christ, that by it he might at the same time manifest his love to men." "Was the Father so angry with men, that unless the Son had died for us, he would not be appeased? No: for the Father had love for us even when we were in our sins." But yet he asserted that "human nature could not be restored unless man paid what for sin he owed to God; and that which Christ ought not to pay but as a man, he was not able to pay but as God; so that there was a necessity that God should be united to man." In the same century, Theophilus, of the Greek Church, said: "The Father was angry; wherefore Christ, being made a mediator, reconciled him to us. How? By bearing what we ought to have borne, namely, death." Thus at length the primitive form of expression, *man reconciled to God*, became reversed, and theology began to teach that *God* was reconciled to man.

St. Thomas Aquinas flourished in the thirteenth century. He was a scholastic theologian of great renown, wrote voluminously, and was of unrivalled authority in the Romish Church down to the time of the Reformation. In his famous work, the *Summa*, he taught as follows: "In consequence of sin man was a debtor to God as a judge, and to the devil as a tormenter. And with respect to God, justice required that man should be redeemed, but not with respect to the devil; so that Christ paid his blood to God, and not to the devil. It was not naturally impossible for God to be reconciled to man without the death of Christ; but this was more convenient, as by this means he obtained more and better gifts by the mere will of God." Again: "God might have remitted the sins of men by his mere will, but it was more convenient to do it by the death of Christ, on account of the various uses which it answered at the same time, especially moral ones, (such as) our being excited to love God, and Christ's example of obedience, humility, and fortitude." But his conclusion was: "The guilt of sin is taken away by the renovating power of grace, and the punishment of Christ as a man making satisfaction to God."

The doctrine of atonement continued in this rather uncertain phase down to the great Lutheran schism, in the sixteenth century. But meantime there arose in the Romish Church the doctrine of supererogation; that is, good works, or righteousness performed by Christ and the saints beyond the absolute requirements of the divine law. St. Thomas and others elaborately demonstrated, in their way, that there was laid up a vast and inexhaustible fund of these extra merits, for which God had been giving the church credit, and that the Pope had received special authority to draw on it, at discretion, for the remission of sins. It was contended that a single drop of Christ's blood was sufficient to redeem the whole human race, so that all the rest was left a legacy to the church to form a treasure, from which indulgences were to be drawn and dispensed by the Roman pontiffs. (See Mosheim.)

Besides this superabundance of Christ's merits, thousands of martyrs and saints had swelled the fund by theirs. Hence arose the scandalous sale of indulgences, which, for liberal sums of money paid into the church coffers, absolved men from the guilt of the darkest crimes, even such as had not yet been committed. This gross abuse roused Luther and his coadjutors to the Reformation.

You may therefore readily understand that those reformers naturally struck for such a form of the doctrine of atonement as would annihilate this malignant fiction of supererogation, and the shameful traffic in indulgences which had been justified on the ground of it. What was the result? The doctrine of the atonement in its most vindictive and abhorrent form. And for this we are mainly indebted to Luther, Calvin, Knox, and their associate reformers of the sixteenth century. The Romanists swung the theological pendulum as far as they could in the direction of mercenary corruption, to fill the Papal treasury, and the reformers, in revolting from their scandalous extreme, pushed it as far as they could to another extreme. Now let us see the shape in which they left the atonement.

First comes the Augsburg Confession, so called, presented by Luther and his followers to the Emperor Charles V., in the year 1530: "Christ died to reconcile the Father to us, and that he might be a true sacrifice for the guilt not only of original sin, but also for all the actual sins of men." The Helvetic Confession more fully expressed the doctrine. It was published in 1536, and approved by all the Protestant churches in Europe. It is therein declared that "Christ took on him, and bore the sins of the world, and satisfied divine justice. God, therefore, on account of the passion and resurrection of Christ only, is propitious to our sins, nor does he impute them to us, but he imputes the righteousness of Christ for ours; so that we are not only cleansed from our sins, but also presented with the righteousness of Christ, and, being absolved from sin, we become righteous, and heirs of eternal life. Therefore, properly speaking, God alone justifies, and only for the sake of Christ, not imputing to us our sins, but imputing to us his righteousness."

But the Synod of Dort put the finishing touch to this metamorphosed doctrine, in 1618: "God is not only supremely merciful, but supremely just. But his justice requires that our sins, being committed against his infinite majesty, must be punished not only with temporal, but with eternal pains, both of body and mind; which pains we cannot escape till the justice of God be satisfied. But when we could not make satisfaction, God gave his only begotten Son to satisfy for us; and he was made sin and a curse upon the cross in our stead."

It was not to be expected that all the reformers would understand, explain, and defend this hypothesis exactly alike. Of course they had various and peculiar notions about it. For instance, Calvin contended that if Christ had not been condemned in a court of justice, his death would have been no satisfaction to divine law. These are his words: "Had Christ been killed by robbers, or in a sedition, his death would have been no kind of satisfaction; but being condemned before a judge, it is plain that he assumed the character of a guilty person." Moreover, he strenuously contended that Christ descended into hell, not to preach to the departed, but actually to suffer the torments of the damned. Said he: "Nothing would have been done by the mere death of Christ if he had not also afterwards descended into hell, where he sustained that death which is inflicted by an angry God on the wicked."

Notwithstanding various personal and sectarian differences about minor details, all the Protestant evangelical sects, and even the Papists, settled down on what we may call the vindictive atonement. If we look into their creeds, we shall find in most of them that it is a fundamental dogma. Hear the church of England: "The Godhead and manhood were joined together; whereof is one Christ, very God, and very man; who truly suffered, was crucified, dead, and buried, to reconcile his Father to us, and to be a sacrifice not only for original guilt, but also for actual sins of men."— Art. II. The Methodists, in their second article, affirm the same. Indeed, all the so-called evangelical denominations substantially agree on this point, and there is no need of additional verbal quotations.

The discussions of the last half century, which have been somewhat vigorously pushed by liberal Christians, have forced the evangelicals, especially the more susceptible of them, to shrink from the coarser statements of the doctrine, to modify and partially disguise its odious features, and to adapt it somewhat to progressive ideas. But the truth is, it is radically erroneous; and candid investigation demonstrates it to be a gross theological corruption of the pure primitive doctrine. It must ultimately be abandoned as such, and the regenerated church must go back to the beautiful and heart-sanctifying original set forth in the unperverted New Testament Scriptures.

What, then, are the principal points of contrast between the primitive and the corrupted doctrine of Christian atonement? The following: —

1. The primitive doctrine makes the atonement reconcile man to God. The corrupted doctrine makes it reconcile God to man, and to be propitious to his sins.

2. The primitive doctrine makes the justice and mercy of God eternally harmonic with each other. The corrupted doctrine makes these divine attributes utterly irreconcilable without punishing a sinless substitute instead of the guilty.

3. The primitive doctrine makes Christ a true representative of God, the Father, in respect to love, justice, mercy, and all divine qualities. The corrupted doctrine makes Christ a second person in the Godhead, who is so much more loving and merciful than

Father, that he consents to suffer infinite anguish to placate the Father's just anger, and so to save sinners.

4. The primitive doctrine makes it the glory of the atonement that Christ, perfectly inspired by the love of the Father in him, gave himself in self-sacrifice to ransom all mankind from sin, selfishness, and moral death, thereby to imbue them with the same spirit, and render them morally Christ-like. The corrupted doctrine makes Christ execute a tremendous process of penal expiation, to change the otherwise inexorable God into a merciful one, who arbitrarily imputes to the saved a righteousness utterly impossible for them to practise or imitate of their own choice; so that they never become Christ-like in their own proper moral character, but only artificially justified saints.

5. The primitive doctrine makes God the Father the spontaneous forgiver of sins under the only conditions which render forgiveness really proper, useful, or salutary to mankind. The corrupted doctrine makes him no forgiver of sins at all, but only an inexorable punisher of all sin, either upon the guilty in person, or their substitute.

6. The primitive doctrine affords the best of guarantees that Christ's atoning work will ultimately redeem and regenerate the whole human race. The corrupted doctrine makes it probable, if not certain, that but a minor portion of mankind will ever be benefited by it.

7. Finally, the primitive doctrine of atonement is easily understandable, consistent, rational, morally practical, and spiritually beautiful. But the corrupted

doctrine is a metaphysical puzzle, inexplicable, incoherent, irrational, morally unpractical, and abhorrently repugnant to godlike minds.

Such is my judgment, and such, I firmly believe, will be the judgment of the regenerated church, when none but those sincerely striving to be morally Christlike shall be deemed its proper members — above all, its consecrated teachers.

Thus we have gone over the historic highways, from the primitive starting-point to the terminus of doctrinal corruption, and are now well informed on this subject of Christian atonement. For my own part, I feel that I occupy a position at once tenable and impregnable. If an arrogant sectarist denounces me as heterodox, — not a believer in the true doctrine of atonement, — I can be calm, for I know better. If the anti-Christian of any school assumes to tell me that I must accept or reject Christianity as the present majority hold it, and that it is of no use for me to distinguish the pure primitive doctrine from its gross corruptions, I know better. Mere assumption, ignorance, and prejudice shall not swerve or disturb me. Proving all things, I will hold fast that which is true and good. My only remaining concern shall be, to profit, spiritually and morally, by the genuine atonement of Christ; to be personally reconciled to the infinite, all-perfect Father; to embrace and follow Christ; to imbibe thoroughly his spirit of loving self-sacrifice, — in fine, to become practically Christlike. Then, as his ambassador, I will beseech my fellow-men to be reconciled to God. These are the sublimest possible attainments, — pure holiness, harmony with Father and Son, unity with all the regenerate; the promotion of universal progress in love, wisdom, and bliss. Who will aspire after and strive for these? Let us all; and the atoning grace shall be sufficient for us.

ARTICLE IV.

ANGELOLOGY, DEMONOLOGY, AND RESURRECTION FROM THE DEAD;
OR, THE DOCTRINE OF SPIRITUAL AND IMMORTAL EXISTENCE.

DISCOURSE XII.

THE PRIMITIVE CHRISTIAN DOCTRINE CONCERNING SPIRITUAL BEINGS.

"Then the devil leaveth him, and behold, angels came and ministered unto him." — Matt. iv. 11.

"If a spirit or an angel hath spoken unto him, let us not fight against God." — Acts xxiii. 9.

"If I by Beelzebub cast out devils [demons], by whom do your children cast them out? Therefore they shall be your judges. But if I cast out devils [demons] by the Spirit of God, then the kingdom of God is come unto you." — Matt. xii. 27, 28.

Rationalistic and Liberal Christians in general have either denied, or seriously doubted, that Jesus and his apostles really held the doctrine of a personal devil in chief, of demons or evil spirits who sometimes obsessed, possessed, and infested mankind in the flesh, of angelic beings manifesting themselves on remarkable occasions to the human senses, and of all kindred spiritualistic phenomena. They grant that the literal record so reads, but contend that Christ only accommodated himself to the errors and prejudices of his times, deeming it unwise to combat them on these points, whilst in fact he knew and inwardly regarded all these phenomena as mere natural ones, having no supermundane origin or character. But our left-wing ultras, from Theodore Parker downward and outward, unable to abide any such special pleading, and utterly discarding the whole New Testament angelology, demonology, and supernaturalism, as merely mythic, have squarely pronounced Jesus an imperfect, fallible, and erring religious teacher, — honest and excellent in some respects, but ignorant and superstitious in others, of which this must certainly be one. Of course his apostles and evangelists must rank still lower. Their conclusion rests on the very positive assumption that the whole system of supernaturalism so called, in all its forms, phases, and details, under any and every religion and philosophy of mankind, is founded on no basis of absolute fact, or credible evidence of reality, but rests on mere myth or superstitious credulity, and therefore must ultimately vanish away with the progress of mind. If such were my own convictions, I would be at no further trouble to rescue Christianity from its corruptions, as I am now endeavoring to do in this series of discourses. But I dissent in this matter radically, not only from these ultra Liberals, but also from those Christian Liberals who explain away the spiritology good and evil of the New Testament Scriptures, on the ground that Christ must have known better, and only accommodated himself, from motives of expediency, to the superstition of his age. I do not believe him to have been morally capable of such a policy, nor that it accords at all with his general character as given in the record. I would prefer rather to think him honestly fallible and mistaken. I utterly reject both assumptions. What, then, is my own position? I will define it.

It is, that the New Testament record on this subject is essentially true in its fair, obvious construction; that Christ and his apostles so held and taught; and that their doctrine was fundamentally correct. There was a period of my life in which I doubted and wavered respecting especially their demonology. But psychological magnetism, clairvoyance, and modern spiritualism, whatever contempt many of the learned manifest towards them, and whatever be some of their abuses, entirely cured my incipient scepticism. They did so partly by important phenomenal facts which I actually witnessed; partly by others, equally or more important, indubitably attested by numerous competent witnesses; and partly by leading me in my investigations to a broad historical knowledge of similar phenomena from the earliest antiquity, in many countries, all down the ages, to our own times. Of this historical knowledge I was previously either ignorant, or so superficially informed, that it had little influence on my judgment. Now, after all my investigations, I am thoroughly settled in my convictions on this subject, and no amount of sensual ignorance, or of learned scepticism, however assumptive and positive, has the weight of a feather against them. To my mind there is a great chain of absolute spiritualistic facts, extending from the earliest historical era to our own times, just as real as any class of materialistic facts, and just as consonant with divine laws, that is, on their own higher plane. I understand comparatively little of that higher plane and its peculiar laws; but the realities of existence, and the phenomenal facts belonging to that plane, are to me unquestionable. And any religion, or philosophy, which ignores them is, in my estimation, radically one-sided and defective, whatever may be its merits in other respects.

But my present chief concern is to set forth fairly the pure primitive doctrine of Christ and his apostles concerning spiritual beings of different classes; and afterwards to show its excellence over earlier and later forms of the same general doctrine. For it was not so much the functional mission of Christ to preach new principles of doctrine, as to separate old truths from commingled errors, and to apply them practically to their legitimate uses. Neither he nor his apostles were metaphysical philosophers, but religious prophets, inspirees, and teachers. In this character they exhibited an emphatic authority and simplicity, not according to the wisdom of human erudition, but rather according to the pungent, sententious wisdom of God. They did not elaborate and explain their conceptions of the spiritual world, and of its denizens thence issuing into this mortal state; but confined themselves to the main characteristics and facts which vitally concern mankind in the flesh. Nor did they demand faith in Satan, demons, angels, or spirits, as indispensably necessary to salvation, acceptance with God, or membership in the Christian Church. They simply declared the truth, warned the people against all satanic temptations and dangers, held to and realized angelic ministrations, experienced wonderful visions, cast out demons, healed all manner of diseases, raised some of the recently dead to natural life, and preached a final complete victory over all the powers of darkness. What, then, was their real doctrine concerning spiritual beings? It was in accordance with the foregoing indications. I will present some of the principal points.

1. They held and taught the reality of a vast spiritual world with various regions of abode suitable for the inhabitancy of different classes of angels, spirits, and demons; and that there all were associated more or less intimately, for the time being, according to their respective kinds and congenialities, whether higher or lower, good or evil. Also, that all human souls consciously survive physical death, and pass, at, or soon after that change, into their appropriate abode in the spiritual world among those of their own sort, there to enter upon such experiences as God has wisely ordained for them, according to their various moral condition and character. The highest, holiest, and most blissful abode of the spiritual regions they called " heaven," " kingdom of heaven," " kingdom of God," and other kindred appellations. The inferior and lowermost, they called " Hades," or hell, " Gehenna," " the prison," etc., etc. Thus much we may verify by numerous passages of New Testament Scripture, of which the following are samples : —

"I say unto you, there is joy in the presence of the angels of God over one sinner that repenteth." Luke xv. 10. "Thinkest thou that I cannot now pray to my Father, and he shall presently give me more than twelve legions of angels?" Matt. xxvi. 53. " In my Father's house are many mansions." John xiv. 2.

"Fear not them which kill the body, but are not able to kill the soul, but rather fear him who is able to destroy both soul and body in hell." Matt. x. 28. "The beggar died, and was carried by the angels into Abraham's bosom. The rich man also died, and was buried: and in Hades he lifted up his eyes, being in torments, and seeth Abraham afar off, and Lazarus in his bosom." Luke xvi. 22, 23. "Ye are come unto mount Sion, and unto the city of the living God, the heavenly Jerusalem, and to an innumerable company of angels," etc. Heb. xii. 23. "Christ was put to death in the flesh, but quickened by the Spirit: by which also he went and preached unto the spirits in prison; which sometime were disobedient when once the long-suffering of God waited in the days of Noah." 1 Pet. iii. 18, 20. "For, for this cause was the gospel preached also to them that are dead, that they might be judged according to men in the flesh, but live according to God in the spirit." Ibid. iv. 6.

2. They held and taught that among the angels and demons of the spiritual world, both good and evil, there is an order of governmental rank, authority, and subordination, analogous to what is universal among mankind and the animals — princes and subjects, chiefs and subservients, presiding spirits and ministering subordinates; and that, by the will of the Father, Christ became enthroned over them all. This appears from such passages as the following: —

"Hereafter ye shall see heaven open, and the angels of God ascending and descending upon the Son of man." John i. 51. "Take heed that ye despise not one of these little ones; for I say unto you, that in heaven their angels do always behold the face of my Father who is in heaven." Matt. xviii. 10. "The Son of man shall come in his glory, and all the holy angels with him." Matt. xxv. 31. Michael, the archangel, is spoken of in Jude, ninth verse, as contending with the devil. The devil, or Satan, is designated as Beelzebub the "prince" or "chief" of the devils, properly, according to the original, demons. Matt. xii. 24–27; Mark iii. 22–27; Luke xi. 15–22. Christ says, he was "a murderer from the beginning," and a "liar." John viii. 44. He calls him "the prince of this world." John xii. 31; xiv. 30; xvi. 11; and Paul calls him "The prince of the power of the air." Ephes. ii. 2. The latter is more explicit on this point than any other New Testament writer, with respect to good and evil powers in the spiritual world, and to Christ's mediatorial enthronement over them all. "Put on the whole armor of God, that ye may be able to stand against the wiles of the devil. For we wrestle not against flesh and blood, but against principalities, against powers, against the rulers of the darkness of this world, against spiritual wickedness in high places;" or, as Noyes renders it, "the spiritual hosts of evil in the heavenly regions." Ephes. vi. 11, 12. Again: "To the intent that now unto the principalities and powers in heavenly places might be known through the church the manifold wisdom of God, according to the eternal purpose which he purposed in Christ Jesus our Lord." Ephes. iii. 10, 11. Again: "He raised him from the dead, and set him at his own right hand in the heavenly places (or regions), far above all principality, and power, and might, and dominion, and every name that is named, not only in this world, but also in that which is to come; and hath put all things under his feet." Ephes. i. 20, 22. Again: "He hath highly exalted him, and given him a name which is above every name; that at the name of Jesus every knee should bow, of those in heaven, and those in earth, and those under the earth; and that every tongue should confess that Jesus Christ is Lord, to the glory of God the Father." Phil. ii. 9–11. To the same effect Peter said: "Who has gone into heaven, and is on the right hand of God; angels and authorities, and powers being subject unto him." 1 Pet. iii. 22.

3. They held and taught the manifestation, communication, and ministration, of good angels and spirits from the other world to mankind in the flesh, and also the manifestation, infestation, and possession of evil spirits; the former for beneficent ends, the latter for maleficent ones. This is obvious from such texts as the following: "Then the devil leaveth him, and, behold, angels ministered unto him." Matt. iv. 11. "And there appeared unto him an angel from heaven strengthening him." Luke xxii. 43. "They had also seen a vision of angels which said that he was alive." Ibid. xxiv. 23. "And, behold, there talked with him two men, which were Moses and Elias; who appeared in glory, and spake of his decease which he should accomplish at Jerusalem." Ibid. ix. 30, 31. Cornelius said, "Four days ago, I was fasting unto this hour; and at the ninth hour I prayed in my house, and, behold, a man stood before me in bright clothing," etc. Acts x. 30. "Are they not all min-

istering spirits, sent forth to minister for them who shall be heirs of salvation?" Heb. i. 14. "I fell down to worship before the feet of the angel which showed me these things. Then saith he unto me, See thou do it not; for I am thy fellow-servant, and of thy brethren the prophets, and of them which keep the sayings of this book: worship God." Rev. xxii. 9.

Now concerning Satan and evil spirits. In Matt. iv. 1, 14, Mark i. 13, and Luke iv. 1–13, we have an account of Satan's appearing to and tempting Christ; in which case the tempter is evidently described as an evil angelic spirit. Next comes Christ's commission to his twelve apostles: "And when he had called unto him his twelve disciples, he gave them power against unclean spirits, to cast them out, and to heal all manner of sickness, and all manner of disease." Matt. x. 1. "After these things, the Lord appointed other seventy also, and sent them two and two before his face into every city, and place, whither he himself would come." "And the seventy returned again with joy, saying, Lord, even the devils [demons] are subject unto us through thy name. And he said unto them, I beheld Satan as lightning falling from heaven." "Notwithstanding in this rejoice not, that the spirits are subject unto you; but rather rejoice because your names are written in heaven." Luke x. 1, 17, 18, 20. The recorded instances in which Christ himself and afterwards his apostles are declared to have cast out demons, and wrought a great variety of wonderful works, are numerous, striking, and unequivocal. And they are too familiar with most of you to need further present specification. I therefore refrain from it.

It seems to me that I have conclusively shown what the primitive Christian doctrine was concerning the spiritual world and spiritual beings, good and evil. But before proceeding to treat of the corruptions of that doctrine, I deem it judicious for me to make some further explanations, and to answer certain objections in relation to particular points involved; because I endorse the primitive doctrine as essentially credible and reasonable, in this as all other articles of faith and practice. I shall therefore devote my next discourse to its more particular explanation and defence, with reference to rationalistic criticisms and objections.

ARTICLE IV.

ANGELOLOGY, DEMONOLOGY, AND RESURRECTION FROM THE DEAD; OR, THE DOCTRINE OF SPIRITUAL AND IMMORTAL EXISTENCE.

DISCOURSE XIII.

THE PRIMITIVE CHRISTIAN DOCTRINE CONCERNING SPIRITUAL BEINGS EXPLAINED AND DEFENDED.

"How can these things be?" — JOHN iii. 9.

In my last I endeavored to set forth the primitive doctrine of Christianity in respect to spiritual beings, good and evil. I am sure my presentation of the doctrine was substantially correct. But as I know that serious doubts and objections have been urged by rationalistic critics as to the truth of the doctrine itself, in which, nevertheless, I myself firmly believe, I proposed to explain and defend it somewhat, before proceeding to treat of its corruptions. This is the business of my present discourse.

Many liberal Christians, besides natural religionists, free religionists latterly so called, and sceptics generally, revolt at the tenet of personal demons, with a chief called the devil, and of demoniac infestations, possessions, and their exorcism, as alleged in the Scriptures. And the fact that Christ and his apostles taught such ideas is beginning to be confidently pleaded as conclusive proof that both he and they were in part the creatures of a superstitious education. If this could be demonstrated, the claims of Jesus to be *the Christ*, and all claims in his behalf, that he is officially the religious Lord and Master of mankind, must be abandoned. But such demonstration has never yet been made, nor, in my judgment, ever can be. I therefore welcome to a fair examination every honest doubt, difficulty, objection, and criticism; being sure that all can be fairly solved. What, then, is there unreasonable, or incredible, in the primitive Christian doctrine concerning demons, a prince of demons, possession, and exorcism?

1. It is felt and said that this entire demonology is inherently repulsive and abhorrent to the moral reason, as well as derogatory to the character of a perfectly good, wise, and powerful God. Answer. Why is it any more so than the existence and wickedness of similar evil beings in this mortal state? The whole history of the human race attests that there has always been a portion of mankind exceedingly perverse, and some of them horribly sinful; that there have always been arch deceivers, seducers, misleaders, and chieftains in every form of wickedness; and that the masses of mankind have always been prone to become dupes to the evil artifices of such misleaders. All this is as undeniable as our own personal existence. Is it repulsive and abhorrent? Nevertheless it is reality. Is it derogatory to the attributes of an all-perfect God? Not unless it is a *finality* of his designs, creation, and government. Primitive Christianity proclaims that it is not a finality, but

shall surely come to an end in the fulness of times; and such also is our highest conception of destined progress.

But it may be pleaded, The present is a rudimental, imperfect, and very gross state of existence; we can partially account for and endure the incarnate demonology, dreadful as it is, of this transitory world, because it will all be transcended in the next state of existence, which will certainly be an immortal and perfect one. I reply: Who knows that our next state of existence will be a perfect one immediately? Who knows that it will not be one of partial imperfection and evil for ages of ages? — one of discipline and slow progress to millions of intelligent spirits for long periods of duration? No one. Why, then, do any of us thus presume and assume? Is it not far more reasonable to take for granted that in the great hereafter there will be many stages of discipline, change, and progression; and that as great differences of moral character and condition await our race after physical death as exist here in the flesh? Is God ever in a hurry? Will our moral natures be suddenly reversed? Will the essential laws of order be changed? Will infants become adults in an instant? or fools wise? or monsters of wickedness saints? Does reason teach us to expect such results? No; but the contrary. Do Christ and the apostles teach us such ideas of the future? Certainly not. Whence, then, do we infer and assume that the first stages of our future existence must be perfect and sinless ones to the whole human race? Only from a childish imagination, wherein the wish is father to the thought. Nor have we any sound reason for even imagining that instant and universal moral perfection at man's entrance on the next life would be as well for the race as would manifold ages of gradual and disciplinary progress. Why, then, says one, do you not push on your reasoning to the endless sinfulness and misery of at least a part of mankind? Because that is no legitimate conclusion, but would utterly contradict and destroy both my reasoning and premises. There must be a *finality* of absolute good, — an unhurried, befitting course of progress to reach that finality, and an eternity of bliss beyond which infinitely transcends all preliminary ages of partial evil. This is the only sound and satisfactory reasoning on the subject, and happily it accords completely with the primitive doctrines of Christianity, as I shall duly show.

Now, then, Christ and the apostles in their demonology do not make the demons, nor their representative chief, officially called the devil, anything essentially different in nature and moral character from the perverse classes of wicked souls here. They do not make the devil a self-existent, creative being; nor his subordinate demons, or angels, to have been originally divine, semi-divine, or celestial beings. On the contrary, they make the gods, demi-gods, and heroes idolized by the heathen to have been largely original human beings; and the demons which infested a class of unfortunate people, often termed "unclean spirits," they held to be the departed spirits of low and evil men, instinctively clinging to this sensual world and aggravating the maladies of persons susceptible to their possession, obsession, or infestation. Nor must we assume, though it may seem so, that they regarded the devil in chief, or his subordinate principalities and powers, as uniformly the very same personal spirits, any more than our human rulers are the same identical persons from age to age; but more probably as successors in office, exercising official authority for the time being, and so successively passing on to other conditions of spiritual existence. In this view, that demon would be Satan, or *the* devil, who at any time was the leading chieftain, or prince of the powers of spiritual darkness.

But here arises another query: Whether spiritual beings, either evil or good, are really associated according to certain laws of affiliation and leadership, as the doctrine before us presupposes. Why not? It is so with the insects, the fishes, the birds, the beasts, and with mankind, here in the flesh. Why not with spiritual beings, whether good or evil? They are real entities, spirit, soul, and body, — only of a more aerial, ethereal, or celestial organization. They have instincts, affections, minds, motives, attractions, and repulsions, on their plane of existence, as we have on ours. How much more rational, then, to conclude that they are gregarious, social, predisposed to combine more or less, and governed by superiors of their own kind, than that they exist isolate, scattered, unassociated, and unled! If there are any spiritual beings of a nature at all akin to beings in this world, whether actually born on this or some other planet, there is probably a strong analogy between them and us in these respects.

2. Next comes the very positive objection, that those spiritual beings, good or evil, and especially the evil demons, cannot communicate with mankind in the flesh, much less ever actually get possession of their physical organisms so as to control them at will; that, in the very nature of things, this is incredible; and that all notions of witchcraft, entrancement, obsession, possession, and exorcism are delusions of some sort, and mere figments of superstition. Answer. As stated in the preceding discourse, I once came near being swallowed up in this egotistic scepticism myself, but was cured by the knowledge and consideration of facts. Mesmerism, psychological magnetism, and clairvoyance, with their strange demonstrations, came to astonish me; then the still more wonderful and multiform spiritualistic phenomena wrought mightily on my convictions; and then I was led to search thoroughly the history of the past, sacred and profane, ancient and continuous, for well-attested similar phenomena. I was satisfied. And now the communication, manifestation, and intromissional operation of spirits, as between the spiritual world and our mortal sphere, with respect to both good and evil spiritual beings, is, to me, as certain a reality as the existence of mankind, though comparatively unfrequent and extraordinary. But this will only prove to many doubters and objectors that I am a victim of delusion; and they will say, "Demonstrate your position by evidence and reason."

Well, then, I will try to do so. But what sort of evidence will weigh with such objectors? Will they accept the sober testimony of witnesses, such as would be deemed perfectly credible, competent, and conclusive on any other subject triable by human judicatories? If they will, I can overwhelm them with a mass of testimony gathered from all ages, countries, and nations, — beginning historically with the most ancient times, and coming down to our own living generation, — embracing millions of the departed, and thousands of our contemporaries. If they ignore or reject all these, as many presumptuously do, what are we to think of their own rationality? Is a man reasonable who feels no respect for such a mass of testimony, which he cannot justly impeach, and to which he can oppose nothing but the plea that he himself has never witnessed such phenomena; that it is too extraordinary to be credited; or that, in his own self-sufficient opinion, nothing of the kind *can* be a reality? I pronounce such a mind positively and pitiably *unreasonable*. For he assumes that his own inexperience outweighs the unimpeachably attested experiences of millions, many of whom were, and are, as competent to judge of the matter as himself, and perhaps more so. Will such persons trust even their own senses? No; some of them boldly declare that they would not; that they are so scientifically settled, as to what is possible and impossible under nature's laws, that anything their senses should attest to the contrary they would promptly and utterly reject.

Again: let me ask, Are such persons reasonable? Is it reasonable for any man to assume that he understands all the laws of nature, — INFINITE NATURE? I think not. Some are disposed to go so far against all **angelogy, demonology, and phenomenal spiritology,** as to say that we cannot rationally credit any alleged fact that is not cognizable by the normal consciousness of mankind in general through their ordinary faculties. Is this reasonable? No. For it throws out of account all that they call abnormal consciousness, abnormal experiences, and abnormal minds; all the seers, prophets, inspirees, and great exceptional geniuses of the whole human race, from the remotest antiquity to our own times. Shall we throw away all the pre-eminent mechanicians, astronomers, philosophers, poets, artists, and transcendents of every kind in every department of human progress, whose perceptions, discoveries, and ideas have risen heaven high above, and shot ages ahead of, the multitude in their common normal consciousness? How many of them died martyrs to their abnormalism! But where would the normal masses now be if they had never been led by these abnormal forerunners? The abnormalists of all sorts are a small minority of mankind, but, all counted, they make up a great host. Is it reasonable to treat them, or any class of them, as less human than the so-called normal multitude? Do they not belong to the human family? Are they unnatural beings? If not, let them be counted in. Let them be deemed God's natural creatures, whose experiences, after all, are legitimate in their own kind, and just as much to be acknowledged real as the flattest common experiences of the multitude. I would call this reasonable.

Others, again, set up natural science as the infallible test of all these spiritualistic phenomena. If they mean *physical science*, whose implements are telescopes, microscopes, the ometers, scalpels, forceps, crucibles, retorts, alkalies, acids, etc., etc., are they reasonable in this? Can men find out God, Satan, angels, demons, souls, all the realities of spiritology, by such means? There is, or ought to be, spiritual science, psychological science, to test these phenomena. If any one has matured such a science, let it be brought forward and put to use. But if such be not available, then let us make the best of honest common sense in judging of undeniable facts, however extraordinary. Meantime let us remember one mental vice, too common among professional scientists, — proud prejudice against light which does not shine from their established candlesticks. In this they are not much above other bigots. What we must come to is, sincere reverence for truth, whether pleasant or unpleasant to our tastes; deference for facts above mere theories; just respect for credible testimony from our fellow-creatures, whether it coincide with our own experience or not; a noble determination to be reasonable in all things, and to exercise our God-given powers of judgment with that modesty which is born of self-knowledge, the knowledge that we know little of what is to be known. This brings me to another objection.

3. That it is repulsive to nature, and derogatory to the glory of a good God, to suppose that he permits mankind to be at all the dupes and victims of demons from the spirit world. Answer. Is it not equally so, that he permits mankind to be the fascinated dupes and victims of arch hypocrites, deceivers, and traitors, operating in organisms of flesh and

blood? That here in this mortal state he permits low, sensual, brutal minds to seduce, infest, infatuate, pollute, and render wretched so many unsuspecting men, women, and youths? That he permits all sorts of delusion, hallucination, bewitchment, insanity, disease, misery, and death? But all these dreadful evils, we know, are permitted. *Why* are they permitted? Doubtless for reasons perfectly honorable to God, and which will be ultimately perfectly satisfactory to us when we understand them in the great hereafter.

But the primitive Christian demonology ascribes nothing to the devil, his angels, or unclean spirits, radically different in nature, principle, spirit, character, or effect, from what darkens the history of mankind as actors and sufferers in the flesh. It only extends the same mental and moral characteristics into those lower spheres, whither so many of our race are continually departing, and whence with the same perverse animus, only in a more subtle manner, they react on kindred spirits in the flesh. On spiritual planes of being they naturally continue to act out their ruling affections till they shall be subjugated fairly to the laws of divine order. Is this unreasonable doctrine? Is it not, on the whole, most reasonable? I must think so. Good spirits bring forth good fruit; evil ones evil fruits, till corrected. It cannot be otherwise in the nature of things. It ought not.

4. It is further objected, that all such doctrines are in their very nature the foster parents of wild,

slavish, and debasing superstitions; therefore they ought to be cut up root and branch, in order to the mental emancipation and progress of the human race. Answer. Not if they are true. This is the point to be settled. Truth must stand; and it can never be the cause of evil. But truth may be misunderstood, perverted, mixed up with error, and abused in manifold ways. Whose fault is this? Not truth's. From whence does it spring? Not from truth, but from rudimental, ignorant, frail, erring human nature. It is just this crude human nature which has perverted and abused all truth, — even the *truth* that there is a God to be worshipped; multiplying gods almost without number, and worshipping all sorts of beings and things most superstitiously. To cure this shall we cut up, root and branch, the doctrine of a God? The French once voted God out of existence, and soon after worshipped the Goddess of Liberty, personated by a pretty Parisian harlot. Mankind have perverted and abused the truth that there is a future immortal state. Does the remedy lie in cutting up, root and branch, the doctrine that there is such a state? What truth or good can be named that mankind have not grossly perverted and abused? Not one. Then let us not make perversion and abuse an argument against any doctrine. But let us go into the merits of the case, and, if we are fairly convinced that any doctrine, principle, or idea is true, let us then do our utmost to guard it against all perversion and abuse. This is our reasonable course. Therefore I so treat the primitive Christian doctrine concerning spiritual beings.

5. Finally, our critics will say, Granting your general premises and reasoning, you let down what you call the primitive Christian Spiritology to a common level with that of the Jews, Persians, Chaldeans, Egyptians, Greeks, Romans, and most other peoples, ancient and modern. Answer. No. I recognize a common basis of spritualistic reality, phenomenal fact, and psychological law, common to all. But I contend that the angelology, demonology, and psychology of Christ and his apostles were eminently free from the errors, perversions, and abuses, more or less prevalent among all the others; and that their spiritual power was higher, purer, better exercised, more orderly, more rational, and more beneficent, than among the others; just as their theology, piety, and morality transcended those of all others, though resting on a common substratum, and similar in certain respects. This is precisely what I contend for, and here the objectors and critics must take issue with me, refute me, or yield to my conclusions. Let no false issues, or evasions, be made, and the truth will come uppermost.

And now, until something stronger shall be presented against my position than has yet come to my knowledge, I shall take for granted that what I have set forth as the pure primitive Christian doctrine concerning the spiritual world and spiritual beings, good and evil, is not only such, but is substantially the truth on that subject. On this ground I shall proceed, in my next discourse, to set forth wherein this primitive doctrine has been corrupted. After that, I shall complete what belongs under the present general head, by taking up the doctrine of the resurrection from the dead in its primitive purity, and treating of its corruptions.

ARTICLE IV.

ANGELOLOGY, DEMONOLOGY, AND RESURRECTION FROM THE DEAD; OR, THE DOCTRINE OF SPIRITUAL AND IMMORTAL EXISTENCE.

DISCOURSE XIV.

CORRUPTIONS OF THE PRIMITIVE DOCTRINE.

"Let no man beguile you of your reward in a voluntary humility, and worshipping of angels, intruding into those things which he hath not seen."— COL. ii. 18.

"There be some that trouble you, and would pervert the Gospel of Christ. But though we, or an angel from heaven, preach any other gospel unto you than that which we have preached unto you, let him be accursed."— GAL. i. 7–8.

IN this discourse I am to treat of the corruptions of the primitive Christian doctrine concerning spiritual beings of different classes. It will be difficult to do justice to the subject in so brief a space, but I will endeavor to present the main facts in condensed statements. The subject naturally opens in two general divisions, namely, Angelology and Demonology. The principal corruptions of doctrine in both these divisions are indicated in one or more of the following specifications: 1. Exaggeration and distortion; 2. Presumptuous philosophizings and heathenizings; 3. Absurd additions and appendages; 4. Gross perversion and abuse; and 5. Terrorism and persecution for alleged spiritualistic criminality. In these various ways the rational and beneficent simplicity of the primitive Christian doctrine, on this as on most other subjects, was gradually superseded by very abhorrent superstitions, many of which disgrace nominal Christianity even in our own so-called enlightened age.

Angelology demands our first attention. I include in Angelology whatever relates to spiritual beings, whether of human or superhuman origin, who have been believed in and reverenced as holding glorious positions in the heavenly world; such as archangels and angels distinctively so called, Mary, the mother of Jesus, the apostles, martyrs, confessors, and saints of the church, glorified after death. All these, together with innumerable less distinguished departed human spirits, belong in the general category of Angelology.

1. Although the primitive Christian doctrine absolutely discountenanced all worship of angels and spirits, it was not long before professing Christians began to fall into it; that is, into a subordinate worship of them. In this they copied, or partially adopted, the ancient customs of the Gentiles, and into which even some of the Jews had fallen. Nearly all the renowned religious sages, both Eastern and Western, had for long ages taught that the one supreme God exercised no direct governing influence out of the inmost heaven, but acted through intermediate gods, angels, and spirits; who, as his vicegerents or deputies, with a large discretion, managed all the affairs of mankind on earth, and in the spiritual world. Plato distinctly affirmed this doctrine, that the Supreme governs only through intermediates, though he

did not originate it. It came from the Egyptians, Hindoos, Chaldeans, and Persians of more ancient times. It was in full vogue during and immediately after the apostolic times; but Christ did not endorse it, further than to the extent of recognizing angelic agencies, ministrations, and manifestations, as among God's more extraordinary methods of government. On the contrary, he and his apostles taught, with the greatest emphasis, that God as the infinite Father is himself everywhere immanent, manifesting himself by his communicable Holy Spirit, in all suitable degrees, to the human mind; eminently through prophetic inspirees, and pre-eminently through his anointed Son. Therefore the Father is to be worshipped in spirit and in truth as really present everywhere and exercising a perfect providence over all human affairs, no less than in those of the remotest heavens and abysses. And when he operates through superhuman ministers he is none the less to be acknowledged. Hence they never encouraged or sanctioned the worship of angels, spirits, prophets, apostles, or even the Son of God himself, except as wholly to the glory of God the Father. But not so our philosophizing Christians of after times. Their Christianity was leavened with Gentile philosophy, and so became a corrupt compound. Hence Justin Martyr, about the middle of the second century, said: "Him (God) and the Son that came from him, and the host of other good angels who accompany and resemble him, together with the prophetic Spirit, we adore and worship."

2. Their semi-deification of the mother of Jesus is a most striking and pitiable illustration of this corrup-

tion. When they had succeeded in deifying the Son into co-equality with the infinite Father, and resolved his birth into the sacred mystery of God incarnated, they must needs elevate the glorified spirit of Mary to a height as near that of the Triune God as possible. And little by little they did so. Prayers began to be offered up to her, and especially for her to make intercession in behalf of the suppliant, in the third century. Also, a sort of oblation in the form of consecrated cakes, called *collyrides*, which, however, some religious teachers disapproved. At length the title "Mother of God" began to be solemnly given her. Thus the celebrated Athanasius, in the fourth century, used such language as the following: "Hear, O daughter of David and of Abraham, incline thine ear to our prayers, and forget not thy people." "Intercede for us, lady, mistress, queen, and Mother of God."

One Anastasius, a presbyter, had the manly decency in a public discourse, about A.D. 428, to protest against this superstitious profanity of calling Mary the "Mother of God," insisting that she should be called simply the mother of Christ. In this he was supported by the famous Oriental bishop, Nestorius. But the corruption had become too deep to be arrested, and great persecution was raised against Nestorius and his sympathizers. The third general council, so called, met at Ephesus, and after much violent debate, in 431, decreed that Mary should be authoritatively called the "Mother of God," and that all who denied her that divine title should be anathematized. Nestorius and his friends were thus put under the ban. A long conflict ensued between contending sections of the church, but the "Mother of God" party triumphed.

It would require volumes to set forth in detail the manifold idolatrous devotionalities sanctimoniously paid by the Romish Church to the "Blessed Virgin." Suffice it to say, that in spite of the dissent of the Greek Church from many of these, and the denunciation of them all by the Protestants, they were still adhered to by the Catholics most tenaciously, and have even been augmented by fresh glorifications.

The Council of Trent, held in the sixteenth century, decreed that "the blessed and immaculate Mary, the Mother of God, is exempt from all sin, actual and original." The present Pope, Pius IX., in 1854, proclaimed the immaculate conception of the Virgin Mary to be an established doctrine of the Roman Catholic Church. Hear an extract from the "Sacred Summons," which convened the present Ecumenical Council, now in session at Rome: "It is already fifteen years since there went forth from Rome the oracle of the definition of the first triumph of the Mother of God over the primeval enemy of the human race; and Mary, in the midst of our tempestuous age, will amply recompense the church and the pontiff by new glories. May the Woman victorious over Satan manifest herself to the Council, in all the splendors of her power; may she crush the devil, and send him howling to the lowest abyss of hell. May Mary thus accomplish the salvation, the might, and the reign of our God, and of his Christ, as it is written in the Apocalypse, 'The great dragon is cast down who seduced the whole world.' Thus may it be, and let Rome and the world joyfully chant the hymn of gratitude to the Virgin Immaculate." Again, from the Pope's "Allocution:" "These words of exhortation, drawn from our inmost heart, may the Almighty and most merciful God, with the intercession of his Immaculate Mother, confirm," etc.

Now, my friends, turn back for a moment from this most astonishing extravagance to the primitive teachings of the New Testament, and ask yourselves what is there said of the mother of Jesus. Pure and good woman as she undoubtedly was, the only laudatory things said of her, and those but few, are contained in Matthew i. 18 to ii. 23, and Luke i. 5 to ii. 52; on which portions of the New Testament record I have heretofore shown that no implicit reliance can be placed. If, however, these were entirely credited, they would afford scarcely the shadow of a foundation for anything more than the appellations, Blessed Virgin, and Mother of our Lord Jesus. All the rest would remain sheer fiction, or assumption. Outside of these unreliable portions of the present received version of our Testament, not even a single allusion is made to the wonderful facts and events therein narrated. Mary, the mother of Jesus, receives no distinctive compliment, not even from her Son. She is not so much as designated a *virgin*, but simply as the *Wife of Joseph*, the *Mother of Jesus*, and *Woman*. Indeed, she is mentioned scarcely half-a-dozen times. At the wedding in Cana of Galilee, where she was present with Jesus, when the wine failed, she said unto him, "They have no wine." His answer was,

"Woman, what have I to do with thee? mine hour is not yet come." John ii. 3, 4. On a later occasion, when he was preaching in a certain house, she and his brethren were reported as outside, desiring to speak with him. But he paid no deference to their desire, and said, "Who is my mother? and who are my brethren?" "Whosoever shall do the will of my Father which is in heaven, the same is my brother, and sister, and mother." Matt. xii. 47-50. As he was bleeding on the cross, his mother, two other Marys, and his beloved disciple John, stood by in sympathetic anguish. He looked down on them, and said, "Woman, behold thy son!" then to John, "Behold thy mother!" "And from that hour that disciple took her unto his own home." John xix. 26, 28.

She is mentioned but once more, which is in the first chapter of Acts, and then merely as abiding in a certain upper tenement, with John and the apostolic community at Jerusalem, who after the ascension continued in prayer and supplication there, as also the brethren of Jesus, awaiting the outpouring of the Spirit on the day of Pentecost. We have no further record of her life, or of her departure into the spirit world. How little could human sagacity have imagined, worthy and beloved as she was, that her glorified soul was to be exalted above all saints and angels, and to receive a worship only second to that of the infinite God, with the paradoxical titles "Mother of God," "Mistress and Spouse of God," "Queen of Heaven," etc.! But just such idolatrous corruptions have been developed, and at this moment they stultify millions of sincere devotees, who expect her, as aforesaid, to "send Satan howling to the lowest abyss of hell"!

3. Let me now briefly refer to the long retinue of martyrs, confessors, and saints, who have been angelized by the church. They have been placed in general communion with the original archangels and angels of heaven; all being ranked in dignity below "the Immaculate Mother of God," and deemed entitled to the third grade of worship. The highest grade is due to the Divine Trinity, the second grade to the Blessed Virgin, and the third to the angels and angelized saints. At an early period the Christians often met at the graves, sepulchres, or memorial places of their departed apostles, evangelists, martyrs, and confessors, to eulogize and pray for them; then regarding them as still unglorified spirits in the Hadean world. Later they came to regard them as in a higher state. At length they brought oblations and valuable offerings in token of their reverential homage, and began to pray to them, imploring their intercession with God in their own behalf and their guardianship over them amid the dangers of life. From this they went on, more and more extravagantly, to dedicate churches and sacred places to them. Then to search for, gather, and revere their mortal relics, or what they were often cheated to believe such, — a skull, a bone, a lock of hair, a handful of dust, or even a rag of cloth that had some time enwrapped a relic. Oh, what pious frauds were imposed on credulous thousands! For no price was too high to pay for a saintly relic. Every church must have in its

sacred vaults something of the kind that had belonged to its patron saint. Every individual, *who could*, must possess one, as an amulet, spell, or charm, for warding off diseases, driving away demons, or securing some miraculous favor. For it was believed that wherever the smallest earthly relic of a saint was, there the saint hovered, and would manifest his presence in behalf of the possessor.

Next came pictures and images of the heavenly angels and saints, set up for reverence in the churches and private sanctuaries. And they were bowed down to, enriched with offerings, and worshipped in the third grade, with the notion that the angel or saint was either present, or at least in some manner appreciated the devotion rendered. By this time it was no longer held that the saint was in Hades, but an inhabitant of heaven, and ready to descend thence at any time to interpose miraculously for the benefit of the devotee. Huge folios would not adequately describe the superstitious abuses which followed from this worship of angels, saints, relics, pictures, and images. The errors, follies, absurdities, evils, and miseries thence developed, were only exceeded by similar pagan ones, which Christianity professed to have abolished, yet has all but repeated under new names and forms. So the Romish doctrine became authoritatively established and sanctioned, as it even now stands in its least offensive language; namely: "That honor and veneration are due to the angels of God and his saints; that they offer up prayers to God for us; that it is good to have recourse to their intercession; and that the relics, or earthly remains, of God's particular servants, are to be held in respect."

But I am trespassing on space and time due to the second general division of my subject,—Demonology. I include in Demonology whatever relates to Satan, infernal angels, and evil spirits of every supposed grade and class. The primitive Christian Demonology became gradually corrupted in the same manner and respects as its Angelology, briefly specified in my opening paragraphs.

1. The converted heathen philosophers soon speculated on the origin and power of the devil, or Satan, and began to magnify his diabolical agency. The Egyptians, Persians, and other religionists of somewhat younger nations, had filled the world with their fabulous notions concerning the origin of evil. According to those still cherished notions, Satan, by whatever name called, was first a pre-eminent Son of the Supreme God, who for some unaccountable reason fell into envy, hatred, and inveterate rebellion against the common Father, and made a tremendous war upon his peers, the equally pre-eminent sons of God, bearing such names as Osiris, Ormuzd, etc., who remained loyal. He was ultimately driven out of heaven with a vast host of his followers, of higher and lower grade, into the lower regions of the universe. Our earth and its adjacent surroundings became a sort of territory open to the invasion and occupancy of both the loyal and rebellious powers. Hence the mixture of good and evil which prevails among mankind; the good gods causing all the good, and the evil gods, with Satan at their head, all the evil. But matter

and the material elements of our world were supposed to be most naturally subject to evil influences, and the devil became a most powerful controller of them; that is, of earthy substances, water, fire, and air. And so he came to be regarded as the chief causator of earthquakes, floods, conflagrations, tempests, plagues, famines, and all the physical calamities that afflicted humanity; as well as of their mental and moral disorders. Indeed, he was made, by this adulterated theology, as nearly the co-equal adversary of the Triune God as he could be and be subject to final overthrow. But even that final overthrow ceased to mean what Christ and the apostles represented it, — a complete subjugation, in the highest spiritual sense, — and was construed into a vindictive endless imprisonment and torment in hell, where still he would reign over his countless dupes, and howl his ever-spiteful blasphemies against the Almighty to all eternity.

In process of time, amid the terrorism of the dark ages and onward, Satan was made the central personage in pulpit oratory, in painting and in dramatic representations. The most horrible and grotesque descriptions were given of his person, — sometimes as in a half-human, half-bestial form, with horns, tail, and a cloven foot; sometimes as a fiery dragon, vomiting flames of sulphur; sometimes as a frightful serpent with deadly fangs, and forked tongue; and always as a shocking monster. Thus the minds and imaginations of ignorant millions were distracted, stultified, and superstitionized in the name of Christianity.

2. But corruptions no less abhorrent gradually disgraced the primitive doctrine relative to demons in

general. Evil angels and spirits of multiform grade, character, and powers, — all servile creatures and subjects of the Supreme Satan, — were conceived to fill the caverns of the earth, the watery depths, and the whole atmosphere. Paracelsus, a famous demonographist, near the close of the fifteenth century, asserted that "the air is not so full of flies in summer, as it is at all times of invisible devils; and that not so much as a hair's breadth is free from them, this side of the moon, in heaven, earth, or waters." Of course, every human being was more or less a prey to them, and every kind of calamity, disease, and suffering was attributed to them. Professional exorcists were recognized by the Council of Antioch, in 341, as a special ecclesiastical order, and in the Romish Church are still one of the four minor orders of its clergy. Holy words, as the names of God, Christ, the Blessed Virgin, and eminent saints, were pronounced; holy water and the sign of the Cross used; psalms, litanies, prayers, and adjurations were recited, all to expel the evil spirit from the possessed. What numberless legends, falsely alleged facts, and strange historical occurrences might I adduce under this head! But I must refrain.

3. Finally, I come to the infatuations and persecutions connected with witchcraft, magic, and kindred developments of Demonology. A grossly corrupt theology, having inflamed and perverted the imaginations of the ignorant multitudes throughout nominal Christendom, now prompted its ecclesiastical organs to insist on fighting the devil and his imps with the pains and penalties of civil government. Civil power was then the tool of ecclesiastical dictation, and things were

carried with a high hand in all western and northern Europe. The Holy Inquisition, falsely so called, and a mercenary host of professional witch-hunters in the various nations, traversed the continent in search of wizards, sorcerers, magicians, witches, and persons in league with the devil. I am now speaking chiefly of what took place from the twelfth to the seventeenth centuries inclusive. Such delusions, infatuations, and cruelties as blacken the annals of those ages, on this subject, can only be appreciated by thorough historians. They seem in our day absolutely incredible, and yet are not to be doubted. The whole population must have been more or less psychologized, and filled with fantasies. But I must not enlarge. A vast majority of the victims who perished in loathsome prisons, in flames at the stake, under painful tortures, and by different forms of capital punishment, were poor, ignorant, friendless persons, and mostly elderly women. Some of them were maddened into confessions of their own guilt, though really innocent; but hosts of them died protesting their innocence. To be suspected and accused was almost sure to be followed by condemnation. The most learned and honorable judges — even a Sir Matthew Hale — could not rise in those times above the superstitious mental atmosphere that universally prevailed. In the reign of Francis I., no less than one hundred thousand victims perished in France, for alleged witchcraft and kindred diabolical crimes. In other countries the evil was equally dreadful. Our forefathers, here in New England, in and around Boston, participated lamentably in this delusion and most unjustifiable persecution. I think I may safely presume, that not less than a million of persons have been put to death in Christendom for this cause since the tenth century, all through mistaken notions of Christian doctrine and duty. But I must close.

Such have been the corruptions of the primitive Christian Angelology and Demonology. And such have been the fruits of these corruptions. Where lies the fault? Shall we charge it on Jesus and his apostles — and discard them on account of the evils committed in the name of their religion? I cannot do so. Shall we charge it on their simple and rational spiritology, so perverted and abused, and say, *Cut it up root and branch?* I cannot do that. Where, then, I repeat, lies the fault? At the door of poor, childish, frail, erring human nature. The world of mankind, as it was, received and treated primitive Christianity, not with a clear understanding of its principles and according to its intrinsic merits, but with weak, prejudiced, and muddy minds, according to the general conditions of incipient rudimental progress. They put its pure doctrines of truth and duty into their own earthen vessels, which were unclean. The natural result was, more or less of contamination and corruption. Therefore let us harshly blame none, even those who seem to deserve it; but make haste to apply our best remedies to the diseased Christendom which surrounds us. Among these is the light of truth, and a consistent exemplification of it in our conduct. That light shows us clearly what the pure primitive Christian doctrine concerning spiritual beings, good and evil, was, and what its corruptions have been. **Let us discriminate** accordingly, winnow out the chaff, and garner the wheat, for wholesome use, into wise and reverential minds. In my next I shall take up the remaining branch of the present article, namely, the Resurrection from the Dead.

ARTICLE IV.

ANGELOLOGY, DEMONOLOGY, AND RESURRECTION FROM THE DEAD; OR, THE DOCTRINE OF SPIRITUAL AND IMMORTAL EXISTENCE.

DISCOURSE XV.

THE PRIMITIVE CHRISTIAN DOCTRINE OF THE RESURRECTION FROM THE DEAD.

"And have hope toward God, which they themselves also allow, that there shall be a resurrection of the dead, both of the just and unjust."—PAUL. ACTS xxiv. 15.

A COMPARATIVELY small minority of mankind have positively disbelieved, or doubted, that there is any personal conscious existence after death. The vast majority have always professed to believe in some kind of future personal existence. Millions have believed in the doctrine of metempsychosis; that is, the transmigration of souls into different states and bodies, through a long succession of changes, pleasurable or painful, until finally purified and reabsorbed into the supreme soul of the universe. Other millions have believed that all human souls pass, at death, into various higher and lower spheres of existence, with a spiritual body of some kind mysteriously extracted from the mortal body, or else formed of ethereal essences everywhere imponderable, which spiritual body experiences refining changes as the soul progresses onward and upward through eternity. This is the doctrine of spiritualistic philosophers of very ancient and of modern times. I understand this to have been substantially the doctrine of the Egyptian, Hindoo, and Grecian spiritualists in remote ages; perhaps of most so-called heathen sages, as it now is, in a more refined form, of Andrew Jackson Davis, the harmonial philosophers generally, and a large majority of our modern spiritualists. This large and complex class of believers in the future immortal existence have never accepted the term *resurrection*, except in a modified sense, as properly significant of their ideas; preferring the terms transition, development, and progression as best expressing their ideas. For they hold that death, and the spirit's evolution into the life beyond, is a strictly natural, transitional, progressional development of human nature; which has been uniformly going on from the beginning of our race, without any distinctive epochs of resurrection, retribution, or demonstration, such as are set forth in the *revealed* religions.

The Persians of the Zoroastrian faith, and perhaps some other ancient religionists, held the doctrine of the resurrection of men's bodies at a great day of general judgment, in which the earth and all things would be subjected to a miraculous purifying conflagration. The Jewish Pharisees held the same doctrine, with certain modifications. So have believed the corrupted Christians generally, and the Mohammedans, but with their respective peculiar modifications. Most of these different religionists have held that the souls of mankind survived their bodies, existed in some sort of intermediate state between death and the resurrection, and then would be reunited with their raised bodies. All such believers have regarded the miraculous reproduction of the body as the essential feature of the resurrection.

A small fraction of professed Christians have strenuously held and taught that there is no such thing as a conscious personal soul separate from the body; that the entire mental consciousness of man ceases at the moment of physical death; and that the resurrection of the body will be the renewal of personal existence. This they hold to be the only ground on which to build the hope of a future existence. Our modern Second Adventists, as well as others of a different creed before them, have tenaciously advocated this notion of the resurrection.

The ancient Hebrews, before their captivity in Babylon, would appear, judging from their Sacred Scriptures, to have had rather indistinct conceptions of man's existence after death. Some have contended that they did not believe in any future state at all. This I deem an error. If I understand their Scriptures, they certainly held that human souls passed at death into the underworld, called in their language Sheol, which is the same as Hades in the Greek. But they seem to have made very little distinction between the righteous and wicked there, and to have believed that all souls were in a very powerless, shadowy, imperfect state of existence. Whether they had any definite, positive hope of an ultimate resurrection out of that state is somewhat conjectural; but that they had at least a vague hope of it is to me probable, if not certain. After the Babylonian captivity, and their intimacy with the Chaldean and Persian religionists, the Israelites evidently formed much more distinct conceptions on this subject, — having obviously adopted, with certain modifications, the then prevalent ideas of the Oriental sacred teachers. The books of the Apocrypha plainly indicate such a change.

I now come to the doctrine of Christ and his apostles concerning the resurrection from the dead, — in other words, the pure primitive Christian doctrine. It is not easy to determine this in all the minute particulars involved; because some of the New Testament language on the subject is ambiguous, and because it is possible that a part of the disciples formed ideas of their own on certain points more or less variant from their Master's. But on the essential points of the doctrine I feel quite sure I can present a correct statement. I will endeavor to do so, according to my own best understanding of the recorded testimony. I think Christ and his leading apostles taught substantially as follows, namely: —

1. That the souls of mankind passed at death into an imperfect state of existence, called Hades, or the underworld, where they were associated with kindred souls, happy or unhappy, until at a certain appointed time they should be clothed upon with a suitable organic ethereal or spiritual body, through which to exercise more complete personal powers.

2. That in the purposes of God every human soul was destined, at the appointed proper time, to be invested with an ethereal or spiritual body, of an in-

corruptible substance and organization, corresponding in identity to the old mortal body, and so be delivered from all the disabilities of Death and Hades.

3. That this resurrection of souls from the primary disabilities of Hades was to be immediately succeeded by a divine dispensation of judgment, retribution, and discipline, of greater or less unrevealed duration, designed to subdue all beings and things to Christ, even the last enemy, Death — so that thenceforth the human race should experience no more evil.

4. That all souls, on attaining to the completeness of the resurrection, would be holy, immortal, and blissful beings, "like unto the angels of God in heaven."

5. That in the divine plan of redemption Jesus Christ was not only made the religious Head, Lord, and Master of the human race, to reign till all things shall be reduced to perfect order, but also their model, exemplar, and forerunner through the resurrection into the glories of the most heavenly mansions.

Before proceeding to the proof that these five cardinal points, as stated, do really present the primitive Christian doctrine of the resurrection, it seems to be proper for me to answer some inquiries which incidentally arise. It may be asked, Did Christ and the apostles make any distinction between *soul* and *spirit?* and did they teach that soul and spirit between death and the resurrection were absolutely without substance of any kind? I understand them to have held a distinction between body, soul, and spirit as the three constituent components of a complete human being: the body as the most external organic dwelling; the soul as the personal, conscious, volitionary, moral agent; and the spirit as the vital principle of individual being. Without the vital principle there could be no sense and no action — no individual living being. Without the soul there could be no personal consciousness, passional loves, motives to action, or moral responsibility. And without an organic body, there could be no complete manifestations of the soul to external natures, or vigorous activity upon, through, and among them. I do not understand Christ and the apostles ever to have conveyed the idea that soul, or spirit, has no kind of substance in itself, or ever exists in absolute isolation from all other substances; but the contrary, only that their own substances are ineffably ethereal and subtile as compared with what we call matter. I infer that what they represented as disembodied spirits or souls were nevertheless shrouded with some sort of covering or shadowy substance, though imperfect in comparison with the proper resurrectional body. As to the terms *soul* and *spirit*, I find them sometimes distinguished from each other in Scripture, but oftener used synonymously, or one of them as including or implying the other; just as they are used in our own times.

Did Christ and his apostles use the term *dead* and its synonymes to signify departed souls in Hades? Yes, in many instances, and never in a sense to signify that any who had passed through death were utterly without life. Did they hold and teach that the great mass of mankind from the beginning of the world, righteous and wicked, remained in the underworld and could not attain to the resurrection before Christ's personal triumph over death and Hades? So I understand their language; that is, that Jesus was actually the first to experience the complete resurrection up to its highest consummation. Others might have preceded him through some of its incipient stages.

Did they hold and teach that an essential distinctive stage of the resurrection was the clothing of souls with ethereal or spiritual bodies, and raising them out of their first disabilities in the Hadean world? So I understand the matter. Did they certainly hold and teach that the resurrectional body was not the identical physical body laid off at death, but an immortal one in its place? Undoubtedly. How, then, was it with Christ's natural body, and his resurrection body? His natural body was probably resolved into its original earthly elements by divine power exercised through him, or in his behalf, during the night preceding his first reappearance to his disciples; and at the same time his spiritual body was formed to clothe him in its stead. At least, it would seem that his natural body was in some manner superseded by a spiritual one, which could be rendered visible and invisible, tangible and intangible, to the senses of his disciples at his own pleasure. How such results were produced, I know not. As little do I know how any spiritual body ever was or can be produced, in place of the gross material body; or how the natural body commences to be formed before birth; or how the soul controls that body during the present life; or how thousands of effects continually taking place are produced. I accept known facts, with or without explanations, and credibly attested facts on the strength of preponderating evidence. Then I account for them as well as I can, or leave them unaccounted for. In this case I adhere to the record, and explain the alleged facts according to my best judgment.

Did Christ and his apostles teach that the first distinctive stage of the resurrection would be succeeded by a divine dispensation of judgment, retribution, and discipline of greater or less unrevealed duration, designed to subdue all beings and things into such a state of moral order as that thenceforth God should "be all in all"? I shall endeavor to prove all this by the testimony on record. But is it a reasonable doctrine, that there should be seasons, crises, and marked dispensations, for the accomplishment of the proposed grand result? Is it not more natural, more philosophical, and more reasonable, to believe, with many ancient religious sages, the Harmonialists, and most modern Spiritualists, that there has been one regular, uniform rebirth into spiritual bodies from the first death till now; and that there is one regular, uniform dispensation of judicial discipline, progress, and development in spiritual excellence onward and upward from everlasting to everlasting?

Answer. It may seem so to many. But Christianity does not so represent things; and I think primitive Christianity, on the whole, the most rational. Why? 1. Because progression without beginning, acme, or end, is utterly incomprehensible, inexplicable, and, so far as we can see, impossible with respect to any finite system of beings and things; certainly with respect to human beings. If it has already required an endless duration of development to make them what they are, what assurance have we that another endless duration to come will essentially improve them? Or, if man's progression had a beginning, but will have no end, what is the sphere of action to be imagined for him in the eternities of futurity? 2. Because, in the history of our world thus far, human progress has not been uniform, or regular; nor have dispensations of judgment, retribution, discipline and reformation, been so; but there have been marked seasons, crises, and periods in respect to all these things. 3. Because great changes in human affairs have nearly always been predicted, heralded, and led by remarkable minds, and consummated only after many ups and downs of action and reaction; seemingly revolutionary circles, and catastrophal vicissitudes. 4. Because the best attested manifestations and revelations which have been received from the spirit-world in modern times do not declare anything like a general, regular, uniform course of things with respect to human discipline, development, and progress; but, on the contrary, declare the most astonishing anomalies and disparities, — some souls remaining for ages almost impervious to progressive influences, some for the time being appearing to retrograde, and others, in more favorable circumstances, bounding forward rapidly in goodness and wisdom. 5. Finally, because such an unrivalled Master of wisdom and righteousness as Christ is more likely to have known and taught the essential truth than those who dissent from him. For these and many other reasons I prefer to adhere to the pure primitive Christian doctrine of the resurrection, as I understand it.

One more rather important inquiry demands attention, which is, Did Christ and the apostles, in their teachings, fix or indicate any time, times, or season, when the resurrection should take place? Answer. I understand them to have taught that no absolute and complete resurrection of any human being ever took place before that of Christ himself; that a resurrection of saints, perhaps incomplete in some respects, took place at or soon after his own; that at the culmination of his mediatorial and judicial authority in the heavenly kingdom, which was also the consummation of the pre-Christian age, termed in our common version of the New Testament "the end of the world," marked by the destruction of Jerusalem and its temple, A.D. 70, Christ was to illustrate his spiritual majesty by commencing an era of general resurrection and judgment, to take instant effect on the then living and dead; and that this era, or day of judgment, would thenceforth continue, in some manner or form, with respect to all mankind, whether of the past or ensuing generations, until all beings and things in heaven, in earth, and under the earth, should be reduced to perfect divine order. I shall have occasion to explain these particulars more fully hereafter, as they come up in their proper connections.

From my foregoing exposition of the primitive Christian doctrine, it will be seen that it embraces all the fundamental excellences of other theories concerning a future immortal existence, with peculiarities of its own which correct their errors, and supply their defects. Such to me seem its merits. Christ did not claim to originate, or first reveal, a future immortal existence, but to illuminate, illustrate, and demonstrate its sublime realities more truthfully and conclusively than had previously been done. In my next I will endeavor to verify the present exposition by the requisite recorded testimony, with suitable explanations.

ARTICLE IV.

ANGELOLOGY, DEMONOLOGY, AND THE RESURRECTION FROM THE DEAD; OR, THE DOCTRINE OF SPIRITUAL AND IMMORTAL EXISTENCE.

DISCOURSE XVI.

THE PRIMITIVE CHRISTIAN DOCTRINE OF THE RESURRECTION FROM THE DEAD VERIFIED AND ILLUSTRATED.

"I saw seven golden-candlesticks, and in the midst of the seven candlesticks one like unto the Son of man, clothed with a garment down to the foot, and girt about the paps with a golden girdle. His head and hairs were white like wool, and his eyes as a flame of fire; and his feet were like unto fine brass, as if they burned in a furnace; and his voice was as the sound of many waters. And he had in his right hand seven stars; and out of his mouth went a sharp two-edged sword; and his countenance was as the sun shineth in his strength. And when I saw him, I fell at his feet as dead. And he laid his hand upon me, saying unto me, Fear not; I am the first and the last: I am he that liveth, and was dead; and behold, I am alive forevermore, and have the keys of hell [Hades] and of death." Rev. i. 12-18.

My proposed business, in this discourse, is to verify, by recorded testimony, the correctness of my statement in the last, formulating the primitive Christian doctrine of the resurrection, and to give such further explanatory illustrations as may seem to be necessary.

I formulated that doctrine in five propositional specifications. The first was in these words: "That the souls of mankind passed at death into an imperfect state of existence, called Hades, or the underworld, where they were associated with kindred souls, happy or unhappy, until, at a certain appointed time, they should be clothed upon with a suitable organic spiritual body through which to exercise more complete personal powers." I explained the distinction made between body, soul, and spirit, and their relations to each other. Also, that the soul was held to be a real personal entity, vitalized by the spirit, and having more or less of substance, organism, consciousness, intelligence, and affectional capability, in its disembodied state. Also, that in many passages soul and spirit were not distinguished apart. I prove the correctness of this first statement by such passages as the following: "Fear not them which kill the body, but are not able to kill the soul." Matt. x. 28. The parable of the rich man and Lazarus is especially pertinent: "The beggar died, and was carried by the angels into Abraham's bosom. The rich man also died, and was buried; and in Hades he lifted up his eyes, being in torments, and seeth Abraham afar off and Lazarus in his bosom. And he cried and said, Father Abraham, have mercy on me, and send Lazarus, that he may dip the tip of his finger in water, and cool my tongue, for I am tormented in this flame. But Abraham said, Son, remember that thou in thy lifetime receivedst thy good things, and likewise Lazarus evil things; but now he is comforted, and thou art tormented." The rest is familiar to you. Luke xvi. 19–31. It may be said that this is a parable, and its terms should be understood as figurative of things in the present life only. Doubtless it is a parable, in respect to the persons, to some of the descriptive imagery, and filling out of the details — like most other parables: for instance, that of the "Good Samaritan," so called. The man who went down from Jerusalem to Jericho, the thieves, the priest, Levite, Samaritan, etc., etc., were fictitious persons; but the places, characters, and principal incidents were real. There were really such places as Jerusalem and Jericho, with a dangerous road between them frequently infested by robbers. There were real travellers from one place to the other, real robbers and robberies, real priests, Levites, and Samaritans, and real moral characters and incidents similar to those represented in the parable. So, in this parable of the rich man and beggar, the places, characters, events, and experiences described were realities, though the persons, minor details, and rhetorical painting of scenery were undoubtedly fictitious. The doctrine, however, is unmistakable. And what is it? That harmless and innocent souls, often wrongfully neglected, despised, and left to suffer in this life, are at death borne by angels to the society of the good in the spirit world, or Hades, and there made comfortable; that unprincipled, covetous, uncompassionate souls, often rich and luxurious in this life, pass at death into the lower spheres of Hades, where they experience bitter remorse and a sense of imprisonment among the justly condemned; that there are abodes in the Hadean world for the just and the unjust of all grades, — the uppermost comparatively paradises, and the lowermost comparatively prisons of distress, impassably separated from each other for the time being; and that the resurrection from those different spheres would elevate their respective classes to a far better state, even though for a season the lowermost should rise only to condemnation and judicial discipline. The point on which I would more especially fix your attention is, that Jesus did not regard even Abraham, favored as he was, as then delivered from Hades; that is, as having already experienced the foreordained resurrection. He was not yet in the glory and blessedness of the "kingdom of God," strictly so called.

The same doctrine appears in the words of Peter, recorded in the second chapter of Acts: "Men and brethren, let me freely speak unto you of the patriarch David, that he is both dead and buried, and his sepulchre is with us unto this day. Therefore being a prophet, and knowing that God had sworn with an oath to him, that of the fruit of his loins, according to the flesh, he would raise up Christ to sit on his throne; he, seeing this before, spake of the resurrection of Christ, that his soul was not left in [Sheol] Hades, neither his flesh did see corruption." "For David is not ascended into the heavens, but he saith himself, The Lord said unto my Lord, Sit thou on my right hand, till I make thy foes thy footstool."

When Jesus said to the penitent malefactor, "To day shalt thou be with me in paradise"(Luke xxiii. 43), he plainly implied that their souls would presently be together in that favored sphere of the Hadean world, where, in his parable, he had represented Abraham and Lazarus to be. The author of the Epistle to the Hebrews, in the eleventh chapter, recounts the names and deeds of ancient worthies, who were expectants of resurrection glory, and then says: "These all having obtained a good report through faith received not the promise, God having provided some better thing for us, that they without us should not be made perfect." The author of the Apocalypse seems to have had a vision of similar import: "I saw under the altar the souls of them that were slain for the word of God, and for the testimony which they held." "And it was said unto them, that they should rest yet for a little season, until their fellow-servants also and their brethren, that should be killed as they were, should be fulfilled." Rev. vi. 9, 11. I think that this whole class of passages must be understood to verify my first stated point.

My second was in these words: "That in the purposes of God every human soul was destined, at the appointed proper time, to be invested with an ethereal or spiritual body, of an incorruptible substance and organization corresponding in identity to the mortal body, and so delivered from all the disabilities of Death and Hades." I explained the three leading ideas contained in this proposition; namely, 1. That the resurrection was to take place at an appointed time, or during some assigned period subsequent to Christ's personal resurrection; 2. That the resurrection body was to be in place of the old earthly body, but not the same body; and, 3. That it was to be an ethereal or spiritual body, of an incorruptible substance and organization. This is provable from a large class of passages like the following: —

"When they shall rise from the dead, they neither

marry, nor are given in marriage; but are as the angels which are in heaven." Mark xii. 25. You will recollect that these words were uttered by Jesus in reply to the Sadducees, who sought to puzzle him with the case of a wife that had had seven brothers successively as her husbands. On that occasion, he paused only to disabuse them of their gross materialistic notions of the resurrection, and to declare the broad truth that its grand ultimate was angelic immortality. In other instances, he makes moral distinctions between "the just and unjust," in the incipient stages of the resurrection. These I shall more pertinently adduce under the next head. Paul treated largely of the resurrection. " But now is Christ risen from the dead, and become the first fruits of them that slept." "For as in Adam all die, even so in Christ shall all be made alive. But every man in his own order: Christ the first fruits, afterwards they that are Christ's at his coming." "But some will say, How are the dead raised up? and with what body do they come? Fool, that which thou sowest [alluding to grain sown] is not quickened except it die. And that which thou sowest, thou sowest not that body that shall be." "So also is the resurrection of the dead. It is sown in corruption, it is raised in incorruption. . . . It is sown a natural [animal] body, it is raised a spiritual body. There is a natural body, and there is a spiritual body." See the whole fifteenth chapter of 1 Corinthians. Again: " For we know that if this earthly house of our tabernacle were dissolved, we have a building of God, an house not made with hands, eternal in the heavens. For in this we groan, earnestly desiring to be clothed upon with our house which is from heaven." 2 Cor. v. 1, 2, etc. Again: "For our conversation is in heaven, from whence also we look for the Saviour, the Lord Jesus Christ; who shall change our vile body, that it may be fashioned like unto his glorious body, according to the working whereby he is able even to subdue all things unto himself." Phil. iii. 20, 21. Here the form of expression seems to imply that the resurrection body would be a transformation of the mortal body; but we must not construe it to mean anything really different from what is plainly declared in the other passages. It means that the resurrection body was expected to be the spiritual one, and a transcendently glorious substitute for the animal body. That Paul held the general resurrection of the then past dead, though near at hand, to be still future, appears from many passages in his epistles, but especially from one in 2 Tim. ii. 17, 18. Therein he denounces Hymeneus and Philetus: "Who, concerning the truth have erred, saying, that the resurrection is past already, and overthrow the faith of some." This was probably written about A.D. 65.

My third propositional point of the primitive doctrine was stated thus: "That the resurrection from the primary disabilities of Hades was to be immediately succeeded by a divine dispensation of judgment, retribution, and discipline, of greater or less unrevealed duration, designed to subdue all beings and things to Christ, even the last enemy, Death; so that thenceforth the human race should experience no more evil." Here are three prominent ideas. 1. That a dispensation of judicial discipline should immediately succeed the resurrection from the primary Hadean disabilities, of greater or less unrevealed duration. It is sometimes called the day, or age, of judgment. 2. That this dispensation is designed to subdue all beings and things to Christ, even the last enemy, Death. And Death, let me remark, as here and in similar passages designated, includes all the consequences of physical and moral transgression. 3. That thenceforth, that is, after the complete subjugation of all beings and things to Christ, the human race are to experience no more evil. The verification of this doctrinal statement, as primitively Christian, is found in a class of passages, of which the following are samples : —

" As the Father raiseth up the dead, and quickeneth them, even so the Son quickeneth whom he will. For the Father judgeth no man; but hath committed all judgment unto the Son." " The hour is coming, in the which all that are in the graves [the region of the dead] shall hear his voice, and shall come forth : they that have done good, unto the resurrection of life ; and they that have done evil, unto the resurrection of condemnation." John v. 21, 22, 28, 29. " When thou makest a feast, call the poor, the maimed, the lame, the blind ; and thou shalt be blessed; for they cannot recompense thee; for thou shalt be recompensed at the resurrection of the just." Luke xiv. 13, 14. " This is the Father's will which hath sent me, that of all which he hath given me, I should lose nothing, but should raise it up again at the last day." John vi. 39.

Peter testified concerning Christ and the dispensation of his judicial rectification of all things: "Whom the heaven must receive until the times of restitution of all things, which God hath spoken by the mouth of all his holy prophets since the world began." Acts iii. 21. Again: the same apostle, referring to the dead in Hades who never in this life heard the gospel, said, Christ "is ready to judge the quick and the dead. For, for this cause was the gospel preached also to them that are dead, that they might be judged according to men in the flesh, but live according to God in the spirit." 1 Pet. iv. 5, 6.

Paul testified, saying: "The times of this ignorance God winked at, but now commandeth all men everywhere to repent; because he hath appointed a day [or dispensation of time] in the which he will judge the world in righteousness by that man whom he hath ordained; whereof he hath given assurance unto all, in that he hath raised him from the dead." Acts xvii. 30, 31. "We must all appear before the judgment-seat of Christ; that every one may receive the things done in his body, according to that he hath done, whether good or bad." 2 Cor. v. 10. "For he must reign, till he hath put all enemies under his feet. The last enemy that shall be destroyed is death." "And when all things shall be subdued unto him, then shall the Son also himself be subject unto him that put all things under him, that God may be all in all." 1 Cor. xv. 25, 26, 28.

The author of the Apocalypse, after describing, in glowing figurative language, the culminating scenes of the great judicial dispensation, amid which not only every rebellious soul received his part in the "lake of fire," but Death and Hades were swallowed up forever, saw, in vision, the ultimate glorious state of creation: "I saw a new heaven and a new earth; for the first heaven and the first earth were passed away; and there was no more sea. And I John saw the holy city, new Jerusalem, coming down from God out of heaven, prepared as a bride adorned for her husband. And I heard a great voice out of heaven, saying, Behold, the tabernacle of God is with men, and he will dwell with them, and they shall be his people, and God himself shall be with them, and be their God. And God shall wipe away all tears from their eyes; and there shall be no more death, neither sorrow nor crying, neither shall there be any more pain: for the former things are passed away. And he that sat upon the throne said, Behold, I make all things new. And he said unto me, Write, for these words are true and faithful." Rev. xxi. 1-5. I consider my third stated proposition of the primitive Christian doctrine abundantly verified. What an ineffably grand and glorious consummation!

My fourth stated proposition was: "That all souls, on attaining to the completeness of the resurrection, would be holy, immortal, and blissful beings, 'like unto the angels of God in heaven.'" The passages already quoted prove my correctness on this point in part, and I need add only the following: "Neither can they die any more: for they are equal [like] unto the angels; and are the children of God, being the children of the resurrection." Luke xx.

36. "The earnest expectation of the creature waiteth for the manifestation of the sons of God. For the creature was made subject to vanity, not willingly, but by reason of him who hath subjected the same in hope: because the creature itself also shall be delivered from the bondage of corruption into the glorious liberty of the children of God." Rom. viii. 19–21. Let it be constantly borne in mind, that the primitive Christian doctrine of the resurrection in its *completeness* always implied, not only physical, but spiritual and moral, perfection; that is, absolute freedom from all sin, as well as death of every kind.

My fifth propositional statement was in the following words: "That, in the divine plan of redemption, Jesus Christ was not only made the religious Head, Lord, and Master of the human race, to reign till all things shall be reduced to perfect order, but also their model, exemplar, and forerunner through the resurrection into the glories of the most heavenly mansions." That this was really a part of the primitive doctrine appears from many passages, of which the following are fair specimens: "The disciple is not above his master, but every one that is perfect shall be as his master." Luke vi. 40. "Thy brother shall rise again. Martha saith unto him, I know that he shall rise again in the resurrection at the last day. Jesus said unto her, I am the resurrection, and the life." John xi. 23–25. "Let not your heart be troubled: ye believe in God, believe also in me. In my father's house are many mansions: if not, I would have told you. I go to prepare a place for you. And if I go and prepare a place for you, I will come again and receive you unto myself; that where I am ye may be also." John xiv. 1–3. "To this end Christ both died, and rose, and revived, that he might be Lord both of the dead and living." Rom. xiv. 9. "And as we have borne the image of the earthy, we shall also bear the image of the heavenly." 1 Cor. xv. 49. "For whom he did foreknow, he also did predestinate to be conformed to the image of his Son, that he might be the first-born among many brethren." Rom. viii. 29. "It became him, for whom are all things, and by whom are all things, in bringing many sons unto glory, to make the Captain of their salvation perfect through sufferings. For both he that sanctifieth, and they who are sanctified, are all of one: for which cause he is not ashamed to call them brethren." Heb. ii. 10, 11. "Which hope we have as an anchor of the soul both sure and steadfast, and which entereth into that within the vail; whither the forerunner is for us entered, even Jesus, made an high priest forever, after the order of Melchisedec." Heb. vi. 19, 20. "Beloved, now are we the sons of God, and it doth not yet appear what we shall be; but we know that when he shall appear, we shall be like him; for we shall see him as he is." 1 John iii. 2. "He is the head of the body, the church: who is the beginning, the first-born from the dead; that in all things he might have the pre-eminence. For it pleased the Father, that in him should all fulness dwell: and having made peace through the blood of his cross, by him to reconcile all things unto himself, . . . whether things in earth, or things in heaven." Col. i. 18–20.

Here I fitly close. I think I have made the pure primitive Christian doctrine concerning the resurrection from the dead sufficiently obvious, by my former statement, and the present verification thereof from the record. Some further illustration of minor points will incidentally be given in my next discourse on the corruptions of this doctrine; for which I trust your minds are now well prepared.

ARTICLE IV.

ANGELOLOGY, DEMONOLOGY, AND THE RESURRECTION FROM THE DEAD; OR, THE DOCTRINE OF SPIRITUAL AND IMMORTAL EXISTENCE.

DISCOURSE XVII.

CORRUPTIONS OF THE PRIMITIVE DOCTRINE OF THE RESURRECTION FROM THE DEAD.

"If the blind lead the blind, both shall fall into the ditch."— MATT. xv. 14.

THE errors and corruptions of Christendom concerning this doctrine of the resurrection from the dead are perhaps more excusable than in respect to almost any other teachings of Christ and his apostles. Why? Because scarcely any primitive Christian doctrine was stated in such figurative, various, and ambiguous terms. For many reasons it was liable to be misunderstood, in some of its bearings, even in the earliest times. The principal stumbling-ground, from the beginning to the present day, has always been, the *meaning* of certain terms, phrases, and statements, in which the doctrine was originally set forth and recorded. A large majority of the Jewish people, in Christ's time, had the same difficulty in understanding the language of those Old Testament Scriptures which predicted the coming of Elias, the

Messiah, and the peculiarities of the Messianic dispensation. Even his chosen disciples had confused and erroneous conceptions on these subjects, — certainly till after his ascension, if not to the end of their earthly lives, in some minor respects. There was a general and intense proneness of mind to confound spiritual and material things; to understand religious terms, phrases, and forms of expression in a secular sense; and to materialize, localize, literalize, mechanize, and traditionize the sublimest spiritual truths. This very proneness of mind has prevailed ever since in the nominal Christian church. Or, if the few have revolted at it, they have generally swung over to the other extreme, and spiritualized things into extreme and improbable senses. But we want "the truth, the whole truth, and nothing but the truth;" and this, by the will of God, we must sooner or later have.

Whoever carefully reads the four gospels must see that Christ often understood Old Testament predictions, doctrines, terms, phrases, and forms of expression, in a very different sense from the popular one, traditionally current among his contemporaries, and always in a higher spiritual and moral sense. He understood the true Messiahship, and indeed everything belonging to the gospel dispensation, in a higher, diviner sense. Consequently he used common language, terms, phrases, and forms of religious expression in a much higher and diviner sense. But mankind understood him then, and have ever since, according to their own generally narrow, carnal, and prejudiced states of mind. To illustrate this, let me, before coming directly to the work in hand, just refer to Christ's understanding of one important event, closely related to his own Messiahship, — the coming of Elias, or Elijah.

He regarded John the Baptist as the predicted Elias. But the Jews did not dream of such a meaning to the prophecy. The learned scribes did not. Even John himself did not regard himself as the promised Elias; for he disclaimed the pretension. John i. 21. Nevertheless, Christ understood him to be Elias. What was the prophecy? You can all read it in the last chapter of Malachi: "Behold, I will send you Elijah the prophet before the coming of the great and dreadful day of the Lord." Turn now to the seventeenth chapter of Matthew, where we have the record of Christ's transfiguration, and the manifestation of Moses and Elias. As they came down from the mountain, "the disciples asked him saying, Why, then, say the scribes, that Elias must first come? Jesus answered, Elias truly shall first come. . But I say unto you, that Elias is come already, and they knew him not, but have done unto him whatsoever they listed; likewise shall also the Son of man suffer of them. Then the disciples understood that he spake unto them of John the Baptist." See also Matt. xi. 7–14. This single case ought to be eminently suggestive to us, in the interpretation not only of Old Testament prophecies, but those in the New, and especially of Christ's own predictions.

I will now proceed to point out some of the principal corruptions which have darkened the primitive Christian doctrine of the resurrection.

1. The first of these consists in misunderstanding

the nature of the resurrection, and assuming that it must relate chiefly to the identical mortal body, miraculously reconstructed and immortalized. The primitive idea of raising the soul from its imperfect Hadean state into an ethereal or spiritual body, which should be a transcendent substitute for the earthly body, though certainly taught and necessarily implied, was obscurely understood, even in the apostolic age. The forms of expression and prevailing habits of thought concerning the resurrection, which were of Persian origin with Jewish modifications, seemed to relate the resurrection body so closely to the animal mortal body, that we need not wonder at the tendency of unspiritual minds to regard them as identical. And this tendency grew worse all through succeeding ages, till it culminated perhaps five hundred years ago. Since then the resurrection of the mortal body, as an article of faith, has lived mainly on traditionary theology and exegesis. It has been decaying slowly for more than a century, but is still cherished by millions in the bosom of the nominal church throughout its several divisions. Of course, nobody ever could make it rational, nor have many tried; but contented themselves by falling back on assumptions of miracle and mystery.

Some Christian teachers, like Origen and the Platonic speculatists, have held that all bodies in the resurrection would be of a globular form, and various fanciful notions on the subject have at different times been broached; but the orthodoxy of the church has rested in the corruption, that the identical bodies of all mankind in their natural form are to be raised incorruptible at the general resurrection. This has been proclaimed from pulpit and press times innumerable, and frequently with declamatory descriptions of the resurrection scene solemnly ludicrous. For instance, preachers who were crude minded enough to take the prophet Ezekiel's parabolic vision of the "dry bones," in his thirty-seventh chapter, as a description of the general resurrection (which plainly relates only to the temporal restoration of Israel), have descanted eloquently on the spectacle of widely scattered bones flying in all directions through the air, "bone to his bone"! It would be unjust to call in question the religious sincerity with which this and a thousand other absurdities have been preached and believed; but it is time that with equal sincerity we should cast away such errors, and understandingly cherish the truth. Religion and reason should never abuse each other.

2. Another great corruption of the primitive doctrine before us consists in misunderstanding the time of the general resurrection, and assuming that it was predicted to take place at the dissolution of our earth and solar system, technically termed the *end of the world*, and *judgment day*. The primitive doctrine positively declared that the judicial coming of Christ and the general resurrection of the then dead were to take place within a generation of time after his ministry and death; which period was termed the *end of the age*, and the beginning of the age to come. Christ said that no man knew the exact day, nor the angels, nor the Son himself, but the Father only. Yet he authoritatively declared, saying: "This generation

shall not pass, till all these things be fulfilled. Heaven and earth shall pass away, but my word shall not pass away." Matt. xxiv. 34, 35; Mark xiii. 30, 31; Luke xxi. 32, 33. The apostles all believed, expected, preached, and wrote accordingly. The "all things," which Christ said should be fulfilled before the then living generation passed away, were called forth in representation by these questions: "Tell us, when shall these things be, and what shall be the sign of thy coming, and of the end of the world [age]?" They include the destruction of the temple and city of Jerusalem, the dispersion of the Jewish nation, the general resurrection of the then dead, and the commencement of a new judicial era or age under the mediatorial administration of Christ, to continue till the subjugation and reconciliation of all things. The general resurrection of the then Hadean dead is not expressly stated in the recorded discourse of Christ now referred to, but is necessarily implied in various forms of expression used, especially by his allusions to the fulfilment of certain predictions in Daniel's prophecy, and by the agreement of the judicial events described with what he says concerning the resurrection in John v. 28, 29, collated with Daniel xii. 1, 2. We must either accept this view of the case, or else conclude that Christ and his apostles very gravely erred in their conceptions, declarations, and expectations respecting the most important of these matters and events. I decide, for myself, that the mistakes have been made by professing Christians since their time.

But how have these mistakes happened? Partly in

the same way that most of the Jewish scribes and their followers mistook the Old Testament prophecies concerning the coming of Elias, of Christ, and the new dispensation; and partly because an important portion of the predicted events took place in the invisible world, whereof they could take no mortal cognizance, and had no just conception. The destruction of the Jewish metropolis, temple, and nationality developed events cognizable by the external senses of mankind, and therefore recordable in the world's history. But the Hadean world, the resurrection of its spirit hosts, the moral majesty of Christ revealing himself amid clouds of angels in his spiritual kingdom, and the inauguration of his perfect dispensation of judicial discipline, were in their very nature invisible to mortal eyes, and not subjects of earthly history. These just views do not seem to have been received, or even imagined, by Christians of the second and succeeding centuries. Christ certainly predicted them in close connection with the signal overthrow of the Jewish hierarchy, power, and national glory; the destruction of Jerusalem and its splendid temple; and the setting up of the "abomination" that should "desolate" the holy place. But then he did so in spiritualistic and figurative language, which unspiritual minds must fain understand in a materialistic sense. He had said, "Immediately after the tribulation of those days shall the sun be darkened, and the moon shall not give her light, and the stars shall fall from heaven, and the powers of the heavens shall be shaken," etc., etc. What, to such minds, could such language mean but the dissolution of heaven and earth

— the literal end of the material world? There was a great mystery about the matter to them, but the probable meaning must be that just such physical events would sometime surely come to pass. Hence clergy and laity have been expecting and postponing them ever since. In our own time the adventists first fixed 1843 as the year of consummation, and since then sundry other dates. Meantime, all the way down from the close of the first century, the second coming of Christ, the general resurrection of the dead, the judgment day, and end of the material world by fire, have been most popular and terrific themes of pulpit declamation. They are slowly dying out in our own age, but are by no means yet extinct, or uncommon, among the terroristic sects. Thus what the primitive doctrine designated as the end or consummation of the then closing theocratic age, order, or dispensation, has been metamorphosed into the dissolution of material planetary nature. The primitive general resurrection, which was to open in the spiritual world coincidently with the destruction of Jerusalem, with respect to the past dead, and continue at Christ's discretion, with respect to succeeding generations, through his mediatorial reign to its triumphant consummation, has been adjourned to the expected dissolution of our solar system. Likewise, the primitive judicial " coming of Christ " and " judgment day " have been corrupted from their original character and meaning into tremendous external, local, and formal displays to take place at the same expected dissolution of all things. And now we find Christianity suffering the consequences of these misunderstandings and corruptions. Its enemies pronounce it crude, inconsistent, and irreconcilable with natural science and even with itself, on these points; to which the great body of its friends, in their confusion of traditionary errors, can make no satisfactorily defensive answer. The only remedy is an intelligent, well-considered return to the pure primitive doctrine.

3. The last great and pernicious corruption, which I have now time to notice, consists in making the resurrection of "the unjust" useless, hopeless, vindictive, and inductive only into a miserable immortality. The primitive doctrine represents the wicked as raised out of their primary low condition in Hades to judgment and condemnation, not to confirm them in ignorance, sin, and misery, but to convince them of the truth, to subdue them to Christ, and to discipline them into a humble confession that he is "Lord, to the glory of God the Father," that finally "God may be all in all." A moral resurrection is always involved in the personal spiritual resurrection. Indeed, raising up and elevating the moral nature is the main and most essential part of the resurrection, as primitively taught. The idea of immortal sinfulness and misery, as an ultimate of the resurrection to any class of human beings, is not to be found in the New Testament. But the corruptionists have made this monstrous notion a part of Christian orthodoxy. For what, according to their notion, are the unjust, or wicked, to be raised from the dead? To better their condition in any respect? No. But to perfect them for an immortality of sin and punishment, — a punishment which is to have no imaginable

good effect except a public, formal display of God's righteous wrath, and this is to do *them* no good. They are more or less unhappy in the underworld; they are hopelessly predoomed at death to an eternity of sin and woe; yet they must be resurrected, soul and body, merely for the purpose of being formally sentenced to immortal anguish. The poet Pollock thus describes their case: —

> "I saw most miserable beings walk,
> Burning continually, yet unconsumed;
> Forever wasting, yet enduring still;
> Dying perpetually, yet never dead.
> Some wandered lonely in the desert flames,
> And some in full encounter fiercely met,
> With curses loud, and blasphemies that made
> The cheek of darkness pale; and as they fought,
> And cursed, and gnashed their teeth,
> And wished to die,
> Their hollow eyes did utter streams of woe.
> And there were groans that ended not, and sighs
> That always sighed, and tears that ever
> And ever fell, but not in mercy's sight.
> And Sorrow, and Repentance, and Despair,
> Among them walked, and to their thirsty lips
> Presented frequent cups of burning gall.
> And as I listened, I heard these beings curse
> Almighty God, and curse the Lamb, and curse
> The earth, the resurrection morn, and seek,
> And ever vainly seek for utter death."

From such and all kindred corruptions of the pure primitive Christian doctrine of the resurrection, let us pray, in the language of the Episcopal Liturgy, "Good Lord, deliver us!"

ARTICLE V.

REGENERATION AND SALVATION.

DISCOURSE XVIII.

THE PURE PRIMITIVE DOCTRINE OF REGENERATION AND SALVATION, AS TAUGHT BY CHRIST AND HIS APOSTLES.

"Verily, verily, I say unto thee, Except a man be born again, he cannot see the kingdom of God." "That which is born of the flesh, is flesh; and that which is born of the Spirit, is spirit." — JOHN iii. 3, 6.

"The grace of God which bringeth salvation to all men hath appeared, teaching us that denying ungodliness, and worldly lusts, we should live soberly, righteously, and godly in this present world." — TITUS ii. 11, 12.

The generation of man is that process which brings him into existence. Regeneration is that process which renders him a truly righteous or holy being. Salvation is the process which delivers from some evil or danger. The salvation proclaimed in the Christian gospel is that process whereby man is delivered from the evils and dangers of sin. It must, therefore, be obvious that Christian regeneration and salvation are very closely related to each other. What, then, is the pure primitive Christian doctrine of regeneration and salvation?

1. That mankind, as flesh-born beings, are naturally first governed by animal, carnal, selfish

motives, hence are averse to purely spiritual, benevolent laws of order, and consequently fall into sin on coming to the knowledge of divine moral requirements. 2. That mankind in general, by reason of their natural animal selfishness, become dead in trespasses and sins, justly condemned by the divine moral law, and so strongly indisposed to true righteousness, without the enlightening, quickening, and sanctifying influences of the Holy Spirit. 3. That by the grace of God his Holy Spirit is universally operating on the souls of mankind, with more or less effect, to induce their regeneration, and when welcomed, cherished, and obeyed, renders them new moral creatures as to their ruling motives, principles of action, and dominant affections, thus gradually transforming them into the spiritual likeness of Christ. 4. That this work of spiritual and moral regeneration always requires faith, prayer, repentance, and earnest endeavor on man's part, and without these is never accomplished, but may be lamentably neglected, hindered, and prevented. 5. That mankind attain salvation from sin and its evils only through regeneration; and until its renewing operation on their moral natures has at least commenced, they abide in spiritual death, under divine condemnation, unreconciled to God, and aliens from his heavenly kingdom, according to their respective degrees of insubordination, sinfulness, and guilt.

That these statements correctly express the essentials of the primitive Christian doctrine concerning regeneration and salvation will conclusively appear from many passages of the record applicable more or less explicitly to my five propositions, either severally or collectively. 1. Mankind are naturally animal, carnal, selfish, averse to purely spiritual, benevolent laws of order, and so, consequently, fall into sin on coming to the knowledge of divine moral requirements. Mark and understand the terms of the statement. It does not assert that mankind are born totally depraved, or actually sinful, or in any sense guilty, any more than the innocent lower animals, but rather like them, only as possessing a latent moral nature which commences its activity after the animal nature has become habituated to rule. Thus, though human infants are all innocent till they come to the knowledge of moral good and evil, they are not *righteous;* because, till then, they make no choice, between right and wrong, any more than the lower animals do. Nor are they otherwise than animally inclined, and so prone to fall into sin when they reach the knowledge of the moral law. Then they readily fall into sin, being more or less averse to the wholesome checks and restraints which that law of purity and unselfishness imposes on their animal desires. Now this is substantially the doctrine of Christ and the apostles, if I can understand their record. Accordingly Christ said, "Except a man be born again, he cannot see the kingdom of God." "That which is born of the flesh is flesh" [that is, flesh-like, or animal, in its nature, desires, and activities]; "and that which is born of the Spirit is spirit" [that is, is spirit-like, or spiritual, in its nature, loves, and activities]. How true! Therefore, mankind, being flesh-born, are animal and selfish before the Divine Spirit calls forth their moral nature to realize the obligations of spiritual law. This is why they cannot perceive, appreciate, and conform to the kingdom of God, until born of the Holy Spirit into the loves of God and man.

Paul treats clearly on this point: "I was alive without the law once [in my infancy], but when the commandment came, sin revived, and I died [that is, I found myself prone to sin, and fell into condemnation.] "For I know that in me (that is, in my flesh), [and my carnal mind thence derived] dwelleth no good thing [no spiritually holy principle of action]: for to will is present with me, but to perform that which is good I find not." Rom. vii. 9, 18. See the whole connection. Again: "We have received, not the spirit of the world [of physical and animal nature], but the Spirit which is of God [the Holy Spirit]; that we might know the things that are freely given us of God." But the natural man [in his animal-mindedness] receiveth not the things of the Spirit of God [being averse to them]; neither can he know them [in their real excellence], because they are spiritually discerned [and appreciated]." 1 Cor. ii. 12, 14. Again: "Walk in the Spirit, and ye shall not fulfil the lust of the flesh. For the flesh lusteth against the Spirit, and the Spirit against the flesh; so that ye cannot do the things that ye would." Gal. v. 16, 17. Once more: "In time past, ye walked according to the course of this world, according to the prince of the power of the air, the spirit that now worketh in the children of disobedience: among whom also we all had our conversation in times past in the lusts of our flesh, fulfilling the desires of the flesh and the mind; and were by nature the children of wrath [subjects of just condemnation], even as others." Ephes. ii. 2, 3. The meaning of these and many similar passages seems very plain, and they are pertinent to my first point. I proceed to the

2. That mankind in general, by reason of their natural animal selfishness, become dead in trespasses and sins, justly condemned by the divine moral law, and so strongly indisposed to true righteousness without the enlightening, quickening and sanctifying influences of the Holy Spirit. This is not asserting that mankind, in their carnal-minded, unregenerate state, are as wicked as they can be, or in any sense totally depraved, or all equally depraved, or not capable of doing right in various respects; but that their ruling loves and principles of moral action are predominantly animal, carnal, worldly, selfish; not spiritually pure, unselfish, and Christ-like; and that their righteousness, whatever it may seem to be, is not the true righteousness which springs from disinterested love to God, man, and the universal highest good. Now the doctrine is, that mankind, through their flesh-born animal-mindedness, and self-worshipping indisposition to divine discipline, are morally incapable of true righteousness without the enlightening, quickening, and sanctifying influences of the Holy Spirit. They are capable *with* this, but not *without* it. So Christ and his apostles emphatically testified.

"This is the condemnation, that light is come into the world, and men loved darkness rather than light, because their deeds were evil." John iii. 19. "Me the world hateth, because I testify of it, that the works thereof are evil." John vii. 7. "Therefore speak I unto them in parables: because they seeing see not; and hearing they hear not; neither do they understand. And in them is fulfilled the prophecy of Esaias which saith, By hearing ye shall hear, and not understand; and seeing ye shall see, and not perceive. For this people's heart is waxed gross, and their ears are dull of hearing, and their eyes they have closed, lest at any time they should see with their eyes, and hear with their ears, and should understand with their heart, and be converted, and I should heal them." Matt. xiii. 13–15. "Ye will not come unto me, that ye might have life." "How can ye believe, which receive honor one of another, and seek not the honor that cometh from God only?" John v. 41, 44.

Paul said: "We have before proved both Jews and Gentiles that they are all under sin. As it is written, There is none righteous, no not one." "They are all gone out of the way; they are together become unprofitable." Rom. iii. 9–12, etc. "Know ye not that the unrighteous shall not inherit the kingdom of God? Be not deceived: neither fornicators, nor idolaters, nor adulterers, nor effeminate, nor abusers of themselves with mankind, nor thieves, nor covetous, nor drunkards, nor revilers, nor extortioners, shall inherit the kingdom of God. And such were some of you: but ye are washed, but ye are sanctified, but ye are justified, in the name of the Lord Jesus, and by the Spirit of our God." 1 Cor. vi. 9–11. Again: "For we ourselves also were sometimes foolish, disobedient, deceived, serving divers lusts and pleasures, living in malice and envy, hateful, and hating one another. But after that the kindness and love of God our Saviour toward man appeared, not by works of righteousness which we have done, but according to his mercy, he saved us by the washing of regeneration, and renewing of the Holy Ghost which he shed on us abundantly through Jesus Christ our Saviour." Titus iii. 3–6. These testimonies are too pertinent and explicit to require comment. I go to the next point.

3. That by the grace of God his Holy Spirit is universally operating on the souls of mankind, with more or less effect, to induce their regeneration, and whenever welcomed, cherished, and obeyed, renders them new moral creatures as to their ruling motives, principles of action, and dominant affections, thus gradually transforming them into the spiritual likeness of Christ. Here are several prominent ideas to be noted. The grace, or unmerited favor, of God originates all the good done. The Holy Spirit, whereby he works, is universally operating, with more or less effect, to induce the souls of mankind to act in the right direction, none being left wholly to themselves. But they must welcome, cherish, and obey the Divine Spirit, not resist, grieve, and quench it. Then it will render them new moral creatures in their ruling motives, principles, and loves, thus gradually transforming their characters so as to make them Christ-like in true righteousness; not leaving them passably moral and civil in some respects, from mere education, or selfish motives, but spiritually upright

from the highest motives of love to God, man, and the universal good. This last is pure Christian regeneration and salvation. It is the great and indispensable work to be wrought in and upon the human soul.

The Logos, really the Holy Spirit in the highest sense, "was the true Light, which lighteth every man that cometh into the world. He was in the world, and the world was made by him [that is, operatively through his agency], and the world knew him not. He came unto his own [entempled in Jesus], and his own received him not. But as many as received him, to them gave he power to become the sons of God, — to them that believe on his name: who were born, not of blood, nor of the will of the flesh, nor of the will of man, but of God." John i. 9-13. "The Spirit of the Lord is upon me, because he hath anointed me to preach the gospel," etc. Luke iv. 18. "It is written in the prophets, And they shall all be taught of God. Every man therefore that hath heard and hath learned of the Father, cometh unto me." John vi. 45. "God so loved the world, that he gave his only begotten Son, that whosoever believeth in him should not perish, but have eternal life." Ibid. iii. 16. "Herein is love, not that we loved God, but that he loved us, and sent his only begotten Son to be the propitiation for our sins. Beloved, if God so loved us, we ought also to love one another." "Love is of God, and every one that loveth is born of God." 1 John iv. 10, 11, 7. "Being born again, not of corruptible seed, but of incorruptible, by the word of God [the Logos], which liveth and abideth forever."

1 Pet. i. 23. "There is no condemnation to them who are in Christ Jesus, who walk not after the flesh, but after the Spirit." "Ye are not in the flesh, but in the Spirit, if so be that the Spirit of God dwell in you. Now, if any man have not the Spirit of Christ, he is none of his." "For as many as are led by the Spirit of God, they are the sons of God." Rom. viii. 1, 9, 14. "Therefore, if any man be in Christ, he is a new creature: old things are passed away; behold, all things are become new." 2 Cor. v. 17. Comments are unnecessary, and I may proceed to the next point.

4. That this work of spiritual and moral regeneration always requires faith, repentance, and earnest endeavor on man's part, and without these is never accomplished; but may be lamentably neglected, hindered, and prevented. God does his part, which is the major part, from beginning to end; but he treats man always as a responsible moral agent, and requires him to perform his minor part; that is, to have confidence in and acknowledge the truth, to seek, pray, strive, and perseveringly endeavor after the good proffered him. Otherwise it could never be truly appreciated and enjoyed by him. This is so plainly taught in so many passages which are familiar to readers of the New Testament, that it seems almost superfluous to quote samples. The same is true of the idea that regeneration is never accomplished without faith, repentance, and obedience on man's part, — never in this world or the future state, and must not be expected; but that there is danger of man's lamentably neglecting, hindering, and preventing it

indefinitely to his own bitter cost. The most delusive and pernicious idea which we can cherish is, that our work of spiritual regeneration, progress, and perfectation, is all to be done for us, by God, Christ, or some power above us. It is true that we cannot frustrate God, or change our final destiny; but on this side of finalities, we certainly can make ourselves very foolish, wicked, and miserable, by resisting God's goodness, poisoning the cup of our own welfare, and retarding our privileged progress. God has wisely left us this liberty to sin, suffer, and repent.

5. Finally, the fifth stated proposition may be regarded as only a more emphatic amplification of the fourth; namely, that mankind attain salvation from sin and its evils only through regeneration; and that, until its renewing operation on their moral natures has at least commenced, they abide in death, under divine condemnation, unreconciled to God, and aliens from his heavenly kingdom, according to their respective degrees of insubordination, sinfulness, and guilt. This is clearly taught in numerous passages, couched in various phraseology, of which the following are specimens: "He that heareth my word, and believeth on him that sent me, hath everlasting life, and shall not come into condemnation; but is passed from death unto life." John v. 24. "And he that believeth not the Son shall not see life, but the wrath [just condemnation] of God abideth on him." Ibid. iii. 36. "Go ye into all the world, and preach the gospel to every creature. He that believeth and is baptized [with the Holy Spirit it must mean] shall be saved, but he that believeth not shall be damned,"

[that is, remain in spiritual death and just condemnation].

Thus it would seem plain that the primitive Christian doctrine of regeneration and salvation contemplates two radically different spiritual and moral states, in one or the other of which all human souls must, for the time being, exist; namely, the unregenerate, sinful, justly condemned state; and the regenerate, righteous, divinely approved state. Mankind were deemed to be primarily in the unregenerate, lost state; then the truly converted to be in the regenerate, saved state; and all not truly converted, of course, to remain in the unsaved, condemned state until subdued to Christ by his mediatorial discipline. But it must be understood that these two radically different spiritual and moral states were held, each of them, to include many various grades of moral standing from lowest to highest. That is to say, in the unregenerate state there are many grades from bad to worse; and in the regenerate state many grades from good to best. The question now remains, Is the doctrine of Christ and his apostles on this subject true, rational, and worthy of our enlightened support? In my next I shall endeavor to show, by proper analysis and elucidation, that it is.

ARTICLE V.

REGENERATION AND SALVATION.

DISCOURSE XIX.

IS THE DOCTRINE OF CHRISTIAN REGENERATION AND SALVATION, AS SET FORTH IN THE PRECEDING DISCOURSE, TRUE, RATIONAL, AND WORTHY OF OUR ENLIGHTENED SUPPORT?

"How can these things be? Jesus answered and said unto him, Art thou a master of Israel, and knowest not these things? Verily, verily, I say unto thee, We speak that we do know, and testify that we have seen; and ye receive not our witness." — JOHN iii. 9-11.

In the preceding discourse I endeavored to set forth the pure primitive doctrine of Christian regeneration and salvation. I believe my statement of it was substantially correct. Before treating of its corruptions, it seems to me that I ought carefully to analyze and elucidate it. Why? 1. Because it is the pivotal doctrine of Christianity, and above all others needs to be understood, appreciated, and acted on. 2. Because it is difficult to understand, appreciate, and practically apply it. And, 3. Because it has not only been grossly abused and perverted by professing Christians, but is now in danger of being nullified by rationalistic moralists, who are prone to regard it as an unmeaning mysticism, rather than a fundamental doctrine. Now, if it is not such a doctrine, the very term regeneration can be little better than one of pietistic cant, denoting some mysterious experience, incomprehensible to human reason even the most enlightened, and thus capable of meaning whatever religious imagination or theological caprice may happen to assume. But if primitive Christianity is justly chargeable with mysticism and cant, or requiring irrational spiritual experiences as necessary to human salvation, then its inevitable grave is already dug. I concede nothing of the kind; and therefore propose to go to the bottom of some searching inquiries into the truth and reasonableness of what I have set forth as the pure primitive doctrine of regeneration and salvation.

1. Is it true and rational to maintain that all mankind indispensably need what Christ and the apostles called regeneration, or being born again, in order to enter the kingdom of heaven, that is, in order to be absolutely holy and happy? Was there some original defect in their creation? Are they generated and born into natural life wrong, or in any sense contrary to God's original design? Certainly not, all things considered, although there have been great human abuses in procreation. They are generated and born according to the order of the fleshly nature and constitution. Is this wrong? No. Is it an evil? No. They are generated and born into natural animal life, like the lower animals, and have all the propensities and passions common to animal nature. Is there anything wrong or evil in this? No. They possess in their constitution important distinctive faculties

and capabilities which the lower animals do not. What are these? Religious, moral, and rational faculties, and the spiritual capabilities of divine inspiration, faith, hope, worship, love, and progress towards heavenly perfection. These faculties and capabilities raise man above the lower animals. They render him a religious being, an accountable moral agent, and of course a sinner the moment he knows his duty and transgresses its requirements. But this religious, rational, and spiritual superiority of man to the lower animals, with all its responsibilities, lies latent in him at first. He has no consciousness of it during his early infancy, for several years. Some attain to it earlier, and some later. Till then, human infants are deemed sinless and innocent, like the animals, even though they manifest dispositions which would be sinful if they knew the moral law. Is not all this obviously true? Yes. Was it not best that God should so constitute man? Undoubtedly. What next in the order of development? Thus far the human being is an innocent animal, unconscious of divine moral law, his higher capabilities latent in him. He is three, four, five, or six years old. He has been subject only to laws which govern beings on the mere animal plane. What are these? The simple natural instincts, affections, and necessities. He craves and enjoys nutriment and whatever gratifies his five senses. He loves self-gratification as it offers itself through those senses. He forms habits of pleasure, and presently has a will of his own. What is that will? It is like that of all the animals, one that insists on self-gratification, more or less modified by his natural affections, by necessity, by circumstances, and by special training, still essentially selfish. Is there any sin in all this? Not yet. It is no sin in the animal to be selfish. That is its nature. But God did not make man to remain and be governed long as a mere animal. How lamentable if he had! His latent religious faculties and capabilities must be developed. Gradually he becomes conscious of them. He finds himself required to love and obey God, and to submit his own will to a higher will, though it sorely crosses his habitual inclinations. He finds himself required to regard the good of others, to love his neighbors as himself, to respect all their rights, to care for their good as his own, to do unto others as he would have them do unto him, and all this, when, for the moment, it seems flatly contrary to self-gratification. Now, how does he act toward God and man? Perfectly right, willingly obedient to this higher law, with a spontaneous, hearty free will? No; if it does not much cross his habitual love of self-gratification, he will perhaps obey the requirement, or, if it comes easy under the circumstances, he will. But otherwise, there will be reluctance, an aversion, a conflict between self and sense of duty, and, presently, sin. Once in sin, he will soon take another step, and another, and another; in which he will find numerous fellow-sinners to keep him in countenance, if not seductively to lead him downward. Meantime, perhaps, he feels some remorse, makes some poor resolutions of reform, falls again through pressure of inclination and temptation, then tries to extenuate his disobedience, then strongly excuses it, then even justifies it nearly or quite, then soothes his conscience by pleading that he is no worse than others, or not as bad, and so finally becomes what is scripturally termed, "dead in trespasses and sins."

Such is the actual origin and history of human sin. Is not the fall into it as natural as it has been animal? Is God in fault for having created the animal nature ignorant of moral law, sensual, and selfish? I think not. Is he in fault for giving to man this animal nature, and depositing in it the ungerminated seed of the religious and rational nature? I think not. Is there anything in the animal nature *per se* evil? I think not. It only requires to be subordinated to and regulated by the moral nature. Is God in fault for so constituting and circumstancing man that the selfish animal nature is developed first, and allowed to acquire habitual activity before the higher nature germinates, thus necessitating a long and painful struggle for victory? This last is the question of questions. The answer depends on three considerations: 1. Did God mean it unto ultimate human good? 2. Are struggle and suffering, to a certain extent, the best means of perfecting humanity's highest good? 3. Has God amply provided all necessary helps for the attainment of humanity's ultimate highest good in passing through this struggle? Primitive Christianity answers these three questions. It answers them in the affirmative. It answers them positively and emphatically. Enlightened reason gives the same answers.

Christ and his apostles declared the world of mankind to be flesh-born, animal-minded, selfish, ignorant, and sinful, — even dead in sins. They declared that God so loved the world that he sent his Son to save it from all its ignorance, selfishness, and sin. And they declared that God's method of salvation through Christ was one of thorough spiritual and moral regeneration, by the operation of the Holy Spirit, concurrently welcomed on man's part with faith, repentance, and sincere endeavors after true righteousness. If God had not loved the world of mankind notwithstanding all its sinfulness, of course it would have perished in its own selfish animality. I say perished; sunk hopelessly down in error, sin, and wretchedness. But he did love it. He loved it in design before actual creation. He has always loved it. He will love it to eternity. "For God is love." Yet there was a wisest and best way to treat mankind in love. Christ came to reveal and illustrate that way. It was a way of salvation from ignorance, carnal-mindedness, selfishness, and sin. It was the way of regeneration. But regeneration was impossible without the operation of that same Holy Spirit wherewith Jesus himself was filled to overflowing. That Spirit must needs enter into man's soul to enlighten his understanding, quicken his religious powers, cleanse his affections, help his infirmities, comfort him with assurances of divine acceptance, and mould him into the moral image of Christ. All this was proffered and promised in the gospel; and sinful man was tenderly entreated to grasp trustingly the helping hand let down from heaven to save him, and to work earnestly for his own salvation under and with the divine regenerating power. Thus the animal in man, which is a hard, bad *master*, would be rendered an orderly and good *servant* to the higher nature. It seems to me that thus far nothing can be truer, more rational, or more worthy of our support, than this pure primitive doctrine of Christian regeneration.

2. But here another important inquiry arises. What is it that regeneration really does for the human soul? How does it commence, through what stages does it proceed, and where does it end? Christian regeneration proposes a threefold perfection as its consummation: perfection of wisdom in the understanding respecting the laws of divine order, so that the soul shall not mistake its duty; perfection of self-discipline and self-sacrifice for righteousness' sake, so that obedience to the laws of divine order shall overrule all contrary motives and influences; and perfection of love to God, to fellow-creatures, to divine principles, and to the highest universal good, so that everything absolutely right and good in thought, desire, temper, word, and action shall be supremely delighted in for its own sake. This consummation of regeneration in every human soul will fulfil man's destiny, according to the purpose of God, as revealed through Christ, — and nothing less than this can. So long as one soul of our race comes short of this, *God will not "be all in all."* And until God is "all in all," the regenerative reign and discipline of Christ will be incomplete. But the Father has ordained that it shall continue till perfectly consummated.

Now, let us come back from the end to the commencement of regeneration. In every soul there must be a moment when regeneration begins. We may not always be able to mark it, but there is such a moment. The kingdom of heaven is like leaven in a mass of meal, and mustard seed in the soil, — small in the beginning, yet having a living principle. What are the signs that regeneration has commenced in any person? There are several. I will mention five.

1. There is a perception and acknowledgment of divine law as rightfully supreme over all that is human. 2. There is a quickened conscience, convicting the soul of sin, and disposing it to confess freely its state of just condemnation. 3. There is a moral principle, of greater or less strength, fixed in the mind to do the understood will of God, in spite of the selfish will of the flesh. 4. There is humility, tenderness of spirit, a felt burden of sinfulness, a deploring of evil propensities, a hungering after higher righteousness, a considerateness of what is due to God and fellow-creatures, and a prayerful seeking for divine help. And, 5. There is a decided interest in what promises human enlightenment, reformation, and progress in real goodness; a growing disposition to put truth and righteousness first, before mere worldly interest, pleasure, convenience, fashion, human applause, and popular opinion. By these signs we can judge, with tolerable certainty, whether regeneration has commenced in our own souls and in those of our neighbors. Every tree is known by its fruits. Regeneration is thus known. The germ may be small, but it will be discernible.

If, on examining myself truthfully, I find that I neither understand nor care much for any divine law, as supreme over all that is human; that I have a dull, easy conscience, and a disposition to contend that I am about wise and good enough; that I have little or no fixed moral principle, and am living mainly as my selfish inclinations lead me, except through fear of civil law or public opinion; that I am self-sufficient, self-willed, inconsiderate of duty toward God and fellow-man, and feel the cross for righteousness' sake to be more burdensome than my own sinful propensities; and that I have little or no interest in the various means of progress in divine wisdom and goodness, but am mainly interested in worldly, sensual self-gratifications, — then I may know that I have not yet entered in "at the strait gate;" that I am in "the broad way" of death; in fine, that the washing of regeneration has not yet commenced in my soul. Alas, what multitudes are in this unregenerate condition, drifting onward they know not whither!

But there are myriads, in whom regeneration has commenced, who have made but small progress in its narrow way toward life eternal, who are mere beginners, very crude and imperfect in their embrace of divine truth and righteousness. Some lack light in their understandings, some warmth in their religious affections, and others are feeble in spiritual power, purpose, zeal, and perseverance. Some go forward rapidly, others slowly, others seem to stand still, or even to retrograde for the time. Few attain to the fulness of regeneration in the present life. But the sublime process will go on, in this or in the next state of existence, under the same laws. In millions it will have to begin there, and continue for perhaps ages. Yet its nature, operations, and effects will remain unchangeably the same in their essentials. Somewhere man must be born again, in order to enter into the full blessedness of the divine kingdom. This is as certain as that he exists.

It may be asked whether the commencement of regeneration, as I have defined it, necessarily requires faith in Jesus Christ and his distinctive religion as a condition precedent. No; its commencement does not; but its consummation *does*. How so? That which we call the Holy Spirit is universally communicable to mankind in some degree. It enlightens more or less every man that cometh into the world. Therefore it may *begin* regeneration in any man, of any nation or people, who welcomes, cherishes, and obeys it. Why, then, not finish the work without Christ? Because this very Holy Spirit is the same that by its pre-eminent inflowing made Jesus the Christ, and must sooner or later lead all to him as its perfect medium and model man. It cannot cause nor allow any soul to hate, despise, or set at nought its own chief Anointed. But why lead all to him sooner or later? Because in him the fulness of this divine Spirit dwells, and through him it gives forth the very highest manifestations of heavenly truth and righteousness, which all need, but can nowhere else find fully embodied and illustrated. Therefore all must bow, and confess him "Lord to the glory of God the Father." His religion is, in fact, the only one which declares the perfect love of God to man without a drawback; which also requires perfect love from man to God and to fellow-man, without the least allowance of self-worship, or of harm even to the worst of enemies. To this all mankind must come, in order to universal and perfect happiness. Consequently complete regeneration, which alone brings them to this, cannot be consummated without the universal acceptance of Christ and his religion. How many millions of sincere, conscientious, pious souls there are, not wise, loving, and good, up to the excellence of Christ-likeness! Either they lack his light, or spirit. Now is not all this true, rational, and worthy of our reverential support? It is so to me. It will some time be so to all human souls.

3. Finally, the inquiry naturally presents itself: If the unregenerate are outside of the kingdom of God, and cannot enter into its blessedness till they become regenerate, where, in God's governmental economy, do they stand meantime? How are they governed? What are their responsibilities? And wherein can they do good at all? Answer. All grades of nature, and all beings, from lowest to highest, are subject to divine laws of some kind, and are properly governed. Mineral nature, vegetable nature, animal nature, human nature, angelic nature, and divine nature, through all their varieties, are thus properly governed. But every grade of nature, and every kind of being, is governed by laws peculiar to its own constitution and condition. God governs unregenerate and sinful men by laws suitable to their condition and needs. They are above the animals both in intellect and moral capacity. They are below the Christ-plane of spiritual and moral order. They cannot, or will not, be governed by his perfect law of love to God, man, and the universal good. Therefore they

are governed by lower laws, which prescribe, or at least allow, lower standards of righteousness. They are governed partly by laws proper for animals, partly by laws proper for intellectual beings without pure moral principles, partly by laws of social relationship, affection, and interest, partly by civil, political and military laws, and partly by refracted moral influences which reach them from a higher plane through the power of truth and public opinion, as crystallized in established institutions, customs, and usages. According to these various lower laws and standards of righteousness, unregenerate mankind are made the best of for the time being on their own plane, and wisely governed, till they can be elevated to the Christ-plane. When they cannot be attracted, persuaded, and educated to act well, or at least to be civilly decent, they are compelled to submit to severe restraint by physical force, or killed outright by those on their own plane. So, through selfish hope of good and selfish fear of evil, — attractive suasion and violent brute force, — the world is kept in such order as it is. Christianity makes no war with this order of worldly society and government, because it is better than what would certainly be a worse state of things without it. Neither does Christianity ignore or denounce anything really right or good which unregenerate men do from motives below its own standard. Yet we must be careful to understand that, as a finality, it is not satisfied with the world as it is, with society as it is, with low standards of virtue and righteousness as they are, nor with the low motives from which the generality of worldly good people do what is externally right. Why not? Because at best all these things are far below its own sublime aim, and leave mankind vastly beneath their high capabilities and destiny. It therefore proposes and insists on regeneration, as indispensable to the glorious result designed by the universal Father. It proposes and insists on regeneration, not according to the genius of military or political revolution, but spiritually by the power of divine truth and love, enlightening the understanding, purifying the heart, and forming the moral character into the likeness of Christ, — so as beneficently to supersede all that is animal, carnal, selfish, and cruel, with all that is spiritual, loving, and heavenly. If Christianity rises not to this unrivalled excellence, its supernal professions are vain. What better is it than the other religions which it claims to transcend? But primitive Christianity certainly does transcend all other religions and philosophies. I have shown in what respects. Its doctrine of regeneration and salvation is therefore most true, most rational, most beautiful, and most worthy of our uncompromising support. Such is my own profound conviction; God grant it may be yours! and may he help us to reverence it accordingly. Next, I shall treat of the corruptions which have disfigured and obscured this doctrine.

ARTICLE V.

REGENERATION AND SALVATION.

DISCOURSE XX.

CORRUPTIONS OF THE PURE PRIMITIVE DOCTRINE.

"Salt is good: but if the salt have lost its savor, wherewith shall it be seasoned." — Luke xiv. 34.

Having stated, analyzed, and elucidated the primitive doctrine of Christian regeneration and salvation, I will now point out several important and pernicious corruptions which it has undergone.

1. It has been corrupted in respect to its cardinal object, necessity, and effect. What was the great object of regeneration and salvation held up to view by Christ and his apostles? Deliverance from sin and induction into true righteousness; translation out of the kingdom of darkness into that of divine light: superseding the tyrannical mastery of the carnal or animal mind with the rightful mastery of the spiritual mind, — in fine, resurrection of the soul out of death in trespasses and sins into that life eternal which inheres in Christ-like wisdom and love. What pressing necessity did they represent there was for this regeneration and salvation? The utter impossibility of man's ever being happy in sin, and the certainty that sin

naturally and inevitably brings forth worse and worse fruits, greater and greater miseries, more and more dreadful death, according to God's perfect laws of order. What great spiritual motive did they hold up to induce and encourage people to seek salvation, exercise repentance, and strive after regeneration? The surpassing love and goodness of God toward the whole world of mankind while yet in their sins, manifested in sending his Son to be the Captain of their salvation, in the gift of his Holy Spirit to enlighten, quicken, and afford them every needed help, and in his readiness to accept them, by the forgiveness of past sins, into free reconciliation and communion with himself. Did they represent that God ever had hated mankind, or ever would hate them, on account of their sins? that he had ever been infinitely offended with them for sin, or ever would be? that he ever was or ever would be implacable toward them? that his vengeance in this world or the next toward sinners was a reason why men should seek salvation? or that they should do so because future endless punishment or annihilation must be their certain doom unless they made their peace with God in this earthly probationary life? No, nothing of all this do we find in the records of the primitive gospel. Sin, death, just condemnation, and woe they made inseparable, as cause and consequence, here and hereafter, with ever-increasing dangers to the impenitent; and they gave no hope of salvation but through faith, repentance, and regeneration; yet never limited the love, grace, or mercy of God, nor made his offended, vindictive justice a motive for religious concern. Their salvation was one from sin as a great prolific evil *per se*, rather than from punishment, hell, or the offended justice of God.

But corruption has given us a very different doctrine of regeneration and salvation, in respect to its principal object, motific necessity, and specific effect. This corruption, like others, began early, but did not take on its most odious features till after church and state became united in the fourth century. Then priestly ecclesiasticism found it convenient to fortify its usurpations by extra-spiritual terror. I cannot give you a ranker specimen of this corruption than in a brief extract or two from a sermon preached in 1741, by the famous Jona. Edwards, "On the Danger of the Unconverted," entitled, "Sinners in the Hands of an Angry God:" —

"The God that holds you over the Pit of Hell, much as one holds a Spider, or some loathsome insect, over the Fire, abhors you, and is dreadfully provoked; his Wrath towards you burns like Fire; he looks upon you as worthy of nothing else but to be cast into the Fire; he is of purer eyes than to bear to have you in his Sight; you are ten thousand Times so abominable in his Eyes, as the most hateful, venomous Serpent is in ours." "This is a Day of Mercy; you may cry now with some Encouragement of obtaining Mercy: But when once the Day of Mercy is past, your most lamentable and dolorous Cries and Shrieks will be in vain; you will be wholly lost and thrown away of God as to any Regard to your Welfare; God will have no other Use to put you to but only to suffer Misery; you shall be continued in Being to no other End; for you will be a Vessel of Wrath fitted to Destruction; and there will be no other Use of this Vessel but only to be filled full of Wrath." Compare this gospel with Christ's and Paul's. You will then see the difference. Compare it with the Sermon on the Mount, parable of the Prodigal Son, etc., etc.

2. Another gross corruption of the primitive doctrine came into popular acceptance in the fifth century. The great St. Augustin, alias Austin, Bishop of Hippo, in Africa, inaugurated it under pressure of his controversy with the celebrated Pelagius. It is the notion of original sin and the fall of the whole human race into a state of total depravity in Adam, considered as their federal head. The assumed practical consequence of that original sin is, that all mankind are born into a state predisposed only to sin, morally incapable of true righteousness, justly under God's wrath and curse, and so "liable to all the miseries of this life, death itself, and the pains of hell forever." This notion has occasioned interminable speculations and controversies in the church, has passed through many phases and modifications, and is still accounted orthodox, in some form, by a vast majority of professing Christians. But even in its most modified phase it is a sheer corruption of the primitive doctrine. Christ and his apostles never held mankind responsible for Adam's sin, or any one's but their own. They never made Adam's sin the cause of man's general proneness to sin, nor taught the doctrine of total depravity in any form, nor of our natural utter moral inability to obey the divine requirements. On the contrary, they plainly taught that mankind, from their first progenitors downward, are naturally generated into the flesh,

are thus first innocently animal-like, or carnally minded, and thence become sinful and guilty on arriving at the knowledge of duty, by refusing to yield their primal selfishness to its justly required cross for righteousness' sake. Accordingly, they preached and made all their appeals to sinners on the ground that they were by nature capable of feeling the moral force of those appeals; that they could give ear, take heed, seek after truth and righteousness, repent, and strive to "enter in at the strait gate,"— in fine, that they had great duties to do in the work of regeneration; that God insisted on their doing them, and was ever ready to afford them all the grace and strength they might need, but never without their consent, seeking, and proper endeavor. All this is truthful, rational, and practical; that is, for God to do the major part, and require man to do his proper minor part. God never treats man as a mere mineral, a mere vegetable, or a mere animal, but always as an individual, responsible moral agent. But hear now the corruptionists:—

"They assert that Adam, the federal head and representative of the human race, was placed in a state of probation, and that, in consequence of his disobedience, all his descendants were constituted sinners; that, by nature, every man is personally depraved, destitute of holiness, unlike and opposed to God; and that, previously to the renewing agency of the DIVINE SPIRIT, all his moral actions are adverse to the character and glory of God; that, being morally incapable of recovering the image of his Creator, which was lost in Adam, he is justly exposed to eternal damnation." These are the words of the Andover Creed.

Yet Dr. Wisner, of the same faith, in stating the doctrine, says: "That men, though thus depraved, are justly required to love God with all their hearts, etc. . and are truly accountable to God for all their actions." So mankind, by the sin of Adam, lost all moral power to love and obey God, yet are justly required to do it on pain of eternal damnation! No such doctrine is to be found in the New Testament. Search for yourselves and see.

3. Another great corruption naturally followed in close connection with the foregoing; which is, that regeneration is an arbitrary and miraculous work of the Holy Spirit, which no man can in anywise seek, promote, prevent, hinder, or effect. Accordingly, the Andover Creed declares: "That no means whatever can change the heart of a sinner, and make it holy; that regeneration and sanctification are effects of the creating and renewing agency of the Holy Spirit." And the Baptist Creed affirms: "That in order to be saved, we must be regenerated, or born again; that regeneration consists in giving a holy disposition to the mind, and is effected in a manner above our comprehension or calculation, by the power of the Holy Spirit." The Episcopalian and Methodist Articles of faith on this point assert essentially the same thing. The corruption amounts to this, that no person ever was, will be, or can be regenerated, in whole or in part, by any choice, seeking, or endeavors, properly his own; because he is of himself totally depraved, and cannot originate even the desire to become holy. But God does the whole work, from beginning to end, by the power of his Spirit. He produces in the sin-

nor all the good feelings, convictions, desires, emotions, and experiences necessary to his new birth; and all this he causes to come to pass at his own sovereign pleasure, in a supernatural, miraculous, and incomprehensible manner. If some are regenerated, God does it, regardless of anything willed or done by them to procure or deserve it. And if many are finally lost, it will be solely because God does not choose to do as well by them as by and for the saved. If this were sound doctrine, Calvinism and Arminianism ought to quarrel no more about free will, election, and reprobation; for man has not a particle of free will to do anything but sin till regeneration commences, and then only to feel, think, and act just as the Holy Spirit impels him. I repeat, that no such doctrine is to be found in the New Testament. This corruption mystifies and confuses the whole subject. It falsifies the moral nature of man, the dealings of God with man, and the dictates of reason.

4. Another corruption of the primitive doctrine limits regeneration to the present state of existence, and to that small portion of mankind who are favored to experience it before passing into the world of spirits; unless, indeed, — as some are beginning to assume, — all infants, dying before actual conscious committal of sin, are regenerated after death, and perhaps the best of the well-meaning heathen. But these exceptional cases of infant and heathen salvation are liberal inconsistencies, which shatter the logic of time-honored doctrinal corruptions, and, if cherished, will, like new wine, burst the old bottles. This, however, is not my present concern. I am thinking

of the millions of millions whom God loves, whom he sent his Son to save, for whose regeneration Christ died, rose again, and reigns in heaven, and who so many grand and solemn declarations predict shall be subdued to divine order, but whom this corrupted doctrine consigns to hopeless sinfulness and ruin. It assumes that nothing will be done to regenerate them beyond this mortal state. Did Christ teach this doctrine,—this dismal frustration of God's purpose, and failure of his own meditatorial mission? Did the apostles teach it? No; but the broad contrary. Whence came it then? From the common source of all these corruptions,—from ignorance, misconception, misunderstanding, false influence, and mistaken theological philosophy.

5. Another early and gross corruption of the primitive doctrine assumes that regeneration is a quickly completed process, consummated and sealed by water-baptism. Instead of regarding it as a work which, being decisively begun, is one of slow growth and gradual progression to its full consummation, and variously more or less so in different individuals,—which certainly Christ and his apostles represented it to be,—the corruptionists suppose it to be completed within a brief period after its commencement,—a few hours, days, or perhaps, in peculiar cases, months. Then the sacrament of water-baptism is to be administered as the sign and seal of its consummation. This corruption came into vogue as early as the third century, and gave such importance to the rite of baptism, that it was superstitiously regarded as the inseparable concluding seal of regeneration. Thou-

sands put off their baptism till the very approach of death, so as to be sure that all their sins were washed away, and their souls perfectly cleansed for heaven. Constantine the Great, the first so called Christian emperor, put off his baptism to the last moment. So did two of his sons. And some left orders to be baptized just after death. Probably many such persons, especially in high worldly life, imagined that they might thus secure a longer indulgence in earthly sinful pleasures, and make sure of immediate bliss in heaven too. After a while this evil practice was discountenanced by the authorities of the church, and went out of fashion. But the notion that baptism was the consummation, or final sign and seal of regeneration, has come down to our own times; and even those sects that discard it, still almost universally hold that regeneration is an instantaneous process whereby mankind are supernaturally changed from sinners into saints. And if anything more is necessary, they distinguish it from regeneration by the term *sanctification;* as if regeneration were anything more or less than sanctification in the degree of its extent.

The evil moral effect of this corruption has been to make people think themselves *graduates* of regeneration when they were nothing but sophomores, — mere beginners in Christian discipleship. Hence joining the church, receiving the sacraments, and conforming to established religious institutions, have become presumptive evidence of the new birth, saintship, and essential preparation for heaven in the future world. Meantime outsiders must be deemed, at best, only decent, unregenerate reprobates. Thus both insiders and outsiders have been more or less deluded, — insiders to believe that they have passed through regeneration complete when they were only in its rudimental stages; and outsiders to conclude that if the insiders have graduated as Christians *they* might as well never enter an institution which turns out such superficial alumni.

But Christ and the apostles made the baptism and church-membership of their converts only a confession of faith in the necessity of regeneration as having commenced their Christian discipleship; and a pledge of submission to all the discipline requisite for its gradual complete consummation. In other words, they inducted their converts into the school of regeneration for a long and thorough discipline, not to set up at once as proficients, experts, and masters of holiness. This is truthful and rational doctrine.

6. Another corruption of the primitive doctrine, closely connected with the foregoing, is that of imputed righteousness, miscalled justification by faith. It is the notion that in regeneration God supernaturally gives the subject faith in the atoning merits of Christ as his substitute, both for keeping the law perfectly, and suffering its full penalty; then, by that faith, or in consideration of it, imputes to him the righteousness of Christ, as if it were his own original worthiness entitling him to eternal life and bliss in heaven. Here three important points are assumed: 1. That Christ obeyed the law, and then was punished for disobeying it in the believer's stead; 2. That belief in this alleged truth is the *special* gift of God, — not a common and normal one; and, 3. That Christ's

personal righteousness, by arbitrary imputation, is transferred to the credit of the believer as his own. Neither of these assumptions has a particle of real warrant from the recorded teachings of Christ and his apostles. Paul used certain expressions concerning the forgiveness of sins, justification by faith, and the efficacy of Christ's righteousness, which in their mere letter may seem to countenance such inferences; but they do not in spirit, and rational comparison with his plainest doctrinal statements.

The New Testament doctrine is, 1. That Christ, the gospel, faith, repentance, and forgiveness of sins, are all gracious gifts and provisions of God for human salvation, — not rewards claimable as deserved by man's prior righteousness. 2. That Christ sinlessly exemplified a perfect righteousness, which was rewarded by his exaltation and glorification in heaven, there to reign until all beings and things shall be spiritually subdued unto him. 3. That he suffered all that he did, even unto death, in the spirit of self-sacrificing love for the regeneration of mankind, — not penally in their stead. And, 4. That faith in Christ, his testimony, and his righteousness is one of the necessary means of uniting men to him in close spiritual intimacy, whereby, as his true disciples, followers, and imitators, they may imbibe his spirit, practise his personal righteousness, be conformed to his moral likeness, and thus be fitted, in joint heirship with him, for that blissful immortality wherein God shall be "all in all." The pure doctrine is as rational as it is morally beautiful and glorious. The corrupt notion is alike irrational, false, and abhorrent.

We need all the gracious gifts associated with Christ to help us out of sin into holy personal Christ-likeness; but none of them to save us from divine chastisement, or to give us credit for any righteousness which we do not make personally our own in veritable practice. The beloved John truly says, "He that doeth righteousness is righteous."

7. There are various other grave errors that amount to corruptions of the primitive doctrine of regeneration. I have now time briefly to notice only two or three of these. One of them is that regeneration consists chiefly in experimental feelings, dreadful emotions of conviction and remorse for sin, horrible fears of deserved punishment, almost hopeless despair of mercy, and then ecstatic rapture of uplifting hope, and the love of God shed abroad in the heart. Now, the substance of these emotional experiences, so far as they are necessary to awaken the religious faculties and give them a decided determination of submission and obedience to God for the future,—that is, a ruling intention to be governed by divine principle, according to one's highest light,—must undoubtedly be deemed indispensable to regeneration. But emotional sensibility depends largely on natural temperament, sympathetic susceptibility, association, and exciting circumstances, as well in religion as in other departments of human experience. In some it is very lively and demonstrative; in others, very calm and undemonstrative; in others, deep, subdued, and silent. It may make a great ado, and amount to little of settled principle; or make little show, and amount to a great revolution of moral character. We

want it in just such degree and quality as will give a man the grand ruling principle and intention to do right according to his highest light, and when he fails therein through frailty, to make him heartily confess and amend. If we can get this result, it is enough. Without this, no amount of feeling and ado is of any real worth. People in the error that awakened conscientiousness, veneration, hope, etc., sincerity, passional religious demonstration, and emotional experiences, have got pure religion, and are truly regenerated, are apt to despise or disparage everything else, and especially to denounce what they call head religion, or what I should call truth in the understanding, as of no account.

At the other extreme is the pernicious error of assuming that truth in the understanding, right belief, opinion, sound rationality, etc., constitute the main desideratum of religion, — making a sound theological intellect the principal sum and substance of what Christ meant by the term "born again." But the pure primitive Christian doctrine of regeneration eschews both these extremes, and combines all the real truth underlying each. It requires light in the understanding, and life in the religious sentiment, — the head right, and the heart right; faith right, and practice right. It illuminates the understanding with the light of divine truth, showing man the grandest principles of faith, hope, and charity; and it quickens the religious sentiment into living vitality and activity, by the Holy Spirit, thereby stimulating the soul's best endeavors to act in accordance with its highest light.

People may be very conscientious, sincere, and full of religious feeling, yet very dark in their understandings, superstitious, bigoted, fanatical, persecuting, and murderous towards dissenters and offenders. Paul was so before he became a Christian. John Newton became deeply religious, even to the most zealous devotional piety, while prosecuting the slave-trade, and did not grow out of his mental darkness for some years. So we have had very pious persecutors, pious slaveholders, and pious warriors drenched in blood. Some need most of regeneration in their hearts, some in their heads, some in their consciences, and some in their moral habits. Christianity insists on regenerating the understanding, that men may know what the highest righteousness requires. But if their religious nature were left dormant, animal and selfish, their heads might be right, and they might theorize soundly, but their conscientiousness, reverence, spirituality, and habitual ruling disposition would remain in slavery to sin. Hence it is that we have fine thinkers, reasoners, and talkers, whose hearts and lives are deplorably unchristian; just as, on the other side, we have very pious, zealous, emotional religionists, who are deplorably unrighteous in very important respects, and some of whom verily think they are doing God service to persecute heretics, and exterminate their enemies. New Testament Christianity gives no support whatever to such errors. Its righteousness is not a partial, superficial, imperfect one. Nor does it countenance any one-sided, half-and-half process of regeneration, but proclaims one which is never finished till the whole heart, understanding, spirit, soul, and body, shall have been set in order and sanctified. Then onward it reaches to the family, to society, and to all human institutions, that in their order they may follow individual regeneration, until all things at length be made morally new, and the kingdoms of this world become the kingdom of Christ, wherein selfishness, sin, and misery shall be known no more.

ARTICLE VI.

DIVINE GOVERNMENT, JUDGMENT, RETRIBUTION, AND DISCIPLINE.

DISCOURSE XXI.

THE PURE PRIMITIVE CHRISTIAN DOCTRINE.

"The Father judgeth no man; but hath committed all judgment unto the Son: that all men should honor the Son, even as they honor the Father. He that honoreth not the Son, honoreth not the Father which hath sent him." — JOHN v. 22, 23.

THE general doctrine that God governs all beings, things, and events, universally and particularly, from everlasting to everlasting, was already received and established in the religious world when Christ entered on his mission. To say nothing of other religions, that of the Patriarchs, Moses, and the Prophets, as developed in the Old Testament Scriptures, explicitly taught and reiterated this doctrine. In truth, it was inseparable from the very idea of a Supreme Being. What, then, was to have been expected of Christ and his apostles in regard to this doctrine? Very much the same as in respect to all the other Old Testament doctrines; namely, that they would recognize it as essentially true, but requiring modification, explanation, and new applications. Let us remember that Christ did not come to reveal and establish absolutely new first principles of religion, but to bear witness to old ones, to be more thoroughly explained and applied in practice. His work was to separate them from human error and corruption, to illustrate their essential excellence, and to give them their legitimate, full application.

Claiming to be the Messiah, or Christ, foreordained from the foundation of the world, long predicted by ancient prophets, and promised in the Old Testament Scriptures as God's pre-eminent representative in the moral government of mankind, he had an office to sustain and a mission to fulfil. His office and mission were not only divine, but *regally* divine. He was to act as King, Lord, Judge, and Saviour, — as the Father's deputy, or vicegerent, — that is, by his authority and in his name. All this he claimed. All this his apostles claimed for him. And all this, correctly understood, is true; else Christianity has no distinctive pre-eminence as a religion. But it must be *correctly* understood, or we shall involve ourselves in utter mental confusion. We must understand, 1. That really God does whatever is done by his authority, whether through Jesus Christ, or any other deputed agent; 2. That Jesus Christ, and every other deputed agent of God, has his own peculiar and proper sphere of official action, outside of which God governs through other instrumentalities; and, 3. That the declared official sphere of Christ's agency is essentially spiritual, religious, rational, and social. He is not King, Lord, Judge, and Saviour over mineral nature, vegetable nature, and animal nature, but over human nature; and not over human nature in matters merely physiological, or merely intellectual, or merely industrial, or merely pecuniary, or merely civil and political, but chiefly in respect to religion, morality, rationality, and voluntary association. Neither does his Christly office interfere with God's laws of order and general providence throughout the universe in any respect not affecting man's religious, moral, rational, and social condition. He is officially concerned with, and only with, what is for or against the good of human beings, as religious, moral, rational, and social beings for time and eternity. Incidentally, indirectly, and by natural consequence, his official operations doubtless affect, and are affected by, matters, things, and events outside of his Christly sphere; because no part of universal being is utterly isolated from the rest. Still, the distinctiveness of spheres throughout boundless immensity is real and practical. Therefore Christ has his peculiar and proper sphere. Now, we want to know the true nature and extent of his Kingship, Lordship, Judgeship, and Saviourship over the human race; that we may not mix up and confound with each other the various agencies and methods by which God governs the universe.

What, then, is the pure primitive Christian doctrine of divine government, judgment, retribution, and discipline? If we can distinguish clearly, in the teachings of Christ and his apostles, between what God does in, by, or through Christ, and what he does otherwise, we shall readily reach the truth. The great system of material cosmic nature — suns and stars, planets and satellites, comets and meteors, — the physical heavens, earth and elements — continued to be divinely governed as from the unknown past. Christ was not invested with their government, neither did he modify, or even explain, their laws. Such was not his office or mission. The same is true of the mineral kingdom, its laws, and phenomena; also of the vegetable and animal kingdoms, with their respective laws and phenomena. None of these were put under Christ's charge. We come next to human affairs. There are important departments of these that were not subjected to Christ's official control, and which never have been, or can be, immediately under his government, though in various degrees affected by his influence. Such is worldly civil government, with its various co-ordinate and necessary institutions. All these have their roots in lower strata of nature, are developed in accordance with other laws, and are operated by different agencies from those of Christ's distinctive kingdom. He was not anointed to prescribe forms of civil government, autocracy, monarchy, aristocracy, democracy, or any imaginable compound of these ocracies; nor to superintend the political, military, financial, and such like institutions, necessary to any form of civil government; nor to teach any governmental science, economy, or policy, whether national or international. Why not? Because all these things were otherwise provided for on the broad plane of ordinary providence. They all originate in, unfold through, and are managed by human genius, under that general government of God which lies below and is morally grosser than Christ's official mediatorial charge. The notion that our milito-civil governments, based as they are on political expediency and destructive force, are or can be Christian governments, or that they belong to the mediatorial kingdom of Christ, is not only anti-Christian, but a most vicious delusion, which has too long prevailed throughout nominal Christendom. Hence our popular paradoxes, — Christian politics, Christian wars, Christian punishments, Christian soldiers, Christian statesmen, etc., etc. These human governments have their necessary place and use in God's government of the world as it is; but to call them and their machinery *Christian* is to nullify primitive Christianity, both theoretically and practically. It is falsifying and confounding important distinctions.

Another of these exceptional departments in human affairs is mere intellectual science, philosophy, literature, and art. Christ came, not to teach any of these, — not to be a titled master of arts, or professor of science, in any branch of mere human erudition. Why? Not because these are not necessary, useful and good in their place; but because God otherwise provided for them, and because something higher than they was indispensable to perfect human happiness. The same is true of the great economical department; I mean the production, management, and distribution of property, — the physical necessaries and comforts of human life. Christ did not come to be a master in agriculture, manufactures, mechanics, navigation, commerce, finance, banking, etc. There is enough of genius, enterprise, and skill in human nature to ensure the ultimate ample development of all necessary property interests. God took care of this matter from the beginning, on planes below that of the purely religious one.

But here was the grand, uppermost desideratum. How to save mankind from the perversion and abuse of all these lower goods, — goods of capability, production, and use, — from bad civil government, bad intellectual science, learning, and art; bad production, acquisition and disposal of property; bad management of everything that concerns human welfare. This grand desideratum is precisely what God has provided for us in, through and by Christ. Man must be raised high enough in the religious, moral, rational, and social scale to love his heavenly Father so perfectly as to do his will with delight at any and every sacrifice of his own will; as to love every fellow human being, even though an enemy, as himself; as to do unto others, without respect of persons, as he would be done unto, — in fine, as never knowingly to disregard any individual's good, or the public good, or the universal good, under any pretext whatsoever. Such is the law of Christ's kingdom. Such is the individual and social righteousness which he taught, enjoined, and exemplified. Such is the church, or voluntary association, he idealized. Such is the humble, holy, loving, peaceful, blissful brotherhood of man which is to be the actualized ultimate of his pure religion. To ensure this, he came into the world, was overflowingly anointed with the Holy Spirit, lived, taught, suffered, died, descended into Hades, rose thence, ascended into heaven, and now reigns in supernal glory. All this, and nothing less, belongs distinctively to Christ's kingdom. Whatever in human politics, in human learning, in human art, or in human economics, is contrary to this, or morally incompatible with it, however useful, or indispensable for the time being, must finally be superseded under the government of Christ. But Christ does nothing by physical violence. He overcomes no evil save with good. He is the Prince of peace.

We have now arrived at an eminence from which we can examine Christ's kingdom with a clear vision. It is not of this selfish world in its structure and genius. He is indeed a King, but not after the fashion of carnal exaltation. His throne is humility, his majesty is love, his sceptre is righteousness, his force is truth, his discipline is just reproof and disfellowship, his *dernier resort* is to let the refractory learn in the school of their own self-procured bitter experience, his triumph the regeneration of his enemies. He is indeed a most perfect Judge. His judgment-seat is set up in the soul of the adjudged, his word of divine wisdom tries their works whether good or evil, and his spirit calmly pronounces the decision with an equity which commands the unreserved acquiescence of conscience and reason. At the same time he is consistently man's Saviour. Because his kingly rule and judicial strictness are purely benevolent, salutary, and salvatory. There is no selfishness in them, no pride of authority, no vindictiveness, no cruelty, no sacrifice of any sinner's good, no disregard of the universal good. They aim only at the fulfilment of his official mission. There is nothing but harmonic Christ-likeness in everything done by him, from the Alpha to the Omega of his dispensations. Through him, mercy and judgment seek the same result.

If I should reduce the pure primitive doctrine of Christianity concerning divine government, judgment, retribution, and discipline, to definite propositions, it would stand nearly as follows: —

1. God exercises, from and to eternity, over all beings, things, actions, and events a perfect government, in accordance with certain immutable laws of order.

2. God's government is exercised and administered largely through various secondary causes and mediatorial agencies, both impersonal and personal, of which he makes use according to his own sovereign pleasure.

3. In one way or another, sooner or later, God duly judges all beings, things, and actions, with reference to their fitness or unfitness to perfect order, and causes a suitable retribution to follow as the proper demonstration of such fitness or unfitness.

4. The divine judgment and retribution are designed not only to demonstrate the fitness or unfitness of beings, things, and actions to perfect order, but to uphold such order, correct disorder, and discipline the erring into true rectitude.

5. Jesus Christ is God's highest mediatorial agent for the administration of divine government, judgment, retribution, and discipline over the human race in this world and that which is to come, but with respect exclusively to their spiritual, religious, moral, rational, and social regeneration and perfectation.

6. Jesus Christ exercises his mediatorial adminis-

trative powers of divine government, judgment, retribution, and discipline, not with an arbitrary personal authority, nor by means of external rewards and punishments, nor by any kind of destructive physical force, but chiefly by means of his declared truth, his distinctive principles, his communicable Spirit, and his manifold moral forces, working in and through the minds of mankind.

7. Jesus Christ will certainly continue to reign in the exercise of these mediatorial powers, forces, and influences, till every human soul shall have been subdued unto him, and thus reconciled to the Father, — who will thenceforth be spiritually "all in all."

The doctrine embodied in these propositions is taught in very positive language, some of which, however, is strongly figurative, and liable to be misunderstood without careful consideration of its structure, connections, and relations to fundamental principles elsewhere plainly declared. But *with* such consideration, minds of sound common sense and decent spirituality may readily apprehend the essential ideas. The particulars in this doctrine most emphasized by Christ and his apostles are the following: That the divine government, providence, and judicial discipline are minute, searching, and complete over individuals, as well as general over communities, and universal over the vast whole; that they are strictly in accordance with the fitness of things, — just, impartial, and equitable, according to works, knowledge, and real responsibility; that judgment and retribution are not instantaneous on transgression, nor uniformly diffused over the whole period of sinfulness, but experienced most intensely in crises, or days of judgment, analogous to harvest seasons following their seed times; that those judgment days occur to individuals, cities, and peoples more or less strikingly in this world, but that the most perfect and conclusive day, or age, of judgment for all takes place after death in the future state; that all divine government, judgment, retribution, and discipline aims at the maintenance, promotion, and complete final triumph of moral order; and that pure benevolence and wisdom characterize all the divine dispensations, tempering judgments with mercies and ultimating all sufferings in a regenerate era of immortal blessedness for the human race.

There was no attempt by Christ and his apostles to philosophize metaphysically on this, any more than on their other doctrines. They declared fundamental and general truths with practical simplicity, leaving to after times the privilege of investigating, analyzing, systematizing, and elaborating the rationale of those truths. This is our privilege, and perhaps our duty; only we are bound to be truthful and just,— never undermining plain first principles for the sake of favorite traditional opinions, or our own ingenious theories. If we look closely at this primitive Christian doctrine, we can but admire its transcendent excellence, in respect to that distinctive feature of it in which Christ stands forth, as, under God, the ruler, judge, and discipliner of mankind. In this official capacity he is the Father's highest Vicegerent and representative, — King of kings, Lord of lords, Judge of judges, and Chief of saviors, — not by a fictitious and constructive divine right, but by a direct absolute divine commission. Yet in his unrivalled official authority there is not a particle of worldly majesty, dignity, power, greatness, awfulness, or terror. He is the humblest of servants, the most self-sacrificing of benefactors, the most devoted of martyrs, the most childlike of teachers, the most truthful of reprovers, the meekest of judges, the most compassionate as well as thorough of disciplinarians, and the most magnanimous of conquerors toward his subjugated enemies. He demands no external homage, imposes no external tribute, and inflicts no external penalty. He exacts nothing selfishly, and seeks nothing but the regeneration, progress, holiness, and happiness of every human being, even his worst enemy. He is the destroyer of nothing that is worth preserving, and the Saviour of all that is worth saving. He has no tenderness for error, folly, and sin, and no harshness for the guiltiest of penitent sinners. He is never false, unjust, or unmerciful. He never despairs, never fails, is never discouraged in his mission. He has all the ages of time and of eternity to accomplish his work in, and will leave nothing undone for which he was made Christ, till all things human harmonize with all things divine. Unto him shall every knee bow in heaven, in earth, and under the earth, and every tongue confess that he is Lord, to the glory of God the Father. And yet, at that moment, he shall stand forth in presence of the universe great and majestic only as the humblest, meekest, purest, wisest, most loving, most harmless Son of God, and brother of the regenerated human race. And our own highest glory will be to be like him in moral character, — the greatest humblest. When we try to conceive of God, not manifested in and represented by this Christ, it is amazingly difficult to regard him as pure love, as the universal Father. He seems an awful Sovereign. We tremble at his power, rather than adore his goodness. To our conception of his laws, government, judgments, and retributions, formed in the light of mere nature and human experience, they seem, at best, more or less arbitrary, severe, inflexible, undiscriminating, cruel, vindictive, and often destructively useless. False religion sometimes only darkens the whole divine horizon. But not so in the light of primitive Christianity, shining in the face of its blessed Prince, as I have endeavored to set forth his Christhood. He shows us the Father, his government, laws, and judgments, for time and eternity, truly and gloriously on the highest spiritual plane. Let us believe, adore, submit, and rejoice.

In my next I shall endeavor to prove that I have not mistaken the pure primitive Christian doctrine on this subject.

ARTICLE VI.

DIVINE GOVERNMENT, JUDGMENT, RETRIBUTION, AND DISCIPLINE.

DISCOURSE XXII.

THE PURE PRIMITIVE DOCTRINE VERIFIED AND EXPLAINED.

"The times of this ignorance God winked at; but now commandeth all men everywhere to repent: because he hath appointed a day in the which he will judge the world in righteousness, by *that* man whom he hath ordained: *whereof* he hath given assurance unto all men, in that he hath raised him from the dead." — PAUL. ACTS xvii. 30, 31.

My last discourse was occupied with a definite statement of the pure primitive Christian doctrine of divine government, judgment, retribution, and discipline. I promised in this to prove that I had not mistaken the primitive doctrine. Much contained in that statement is so obviously correct that no one will call it in question. It would be superfluous to array testimony and illustration in support of undisputed propositions. I will, therefore, confine myself to points of a questionable nature, about which there are honest differences of opinion.

Of the seven propositions in which I presented my statement of the doctrine, I think the first four will be generally acknowledged sound, with exceptions, if any, too slight to require my present consideration.

The fifth, sixth, and seventh involve important points likely to excite more or less dissent. These I will consider in their order. The fifth was in these words: That Jesus Christ is God's highest mediatorial agent for the administration of divine government, judgment, retribution, and discipline over the human race in this world and that which is to come, but with respect exclusively to their spiritual, religious, moral, rational, and social regeneration and perfectation. What are the points which will excite dissent in this proposition?

1. Those who believe in the strict Deity of Christ may object to the term "highest mediatorial agent," as implying the absolute inferiority and subordination of the Son to the Father. All I need say, in answer to this is, that Jesus and his apostles unequivocally represent the case in this light, — positively declaring, again and again, in various forms of expression, that he did not come of himself, or speak in his own name, or act by his own authority, but as sent, commissioned, and authorized by God the Father. To prove this, is unnecessary to any intelligent reader of the New Testament. And they who are ingenious enough to construe the plain declarations of this sort, so abundant there, into harmony with their theology, may as easily dispose of my term "highest mediatorial agent."

2. Some will contend that Christ's regal power and authority are unlimited; that they not only extend to all human nature, but to the whole material universe, animate and inanimate. Here they can plead at least the *letter* of Scripture in certain passages,

such as the following: "All things are delivered unto me of my Father." Matt. xi. 27; Luke x. 22. "The Father hath committed all judgment unto the Son." John v. 22. "All power is given unto me in heaven and in earth." Matt. xxviii. 18. "Jesus Christ, he is Lord of all." Acts x. 36. "It pleased the Father that in him should all fulness dwell." Col. i. 19. "Whom he hath appointed heir of all things." Heb. i. 1. If such passages, with their comprehensive phraseology, were not necessarily restricted in their meaning by the context, the nature of the case, and other plain declarations, they would prove that Christ's mediatorial sphere is absolutely unlimited. But we know that their meaning is thus restricted. They relate particularly to his spiritual kingdom and authority, the nature of which is defined in a multitude of passages, of which the following are samples: "The Spirit of the Lord is upon me, because he hath anointed me to preach the gospel to the poor; he hath sent me to heal the broken-hearted, to preach deliverance to the captives, and recovering of sight to the blind, to set at liberty them that are bruised, to preach the acceptable year of the Lord." Luke iv. 18, 19. "God so loved the world that he gave his only begotten Son that whosoever believeth in him should not perish, but have everlasting life. For God sent not his Son into the world to condemn the world, but that the world through him might be saved." John iii. 15, 16. "The Son of man is come to seek and to save that which was lost." Luke xix. 10. "Ye are from beneath; I am from above; ye are of this world; I am not of this world." "Who art thou? . . . The same that I said unto you from the beginning. I have many things to say and to judge of you: but he that sent me is true; and I speak to the world those things which I have heard of him." . . . "I do nothing of myself; but as my Father hath taught me, I speak these things." John viii. 23, 25, 26, 28. "The kingdom of God cometh not with observation: neither shall they say, Lo here! or, lo there! for, behold, the kingdom of God is within you." Luke xvii. 21. "My kingdom is not of this world: if my kingdom were of this world, then would my servants fight, that I should not be delivered to the Jews: but now is my kingdom not from hence." "To this end was I born, and for this cause came I into the world, that I should bear witness unto the truth. Every one that is of the truth heareth my voice." John xviii. 36, 37. "Then opened he their understanding, that they might understand the Scriptures, and said unto them, Thus it is written, and thus it behoved Christ to suffer, and to rise from the dead the third day: and that repentance and remission of sins should be preached in his name among all nations, beginning at Jerusalem." Luke xxiv. 45–47. "He that descended is the same also that ascended up far above all heavens, that he might fill all things. And he gave some, apostles; and some, prophets; and some, evangelists; and some, pastors and teachers; for the perfecting of the saints, for the work of the ministry, for the edifying of the body of Christ: till we all come in the unity of the faith, and of the knowledge of the Son of God, unto a perfect man, unto the measure of the stature of the fulness of Christ." Ephes. iv. 10–13. This class of passages settles the question as to what the nature of Christ's mediatorial kingdom is, and so what is meant by the *all things, power, judgment,* and *fulness* wherewith the Father has invested him as his vicegerent.

In accordance with such passages, I confine Christ's mediatorial agency, not only to the human race, but exclusively to what concerns their spiritual, religious, moral, rational, and social regeneration and perfectation. What do I mean by the term *spiritual?* That in human nature which is above the animal plane. What by the term *religious?* Conscientious obligation toward God. What by the term *moral?* Dutifulness toward one's self and fellow-creatures. What by the term *rational?* The exercise and right use of reason. What by the term *social?* The relationship of human beings in reciprocal personal intercourse, in the family connection, in select friendship, in the church, and in all kinds of voluntary association, that is, all kinds of society not sustained in the last resort by destructive physical force. All grades and forms of human association on the milito-civil and political plane belong to another department of divine government and providence, grosser than that of Christ; because they depend mainly on temporal expediency, penal coercion, and the *dernier resort* to destructive physical force. God orders and overrules all these for the universal good by means adapted to their nature. The same is true of all other departments below the Christ-plane, such as the mere intellectual, industrial, commercial, and financial. The inherent genius, instinct, and enterprise of human nature originate and develop these on their own basilar planes. Christ's vicegerency, or mediatorial agency, is above all these lower spheres of human interest and action, but does not assume direct control over them, nor immediate interference with them; much less does it depend on the use of their institutional machinery to execute its own distinctive work.

3. Here arises another very important issue of dissent. Many will strenuously contend that I am certainly wrong on this point; that, in truth, human government, human learning, human industry, human commerce, human finance, and all departments of human concern are included in Christ's mediatorial kingdom, and are superintended absolutely by him. What is the precise question in dispute? It is not whether Christ's official sphere of divine government is above all these; for I affirm that it is heaven-high above them. It is not whether Christ's mediatorial administration affects all these inferior departments of human concern indirectly so as to enlighten and modify them; for I have stated this as a truth, and sincerely hold it. Nor is it whether the mediatorial reign of Christ will gradually and ultimately do away everything evil in these lower departments; for this I continually assert and reiterate. The question really at issue is, whether God has committed to Christ, as his mediatorial vicegerent, all departments of human concern, including certainly what are commonly called the world's civil governments and their concomitant institutions? or especially and exclusively the spiritual, religious, moral, rational, and voluntarily social concerns of human nature? I deny the former, and

affirm the latter; my opponents, the reverse. Let us appeal to the record.

Did Jesus or his apostles ever claim, court, or depend on the governments of their time to promote their cause and mission? Never. Did they ever seek to manage or participate in the machinery of those governments? Never. Did they ever give any precept or advisory instructions to Christians, of their age or any coming age, to seek the management of governmental machinery? Nothing of the kind is on record. Did they not give many positive injunctions for humility, forgiveness of offences, love to enemies, abstinence from all inflictions of personal harm, and the practice of universal good will, which human governments have always repudiated or nullified, as under many circumstances utterly impracticable on their plane, and which no individual can obey if acting in strict allegiance to them? This is as certain, both from the letter and spirit of New Testament Scripture, as that the sun shines on the earth at noonday. Did not Christ directly and solemnly warn his disciples against expecting the aid or favor of worldly governments, himself setting the example? Yes. "Behold, I send you forth as sheep in the midst of wolves: be ye therefore wise as serpents, and harmless as doves. But beware of men; for they will deliver you up to the councils, and they will scourge you in their synagogues; and ye shall be brought before governors and kings for my sake, for a testimony against them and the Gentiles." Matt. x. 16–18. Why did he not add: But as soon as you can command influence enough, get the political control and management of these governmental institutions, turn the tables on your opposers, and use their power in the interest of my kingdom; for all these coercive instrumentalities are rightfully mine? Was this omission because he knew too little, or because he was too wise? The latter, in my judgment.

Again: when Satan offered him all the kingdoms of the world, why did he not promptly reply that God had already put them in his possession? When the people were ready to take him by force and make him a king, why did he escape into the solitude of a mountain? John vi. 15. When one said, "Master, speak to my brother, that he divide the inheritance with me," why did he reply, "Man, who made me a judge or a divider over you?" Luke xii. 13, 14. When asked about tribute to Cesar, why did he answer, "Render therefore unto Cesar the things which are Cesar's; and unto God the things that are God's"? Matt. xxii. 21. When arraigned before Pilate as a pretender to temporal royalty, why did he emphatically declare that his kingdom was not of this fighting world? John xviii. 36. When, after his resurrection, his disciples demanded, "Wilt thou at this time restore again the kingdom to Israel?" why did he answer, "It is not for you to know the times or the seasons, which the Father hath put in his own power"? Acts i. 6, 7. The conclusion to which all these considerations lead us is, that my position is impregnable, and that milito-political Christianity, which forever itches to manage secular governments for the promotion of righteousness, has no warrant in the New Testament.

My sixth propositional statement was, That Jesus Christ exercises his mediatorial administrative powers of divine government, judgment, retribution, and discipline, not with an arbitrary personal authority, nor by means of external rewards and punishments, nor by any kind of destructive physical force, but chiefly by means of his declared truth, his distinctive principles, and his manifold moral forces, working in and through the minds of mankind. Some will controvert the correctness of this statement, and they can quote certain literal phrases of Scripture which seem to support them. But I contend that all such phrases are of a figurative nature, and are necessarily qualified into agreement with my statement by passages which unequivocally define the radical peculiarities of Christ's government. Of such passages the following are samples: "There shall come forth a rod out of the stem of Jesse, and a branch shall grow out of his roots. And the Spirit of the Lord shall rest upon him, the spirit of wisdom and understanding, the spirit of counsel and might, the spirit of knowledge, and of the fear of the Lord; and shall make him of quick understanding in the fear of the Lord. And he shall not judge after the sight of his eyes, neither reprove after the hearing of his ears. But with righteousness shall he judge the poor, and reprove with equity for the meek of the earth: and he shall smite the earth with the rod of his mouth [his word of truth], and with the breath of his lips [his just reproofs] shall he slay the wicked [spiritually, not with carnal weapons]. And righteousness shall be the girdle of his loins, and faithfulness the girdle of his reins. The wolf also shall dwell with the lamb, and the leopard shall lie down with the kid, etc., etc. They shall not hurt nor destroy in all my holy mountain; for the earth shall be full of the knowledge of the Lord, as the waters cover the sea." Isa. xi. 1–9. "Behold my servant, whom I have chosen; my beloved, in whom my soul is well pleased: I will put my Spirit upon him, and he shall show judgment to the Gentiles. He shall not strive, nor cry; neither shall any man hear his voice in the streets. A bruised reed shall he not break, and smoking flax shall he not quench, till he send forth judgment unto victory. And in his name shall the Gentiles trust." Isaiah, quoted Matt. xii. 18–21. "Take my yoke upon you, and learn of me; for I am meek and lowly in heart; and ye shall find rest unto your souls. For my yoke is easy and my burden is light." Matt. xi. 29, 30. "Who is greatest in the kingdom of heaven? And Jesus called a little child unto him, and set him in the midst of them; and said, Verily, I say unto you, Except ye be converted, and become as little children, ye shall not enter into the kingdom of heaven. Whosoever therefore shall humble himself as this little child, the same is greatest in the kingdom of heaven." Matt. xviii. 1–4. "There was a strife among them, which of them should be accounted the greatest. And he said unto them, The kings of the Gentiles exercise lordship over them; and they that exercise authority upon them are called benefactors. But ye shall not be so; but he that is greatest among you, let him be as the younger; and he that is chief, as he that doth serve. For whether is greater, he that sitteth at meat, or he that serveth?

Is not he that sitteth at meat? But I am among you as he that serveth. . . And I appoint unto you a kingdom, as my Father hath appointed unto me, that ye may eat and drink at my table in my kingdom, and sit on thrones, judging the twelve tribes of Israel." Luke xxii. 24–31. "Ye call me Master and Lord: and ye say well, for so I am. If I then, your Lord and Master, have washed your feet, ye also ought to wash one another's feet. For I have given you an example, that ye should do as I have done unto you." John xiii. 13–15. "If any man hear my words, and believe not, I judge him not: for I came not to judge the world, but to save the world. He that rejecteth me, and receiveth not my words, hath one that judgeth him: the word that I have spoken, the same shall judge him in the last day. For I have not spoken of myself; but the Father, which hath sent me, he gave me a commandment, what I should say, and what I should speak." John xii. 47–49. "For the word of God is quick and powerful, and sharper than any two-edged sword, piercing even to the dividing asunder of soul and spirit, and of the joints and marrow, and is a discerner of the thought and intents of the heart." Heb. iv. 12.

Thus we have a clear view of the nature of Christ's mediatorial kingdom, of its spiritual order, and of the manner in which he exercises his judicial authority. We see how radically different all the distinctive peculiarities of his government are from those of this world's governments. There is no pompous personal display of dignity, power, and authority; but a child-like simplicity, a servant-like humility, a benign meekness, and absolutely not a particle of that external grandeur which commands the admiration and awe of our mortal millions. Here is the true King of kings; yet it is his chief glory to wash the feet of his poorest subjects. He sits on a throne; but it is not one of ivory, overlaid with gold, and inwrought with precious stones. Can you imagine what or where it is? He wears a crown; yet it costs no one but himself a moment's toil, or pain, or a drop of blood. What is it? He holds a sceptre before which archangels bow with reverence. What is it? He is robed in peerless majesty; but it is wholly spiritual. What is it? He never taxed his subjects a mill; yet he has enriched them all. His word is the law of the infinite God; but he himself first obeyed it most implicitly, under the strongest temptations, and with the greatest self-sacrifice. And now he only requires us to imitate his example, with the promise that he will help our infirmities. He is the strictest of judges, the most uncompromising of reprovers, and the most thorough of disciplinarians; but always for the highest good of the sufferers. He wields the keenest of two-edged swords; but he slays only sin, evil, and death, that is, sinners in respect to their love of sin, — not as created beings. He is to be the conqueror of the whole world; but only to reconcile it to God, and harmonize it with heaven. The better I understand him, the more profoundly I reverence him, as the highest Son of man, Son of God, Lord, Judge, and Saviour of the human race. And thus the more I am weaned from all worship of this world's martial, political, and literary idols, which cost it so much, and serve it so little. But infinite

Wisdom has a place and a use for all things, on their own plane : —

> One God supreme o'er boundless Nature reigns,
> Embracing countless spheres in one domain;
> But governs each through agencies and laws
> Befitting best its plane of pregnant cause, —
> Material globes in solar systems bound,
> All vegetable life in planets found,
> All animals that creep, or swim, or fly,
> And human souls that people earth or sky.
> The grosser natures, grosser powers obey,
> And finer ones a finer, gentler sway.
> Terraqueous worlds by raging elements are trained,
> And brutal nations oft by war restrained;
> Whilst frenzied patriots crush mad tyrants out,
> And rash iconoclasts old idols scout;
> But Christ, the Father's noblest Son, appears,
> Vicegerent of a realm above these spheres.
> Behold in deep humility his throne, —
> His majesty by perfect meekness shown,—
> His crown divine, self-sacrificing love, —
> His regal emblem Heaven's descending Dove, —
> His sceptre Justice, Truth, and Mercy twined, —
> His law all laws of righteousness combined, —
> His kingdom human souls redeemed from sin,
> A world made Christ-like by his discipline.

ARTICLE VI.

DIVINE GOVERNMENT, JUDGMENT, RETRIBUTION, AND DISCIPLINE.

DISCOURSE XXIII.

THE PURE PRIMITIVE DOCTRINE FURTHER VERIFIED AND EXPLAINED.

"According to the working whereby he is able even to subdue all things unto himself." — PHIL. iii. 21.

BEFORE I can proceed, with propriety, to point out the corruptions of the primitive doctrine now under consideration, my seventh propositional statement of that doctrine remains to be verified, and also an important objection to the sixth answered. This objection belongs in immediate connection with my preceding discourse, and therefore comes first in order. The objection may thus be stated: Notwithstanding all your quotations of Scripture, and your reasonings therefrom in support of your sixth propositional statement, there are many positive texts of Scripture to the contrary, which must not be ignored, or set at nought. Let us find the points of this objection. My sixth statement was, That Jesus Christ exercises his mediatorial administrative powers of divine government, judgment, retribution, and discipline, not with an arbitrary personal authority, nor by means of external rewards and punishments, nor by any kind of destructive physical force, but chiefly by means of his declared truth, his distinctive principles, and his manifold moral forces, working in and through the minds of mankind. The capital points of the objection are indicated in the clauses, "arbitrary personal authority," "external rewards and punishments," and "destructive physical force." I make the pure primitive doctrine to have been, that Christ exercises his mediatorial administrative powers *without* arbitrary personal authority, without external rewards and punishments, and without any kind of destructive physical force; but chiefly by means of his declared truth, his distinctive principles, and his manifold moral forces, working in and through the minds of mankind. The objection asserts that many positive texts of Scripture teach the contrary, that is, teach that Christ exercises his official powers *with* an arbitrary personal authority, by means of external rewards and punishments, and by destructive physical force, — at least to a large extent. I call this an important objection; because, if true, it overthrows nearly all my cardinal ideas of Christ, his office, and his religion; and, if false, our popular Christianity, which I pronounce corrupt, must be regenerated from centre to circumference.

Now, at the outset of my answer, let there be no misunderstanding of the precise points at issue. What is "arbitrary personal authority"? Authority exercised at mere personal will and discretion, — not subject to prescribed principles and rules, — despotically and absolutely, without accountability to any higher authority, or the sanction of any governing standard. I affirm that Christ did not claim, or pretend to exercise, any such arbitrary personal authority. The objector affirms that he did. What are external rewards and punishments? Material or physical ones,—such as are enjoyed or suffered chiefly in the external person, not within the mind, the spirit, the rational and moral nature. I affirm that Christ did not claim to govern, judge, and discipline mankind by means of external rewards and punishments. The objector affirms that he did. What is destructive physical force? Any force which destroys, kills, or injures the body, or organic person, or constitutional being. I affirm that Christ did not claim to exercise, or threaten to use, any kind of destructive physical force in the administration of his mediatorial government. The objector affirms that he did. These are the points in question. So we join issue. I admitted, in my last discourse, that certain literal phrases of Scripture could be quoted seemingly against me, but contended that all such phrases are of a figurative nature, and are necessarily qualified into agreement with my statement by other passages of unmistakable meaning. On this I shall insist. For it is not the literal phraseology and *seeming* meaning of Scripture which settles any question, but the real intent and meaning of its language, understood in its proper connection, relation, and spirit. Christendom boils like a caldron with conflicting dogmas and opinions, formed erroneously out of the mere literalism of the Bible, regardless of its spirit and essential principles, which by themselves no sound mind can seriously deny or mistake. But to the texts which the objector will plead against me: "Thou art my Son; this day have I begotten thee. Ask of me, and I shall give thee the heathen for thine inheritance, and the uttermost parts of the earth for thy possession. Thou shalt break them with a rod of iron; thou shalt dash them in pieces like a potter's vessel." Psalm ii. 7–9. "Sit thou at my right hand, until I make thine enemies thy footstool. . Rule thou in the midst of thine enemies." "The Lord at thy right hand shall strike through kings in the day of his wrath. He shall judge among the heathen, he shall fill the places with the dead bodies; he shall wound the heads over many countries." Ibid. cx. 1–6. "Did ye never read in the Scriptures, The stone which the builders rejected, the same is become the head of the corner?" . . "Whosoever shall fall on this stone shall be broken: but on whomsoever it shall fall, it will grind him to powder." Matt. xxi. 42, 44. Ay, says the objector, such texts have the true ring in them. They have a refreshing tone; not that of your sickly, effeminate, moral suasion, non-resistance, and mere spiritual influence, — all love and no destructive vengeance; but of absolute personal authority, power, and crushing "indignation that devours the adversaries." Christ sits at Jehovah's right hand, in awful majesty; his foes lie prostrate, and are made his footstool; he rules in the midst of his enemies with a rod of iron, and dashes them in pieces; he strikes through hostile kings in his wrath, and fills the battle-field with dead bodies; yea, he wounds the heads of the rebellious, and grinds them to powder. This is the Christ for me; whose nod is law, whose rewards and punishments are external enough to mean something, and whose omnipotent power crushes out all opposition with utter physical, as well as moral and spiritual, destruction! Even so; he is the Christ of all Christians in whom the animal predominates; of all Christians who worship despotic power more than meek goodness; of all Christians who are ambitious to be greatest in the kingdom, and, like the two foolish disciples, aspire to sit on either hand of Christ in glory; of all Christians who, when slighted or thwarted, are ready to say, " Lord, wilt thou that we command fire to come down from heaven and consume them?" of all Christians who establish inquisitions, resort to the manifold cruelties of persecution against heretical opposers, torturing them on the rack, hanging them on gibbets, and confiscating their temporal goods to the ruin of their widows and orphans; of all Christians who marshal armies, drench the earth with blood, and make the air resound with groans; who sanctify the sword with prayers, and make it the defence of the church, or, still worse, their chief instrument in the conversion of the heathen; and who cap the climax of their religion with the grim caricature of a Christ and his favorites celebrating his triumphs to all eternity over the masses of the human race forever utterly ruined by his destructive power! This is the sort of Christ for whom the proud and vindictive Jews were looking, when the lowly Galilean appeared, to their disgust, — the beau ideal of such a Messiah as the high priest, scribes, Pharisees, and rulers wanted. They would have joined him at once in full force, and even Herod would have hastened to bargain with him for some high subordinate place near his throne. Would they have conspired against such a Christ? Would they have pretensively arraigned him as a blasphemer and seditionist; mocked him, scourged him, and crucified him between two thieves? Never. Or if they had attempted it, he would have summoned his "twelve legions of angels," and swept Jerusalem with the besom of destruction; not sublimely prayed, "Father, forgive them, for they know not what they do."

But says the objector, There stand the texts; what will you do with them? Will you spiritualize them away into nothing? No; I will spiritualize them into their true meaning, as the Holy Spirit intended, — into harmony with those plain passages which I quoted in support of my statement in the last discourse. What is the "right hand" of God? Has he an organic body with members like ours — *literally?* Is the infinite Spirit an organized person, seated on a literal, local, material throne? No; he fills boundless immensity, and is an invisible, omnipresent Spirit. His right hand signifies spiritual and moral approbation, exaltation, honor, and glory. Christ sits at that divine, spiritual, and moral right hand. Whoso heareth, let him understand. "Until I make thy foes thy footstool." What! literally, physically, their prostrate bodies made his footstool? Sensual absurdity! The meaning is, that their minds, hearts, wills, souls, should be spiritually and morally subdued to him, so that they should be perfectly humble, submissive, and willing to obey him. "Thou shalt break them with a rod of iron," "thou shalt dash them in pieces." What! literally break them with a literal rod of iron? literally "dash them in pieces"? Brutish conception! Truth is his rod of correction. Iron signifies strength. Truth is ten thousand times stronger than iron. It convicts minds, and subdues wills, which literal iron never could. Thus you see that Christ "breaks," and "dashes in pieces," and "grinds to powder," not literally the external persons of his enemies, but spiritually and morally their stubborn wills, the hateful dispositions of their minds that oppose him. He slays, not the bodies or external persons of his foes, but their hostile wills and feelings; his wrath is not the literal wrath of man, but the heart-searching, inflexible reproof of pure justice; and he wounds the heads of his refractory subjects through their conscience and reason, by the force of his spiritual two-edged sword. Thus he convicts, subdues, and saves sinners, as Joseph did his wicked brethren. Behold that beautiful type and forerunner of Christ! How did he smite and strike through his envious, cruel persecutors? How did he wound their heads, slay them, and grind them to powder? How did he make his foes his footstool? Even so will Christ. One such destruction of enemies, whereby they are pierced with just and salutary remorse, and subdued into humble, penitent, grateful, adoring friends, transcends in power and glory all the battles of renowned warriors since the world began.

But the objector is not yet satisfied. He insists on my meeting other passages of terrific Scripture:

"Whose fan is in his hand, and he will thoroughly purge his floor, and gather his wheat into his garner; but he will burn up the chaff with unquenchable fire." Matt. iii. 12. "Fear him who is able to destroy both soul and body in hell." Ibid. x. 28. "The angels shall come forth, and sever the wicked from among the just, and shall cast them into the furnace of fire: there shall be wailing and gnashing of teeth." Ibid. xiii. 49, 50. "Ye serpents, ye generation of vipers, how can ye escape the damnation of hell?" Ibid. xxiii. 33. "When the Son of man shall come in his glory, and all the holy angels with him, then shall he sit upon the throne of his glory. And before him shall be gathered all nations: and he shall separate them one from another, as a shepherd divideth his sheep from the goats. And he shall set the sheep on his right hand, but the goats on the left. Then shall the King say unto them on his right hand, Come, ye blessed of my Father, inherit the kingdom prepared for you from the foundation of the world." "Also unto them on the left hand, Depart from me, ye cursed, into everlasting fire, prepared for the devil and his angels." "And these shall go away into everlasting punishment: but the righteous into life eternal." Ibid. xxv. 31–34, 41, 46. "For we must all appear before the judgment-seat of Christ, that every one may receive the things done in his body, according to that he hath done, whether it be good or bad." 2 Cor. v. 10. "The Lord Jesus Christ shall be revealed from heaven in flaming fire, taking vengeance on them that know not God, and that obey not the gospel of our Lord Jesus Christ: who shall be punished with everlasting destruction from the presence of the Lord, and from the glory of his power." 2 Thess. i. 7–9. "There remaineth no more sacrifice for sins, but a certain fearful looking for of judgment and fiery indignation, which shall devour the adversaries." Heb. x. 26, 27. Will these texts suffice as a specimen of the class relied on to disprove my position?

Yes, answers the objector, and what can you say of them?

I can say that, if they must be understood according to the mere sound and strict letter of their phraseology, they flatly contradict, not only my position, but the whole host of testimonies whereof I adduced striking samples, in my last discourse, to illustrate the true nature of Christ's kingdom, authority, and governmental administration. I can say that if they must be thus understood, Christ will prove to be the destroyer, rather than the Saviour, of the world; that his declared meekness, lowliness, and mercifulness end in despotic power, vengeance, and cruelty; that all his sublime precepts to his disciples, enjoining them to be as little children, to love their enemies, bless those that curse them, do good to those that hate them, to forgive offenders till seventy times seven, to imitate his own example, and to be merciful as their Father in heaven is merciful, are just such unmeaning absurdities as his degenerate church has made them for the last sixteen centuries; and finally that such a Christ would be one that I could never love, honor, or follow. But I can say, on the contrary, with the utmost positiveness and assurance, that these texts are *not* to be understood according to the mere sound and strict letter of their phraseology. Their authors never meant them to be understood thus literally. They are all more or less figurative, and most of them intensely so. Material and temporal things are made metaphorically significant of spiritual and moral realities. Their true meaning can be deduced only by due consideration of their relation to the essential spirit and principles of Christianity. We know very well that they teach Christ's personal authority to execute divine judgment and retribution; that in so doing he was certain to make a just and broad distinction between the righteous and the wicked; that he was sure to render unto every individual according to works and character; and that all this was to subserve some important end for the triumph of his mediatorial government. All this I undoubtingly believe and contend for.

The questions really at issue are: 1. Does he exercise *arbitrary* personal authority in executing his official power? 2. Does he execute judgment by means of external rewards and punishments? 3. Does he resort to destructive physical force? And, 4. What are to be the actual results of all his judicial dispensations? My position is the same as before. The objector's is unchanged. One of the most important terms in these texts is fire. Will the objector, or any person of common sense, insist that literal material fire was meant? I think not. Then what was meant by this term? Evidently spiritual and moral *fire*. What is that? Just judgment. What is just judgment? Truth and justice convicting the soul of sin. Why is just judgment metaphorically called *fire?* Because it is the nature of fire to consume whatever is consumable, and to purify what is unconsumable, or, by melting, to fit it for new uses. Therefore Malachi predicted that Christ should "sit as a refiner and purifier of silver." iii. 3. And John the Baptist declared that he should "baptize with the Holy Spirit, and with fire" [just judgment]; that he should "thoroughly purge his threshing-floor, gather the wheat into his garner, and burn up the chaff with unquenchable fire" [just judgment], whose nature it is to consume all that is sinful, evil, or worthless. *Wheat* and *chaff* are metaphorical words, denoting what is valuable and what worthless; that is, what constitutes good and bad moral character in accountable beings. But inside of moral character is the being itself, which God created good. The fire is not designed to consume this, but to melt and purify it for a better use and state. The good moral character it only brightens. The bad it utterly consumes; so that a wicked man, *as wicked*, ceases to be; yet the man does not cease to be. He only ceases to be a wicked man. The chaff is consumed. Paul states the case pertinently: "Every man's work shall be made manifest: for the day shall declare it; because it shall be revealed by fire [just judgment], and the fire shall try every man's work of what sort it is. If any man's work abide which he hath built thereupon, he shall receive a reward. If any man's work shall be burned, he shall suffer loss: but he himself shall be saved; yet so as by fire." 1 Cor. iii. 13–15.

Similar metaphorical phraseology is used in the precept, "If thine enemy hunger, feed him, if he thirst, give him drink: for in so doing thou shalt heap coals of fire [just judgment and purifying convictions for sin] on his head." "Be not overcome of evil, but overcome evil with good." Rom. xii. 20, 21. Is this Christ's principle and method of action, or not? I say it is; and that none of these alleged texts really mean anything to the contrary. It is perversion and presumption to make them mean the contrary.

"Fear him who is able to destroy both soul and body in hell," — Gehenna, or Gehenna fire. Gehenna, or Gehenna fire, denoted in Christ's day, figuratively, the severest kind of just judgment to which mankind were liable. But it is still just judgment, and has the same use as before stated.

The terms destroy, destroyed, destruction, etc., in such passages, do not denote utter annihilation, nor hopeless endless misery, but the utter subjugation of sinners, rendering them, as sinners, utterly powerless, utterly helpless, and utterly wretched for the time being, with nothing to hope for except through the undeserved mercy of their Judge. Hear the word of the Lord: "Thou turnest man to destruction; and sayest, Return, ye children of men." Psalm xc. 3. "He sent his word, and healed them, and delivered them from all their destructions." Ibid. cvii. 20. "O Israel, thou hast destroyed thyself; but in me is thine help." Hosea xiii. 9. Here we get the true idea of *how* God, or Christ, will destroy the wicked in the hell-fire of just judgment; of their being severed from among the just, and cast into "the furnace of fire;" of the certainty that those metaphorically called "serpents" and "vipers" cannot escape their deserved condemnation; of the nature of the "flaming fire," and vengeance in which Christ should "be revealed;" and of the "fiery indignation which should devour the adversaries." *Just judgment*—the spiritual fire that burns up all evil, melts all obdurate metals, and purifies for better uses all that survives its dross — explains the whole judicial administration of Christ. Is it not abominable to take up oriental metaphors, hyperboles, and figurative phrases, without regard to the manner of expressing ideas, and understanding of the words when they were written, reduce them to our flat, matter-of-fact use of language, and then assume from them that God is a monster of cruelty, and Christ a vindictive despot? As if the wrath of God were madness, and the vengeance of Christ implacable revenge against his enemies! We read that "God is a consuming fire," but still more emphatically, that he "is love." Is he not both? A consuming fire in respect to just judgment against sinners as such, and love toward all his offspring as eternally seeking their highest good? Certainly. We read that Christ is the Lamb of God that taketh away the sin of the world, and also of "the wrath of the Lamb," who will render judgment to all according to their works, make his foes his footstool, and subdue all things. Is not all this true? Why, then, do we imagine his lamb-wrath to be tiger-wrath, and him to be a sort of omnipotent Nebuchadnezzar, with a literal furnace of fire into which to cast his offenders? Why not accept him as the transfigured antitype of Joseph?—who, when his guilt-stricken brethren trembled as under sentence of death before him, revealed his great heart, saying, "I am Joseph your brother, whom ye sold into Egypt; be not grieved nor angry with yourselves that ye sold me thither: for God did send me before you to preserve life." And when, years later, they still felt that he might hate and punish them, and bowed down to implore his forgiveness, he said, with tears of generous love and pity, "Fear not, for I am in the place of God. Ye thought evil against me; but God meant it unto good." Will we have such a Christ? Or will we have one who is the intensified antitype of some vindictive Asiatic monarch, whose throne is a mountain of human skulls, and his palace vaulted beneath with dungeons of despair?

Ah, says the objector, you argue plausibly, but you forget the "everlasting fire," the "everlasting punishment," and the "everlasting destruction." No, no. The fire of just judgment is as everlasting as divine truth and justice, yet, though unquenchable, it consumes nothing but error, sin, and evil. That which is worth preserving, it melts, purifies, and blesses. The punishment is therefore everlasting in its good effects. It is a part of that "effectual working whereby Christ is able to subdue all things unto himself." This will be an everlasting subduing, which will never need to be repeated. And so will the destruction be an everlasting destruction, putting an eternal end to all rebellion and sin. Thus will my seventh proposition be proved and fulfilled; namely, Jesus Christ will certainly continue to reign, in the exercise of these mediatorial powers, till every human soul shall have been subdued unto him, and so reconciled to the Father, who will thenceforth dwell spiritually "all in all."

As it is written, "He must reign till he hath put all enemies under his feet. . . And when all things shall be subdued unto him, then shall the Son also himself be subject unto Him that put all things under him, that God may be all in all." 1 Cor. xv. 25, 28.

ARTICLE VI.

DIVINE GOVERNMENT, JUDGMENT, RETRIBUTION, AND DISCIPLINE.

DISCOURSE XXIV.

CORRUPTIONS OF THE PURE PRIMITIVE DOCTRINE.

"The time will come, when they will not endure sound doctrine. . . And they shall turn away *their* ears from the truth, and shall be turned unto fables." — 2 TIM. iv. 3, 4.

HAVING carefully presented the pure primitive Christian doctrine of divine government, judgment, retribution, and discipline, in accordance with my best information and conviction, I now proceed to point out some of the principal corruptions which have darkened and perverted it.

1. Perhaps the earliest of these corruptions was the materializing, or literalizing, of the doctrine, — construing the strong figurative language through which Christ and his apostles frequently taught it, in an external sense, contrary to its intended spiritual meaning. It was natural for people to fall into this error then, as it is even now; because the animal, carnal, sensuous mentality is first developed in mankind, and is transcended by the higher spiritual mentality only after much regenerative discipline and

rational cultivation. It is far easier for the general masses of our race to understand and bow to arbitrary personal authority, than purely spiritual and moral authority; to understand and appreciate external glory, power, government, and retribution, than spiritual and moral; to conceive of divine "wrath" "indignation," and "vengeance," as *human*, only intensely more dreadful, and to construe such terms as "fire," "hell-fire," "everlasting fire," "a furnace of fire," etc., etc., in their literal, rather than in their true spiritual, sense. Christ stood on the high spiritual and moral plane. It was his special office and mission to lift us all up to that plane. But he could not do this, in an orderly manner, without adapting himself more or less to the unspiritual conceptions of mankind on their lower plane. This occasioned a perpetual struggle for the elevation of his apostles and first followers. If he spoke altogether in language nakedly spiritual, they could hardly appreciate his meaning; and if he used strong figurative expressions, they were prone to understand him in a gross literal sense, so that he was obliged to explain his real meaning. When he said, "Except a man be born again," etc., Nicodemus exclaimed, "How can a man be born when he is old? Can he enter the second time into his mother's womb, and be born?" John iii. 4. Then Jesus had to explain his spiritual meaning to that "Master of Israel." When he said, "It is easier for a camel to go through the eye of a needle than for a rich man to enter into the kingdom of God," his "disciples were exceedingly amazed, saying, Who, then, can be saved?" He looked at them a moment almost in astonishment, and said, "With men this is impossible; but with God all things are possible." Matt. xix. 24–26. Once more; he said, "Except ye eat the flesh of the Son of man, and drink his blood, ye have no life in you," etc. This shocked even his disciples, many of whom said, "This is a hard saying; who can hear it?" And he was obliged to give them his spiritual meaning: "It is the Spirit that quickeneth; the flesh profiteth nothing: the words that I speak unto you are spirit and are life." John vi. 53–63. Feed on them.

While it was easy to fall into this error, and for the vast majority of nominal Christians to cherish it, even as they have down to our own age, it has proved a pernicious corruption. It has been food for fanaticism, superstition, unholy ambition, and declamatory proselytism. It has turned Christ into a celestial autocrat, heaven into a palatial metropolis, and hell into a vast dungeon of physical torture. And thus it has debased Christianity into a religion of wild imaginations, irrational hopes, and absurd fears; belittling its sublime principles, motives, and righteousness, in the mistaken conception of millions, into petty competition with those of the inferior religions, older and younger, which have divided the reverence of the world. There have been enlightened, wise, and good minds, in all ages of the church, who saw and deplored this corruption; but they were too few and far between to withstand its noise, popularity, and brute force. It will eventually be outgrown and shaken off, but only as a higher degree of mentality, spirituality, and rationality prevail.

2. Another and kindred corruption, which took early root downward and has borne grievous fruit upward certainly for nearly sixteen hundred years, is the notion that Christ administers the whole government of the universe in every department of creation, either in place of God, or as really himself the supreme God. This erroneous notion ignores Christ's official mediatorial specialty, as defined and limited by the primitive doctrine, resolves him virtually into the only God, makes him the executor of all physical as well as moral laws and retributions, and, of course, holds him to be the superintending head of all human governments, to institute, uphold, and put them down, at discretion, by his personal administrative providence. Hence he became, in the mistaken conception of most professing Christians, the Supreme Dictator and Arbiter of all civil, political, military, and governmental affairs on earth, — by whom kings reign, princes decree justice, and the whole machinery of legislation, penal infliction, and warlike force operates. On this basis the church assumed to be the superior, the counsellor, and, to a great extent, the director of the state, wherever the twain could be united; all in the name of Christ. When the church said, Make war against those heathens, or infidels, or heretics; go on a bloody crusade against them; dash them in pieces; crush them out, and destroy them, — it was all to be done in the name and by the authority of Christ, — all consecrated with Christian prayers and benedictions. This horrible abomination has rolled on in blood now for long centuries, metamorphosing the Prince of Peace into a Deific Dragon,

who is sure to triumph by the destructions of eternity, if not here in time. Behold his pretended Vicar at Rome, assuming to rule both by spiritual and temporal power, thundering his anathemas against all opposers, and supported by brigades of mercenary soldiers! He does all this in the name of Christ. And the same thing is done, directly or indirectly, under one pretext or another, throughout Christendom. Is this the Christianity of Christ and the New Testament? No more than Mohammedanism is. It is a gross and shameful corruption, which the Son of God from heaven abhors, and will ere long purge away by his fire of just judgment.

3. Another and kindred corruption of the primitive doctrine is, that the judgments and retributions of Christ are penal ends and finalities, — not disciplinary means of subduing offenders and enemies to his spiritual authority. The notion is, that he disciplines his elect, his church, his saints, for their good, at least in this present life, by various salutary and beneficent chastenings; but that he treats all the rest of mankind, who die outside of these limits in unbelief and sin, as incurable criminals, hopeless offenders, and unpardonable rebels, or enemies. As such he will not regard their good, nor aim at their reformation, but make mere penal sufferers of them, — dreadful examples of his just vengeance, to vindicate divine law and order, either by subjecting them to endless misery, or annihilating them outright, or, at the least, leaving them as voluntary reprobates and utter aliens from his favor forever.

Just consider the horrible import of this corruption.

It is plethoric with manifold nullifications of primitive Christianity, and involves results and conclusions which rob Christ of all his spiritual glory. Ancient heathenism taught the final bliss of all human souls, after ages of ages of retributive and disciplinary transmigration, by absorptive reunion with the Supreme God. Have we a Christ and Christianity with a worse ultimation than this? The Zoroastrian religion proclaimed one Infinite, All-perfect God, with two sons, one of whom became his vicegerent, and the other a mighty rebel, or devil. Both were creators, and had hosts of angels at command. Ormuzd wrought only good, and Ahriman, his rebel brother, only evil. But Ormuzd is to triumph completely at the end of twelve thousand years, purify the world of all evil by fire, subdue his satanic brother with all his angels, and convert them into devoted friends. Have we a Christ and Christianity inferior to this Persian heathenism? Buddhism has four hundred millions of adherents, who have the credit of never propagating their religion by fire and sword, as corrupt Christianity has often done. Buddhism, notwithstanding its painful and long-continued transmigrations, declares the final return of all souls to their Divine Source, and gives them perfect rest in his bosom. Have we a Christ and Christianity whose consummative glory is to be the happiness of a favored few, and the confirmed reprobation and hopeless ruin of the countless many? Must we degrade Christianity into a rival of Pharisaic Judaism and Mohammedanism, in respect to its retributions and their results? Is our Christ to be revenged on his murderers after such a fashion?

Is he to subdue his enemies in even a worse sense than the great Tartar warrior, Tamerlane, did the Grand Turk, Bajazet I., whom he confined in an iron cage, such as the vanquished despot had proposed for him? There the miserable Turk, with a still proud, defiant, and unconquered will, dashed out his own brains against the iron walls that confined him. Is even this poor privilege to be denied to Christ's enemies? These questions suggest their own answers, and protest with irresistible moral force against the gross corruptions I am denouncing

And does not the whole New Testament record present a like protest? Jesus Christ is there set forth as the very Prince of peace, love, meekness, forgiveness, and lowly service. Is he to resolve himself, as King and Judge, into the Prince of war, of vengeance, of stern, inexorable despotism, and of implacable penalism? He there preaches and exemplifies the very perfection of love to enemies, and the overcoming of evil with good. Was this mere sentimentalism, spasmodic rhetoric, or, meaner still, the soft disguise of politic weakness, only to be worn till he could gain power to crush his foes by destructive force? And when this Lamb of God should reach his prime, was he to become a Ram of hard-headed violence, reversing all his merciful precepts and examples? On that record he is exhibited in the true greatness of humility, the godlike dignity of meek and truthful benevolence, preaching and practising the universal neighborhood and brotherhood of man. Is he to consummate his career as the Head of a Caste, whose glory it is to love and pamper its own elect, but to despise, enslave, and forever trample under foot the reprobate? There we find him declared to be the Saviour of world. Is he to prove himself the destroyer of the world, except a mere fraction of converts graciously plucked as brands from the unsavable mass? There it is proclaimed that he was filled with the divine fulness, in order to reconcile all things to God; that he shall reign till all be subdued unto him; that every tongue shall confess him Lord to the glory of the Father; and that he shall make all things new. But this corruption throws its "blackness of darkness" over all these supernal prospects. How? By assuming that Christ cannot fulfil his official mission, as King and Judge of mankind, without reversing his characteristics as Saviour, Teacher, Exemplar, and merciful High Priest, — without resolving himself into the Eternal Punisher of all who leave this mortal state of existence in unbelief and sin. It will not allow that his rewards and punishments are to be according to works, and so made a salutary means to the one great benevolent end of his Christship, universal holiness and happiness; but gloomily insists that they are *ends, finalities,* of the divine government, in which the universe is to settle down to all eternity; the few rewarded with heaven, the countless many destroyed or rendered confirmed reprobates forever! It will have it that this is all Christ and his religion are to accomplish! This is the transcendent excellency and glory of Christianity! Ah, of a Christianity perverted, and darkened, and blighted by gross corruptions!

Is it any wonder that such a Christianity propagated

itself for ages among the heathen by fire and sword? Any wonder that it provoked the fire and sword of Mohammedanism, till robbed of a third of its early domain? Any wonder that it so long suppressed heresy by the tortures of the inquisition, fagots, and cruel penalties? Any wonder that the nominal church is rent into selfish and combative sects? Any wonder that its largest division has a spirito-temporal monarch, whom it is presumptuously proclaiming infallible, and whose tottering throne has to be sustained by drilled warriors? Any wonder that even the better sects still cleave to the governmental sword of worldly power to abolish wrong, establish right, and promote human progress? Any wonder that mere science, learning, civilization, politics, and moral philanthropy are taking the lead, and obliging Christianity, such as it is, to play the servile handmaid to their schemes? Any wonder that so few professing Christians perceive the radical difference between primitive Christianity and ordinary political civilization, — that is, between pure moral forces and a system of temporary expediency backed by deadly physical force? Finally, is it any wonder that so many intelligent persons have little faith in, and respect for, Christianity, in any of its present forms, or that multitudes of common people are indifferent to its ministrations, finding their chief interest and pleasure in material things? So it now is, and so it must be, with increasing momentum, till the axe of reform shall be laid at the root of the tree, all corruptions hewn away, and pure primitive Christianity, both doctrinal and practical, made to bud, blossom, and bring forth fruit according to its own legitimate excellency. Then, if God is shown to be really our Father, we shall know what we must be as his children. If all mankind are shown to be our brethren and sisters, we shall know how we must treat them as such. If Christ is shown to be really our spiritual Lord, Exemplar, Judge, Discipliner, and Saviour, we shall know that he never frustrates his mission by acting in one official capacity utterly contrary to what he does in another; but is a self-consistent, harmonic, and triumphant Christ. Then shall we know that there is no such thing as being true and full Christians without being Christ-like in spirit, principle, conduct, and moral character. And then dawneth the long-predicted era of fraternal love and peace for the human race, ripening at last into the final universal triumph of good over evil.

> O Love, all triumphant, thou Soul of the Highest,
> Whose Wisdom ensureth the end thou desirest,
> The wheels of thy chariot, majestic and glorious,
> Are rolling serenely, forever victorious!
> Reign on in thy beauty, meek Prince of salvation,
> Till thy work be accomplished in full consummation,
> And the last conquered sinner, subdued in contrition,
> Be welcomed by angels to life's grand fruition.

ARTICLE VII.

THE FINAL DESTINY OF MANKIND.

DISCOURSE XXV.

THE PURE PRIMITIVE CHRISTIAN DOCTRINE OF MAN'S FINAL DESTINY.

"Having made known unto us the mystery of his will, according to his good pleasure, which he hath purposed in himself: that in the dispensation of the fulness of times he might gather together in one all things in Christ, both which are in heaven, and which are on earth, even in him." — Ephes. i. 9, 10.

WHAT do I mean by the final destiny of mankind? Their designed ultimate condition, or state, in the universe, so far as the human mind can now form definite conceptions. The human mind can form three definite conceptions of its own ultimate condition, or state, namely, that it will be holy and happy; that it will be sinful and miserable; that it will cease to exist as a conscious entity. Beyond these three definite conceptions the human mind may have many speculative ideas, but they must of necessity be vague and fanciful. Thus some talk beautifully of endless progress, and others of successive grand cycles; but whatever of truth there may be in such doctrines, they are at present too inconceivable to be made the basis of moral action. And I hold that no theoretical doctrine whatever is of much use which has not some strong legitimate practical influence as a spring of positive human action. Fruits prove the *worth* as well as the *kind* of every tree.

Assuming, then, that the final destiny of mankind must be holiness and happiness, sinfulness and misery, or annihilation of conscious individual entity, must we not also assume that the finality, whichever it be, was designed by our Creator from the beginning; that is, from such moment in the past as the work of human creation was commenced, or, if you please, planned? I think so. I think primitive Christianity so teaches. Certainly it most positively represents God as possessing and exercising all the essential attributes of mind, — of rational and moral personality (not corporeal organic personality); that is, as being an all-perfect Spirit, in respect to consciousness, intelligence, love, wisdom, moral rectitude, desire, will, purpose, and action. The notion that God has no consciousness of his own existence, or that of finite entities; that the First Cause is without mind, affection, will, purpose, design, and voluntary action, — a mere plexus of necessitating forces, principles of vitality, or blind instinctive laws; is totally contrary to the teachings of Christ and his apostles, as, in my judgment, it is to natural reason.

Therefore I am obliged to conclude that whatever shall prove to be the final condition or state of mankind was foreseen and purposed from the beginning. Foreseen, it must have been by the all-perfect Mind; and, if foreseen, it must somehow have been either willed *per se*, or accepted, calculated on, and provided for, as inevitable and best, all things considered. Practically the actual result must be tantamount to a deliberate design of God, or what Peter termed "the determinate counsel and foreknowledge of God."

Taking this ground, which seems to me to be the only tenable one, we must understand that this subject of man's final destiny has a moral importance far greater than that of mere speculative theology. It radically affects the very foundation of religion, and especially the standard of personal righteousness in all its practical bearings. How so? Because God's destiny of man determines, more or less conclusively, his own standard of righteousness and moral character; which standard must be the absolute one for us, and which moral character must fashion ours. But is this certainly so? Undoubtedly. A little serious reflection must convince the honest mind. To be godly, or godlike in spirit, principle, and action,— that is, to be perfect, in these respects, as our heavenly Father is perfect,— is the grand moral ultimate proposed and enjoined by primitive Christianity. Perfect love to God and man — the grand mainsprings of piety and morality — are enforced by the fundamental truth, that God himself is love toward his creatures, even "the unthankful and evil." Therefore is the sublime obligation to love God with all our capabilities, and our fellow-humans as ourselves, pressed home upon us as indispensable. It is also made plain to us, that love, unlike hatred and indifference, worketh no evil to its beloved, but good. It is true, that love works under different and sometimes almost opposite conditions. God's love and ours towards a rebellious, repellant sinner has to struggle, for the time being, against antagonistic forces. Congeniality and sweet communion of soul cannot exist till those forces shall be overcome. What, then, is it that God loves, or that I ought to love, in such a sinner? That precisely which is lovable in a cross, wayward child. His inherent capabilities of becoming penitent, wise, and good under the right treatment and discipline. For the love of these capabilities God seeks every sinner's reformation and highest good, in the use of all suitable means. And so ought I. Still there is no congeniality, agreeable fellowship, or sweet communion, between the parties. But if the pure divine love be absorbed by the moral capabilities of the once repellant party, so as to dwell and rule therein, then the same element blends both parties into happy unison. Thus love would consummate that holy union for which Christ prayed, " that they all may be one, even as we are one." This just view of the different conditions under which love operates, explains how it was that, " for the great love " wherewith God loved us, before we loved him, " even when dead in trespasses and sins," he provided for our salvation; also how it is that we are enjoined to love our enemies; and also how, in the higher class of cases, the communion of a common love makes the heaven of a holy fellowship. God loves a hateful sinner (whom he must rebuke) for the sake of the good capabilities in him which he is perverting and abusing. And when, through regenerative discipline, that sinner becomes penitent, welcoming the love of God to be shed abroad in his heart, he is a thousand times more lovable, because his good capabilities are full of the divine love, and have cast off their hateful perversions. He is then not only lovable for his good capabilities, but much more for his actual good attainments. So must it be between the truly godly man and his enemy. While an enemy, he loves him for the sake of his good capabilities, and in spite of all the evils which he must rebuke. But when this love has overcome those evils with good, and at length changed him into a devoted friend, they love each other as brothers in the blissful unity of the Holy Christ.

Now I approach the exact point. Suppose a human being whose final destiny is sinfulness and misery, or, if you please, annihilation. And you may suppose him to be as wicked as you can imagine. Why did God bring that being into existence with such a foreseen destiny? Did he do it under the pressure of some disagreeable necessity, or fate, behind himself? If so, he is not the absolute and supreme God. There is a mysterious and prior Cause behind and above him. And if so, we have no reliable assurance that he will not be thwarted in all that his benevolence wills. That other, greater Causator is the real God, to whom he and we must all bow. Away with such a notion! Then it was of *choice* that he gave existence to this hopeless reprobate. This must be the ground to take in making the supposition suggested. Did God create such a wretch in love? If so, what better is love than hatred, or, at best, than cold indifference? Not at all. Then the very term love is a misnomer and a cheat. It seems to mean something good, but is a hateful fraud on the understanding. Away with such a presumption! But if God created this foreseen and, of course, designed, hopeless reprobate from choice, cursing him unto a cursed existence, can he love God? Ought he to love him? Is it not a cruel mockery of his reason and moral nature to command such a creature to love such a Creator? Is it not downright tyranny? Is not obedience, in such a case, a moral impossibility? Undoubtedly. Step a little further, and ask if any *holy* man or angel could love such a Creator with all his heart, all his mind, and all his strength: nay, more, ask if he ought! Yes, says one, he can and ought, because he himself is loved and made a favorite by his God. Perhaps; that is, granting that such a God can be called holy, and his favorites holy. But this must let down holiness to the low standard of publicans and sinners, which Christ contemned. "If ye love them who love you, . . do not even the publicans so?" "For sinners also love those that love them." This may answer for a selfish being, but not for a holy one. Besides, if my God be morally capable of tyranny, malignity, and cruelty to my fellow-being, how can I be sure that he will not some time make me a like victim; and if me, millions of others? But worse than all this,— if love, goodness, and moral perfection be really such as this in my God, should it not be the same in me, and in all his children? Are we to be more pure than our Maker, more just than our God, more merciful than our Father in heaven? Is the stream to rise higher than the fountain, the branch to be greater than the trunk, the child to be better than his parent, the worshipper to be holier than his God? This is not the doctrine of primitive Christianity, which enjoins that we "be followers of God as dear children, and walk in love;" that we be "led by the Spirit of God, and so become the sons of God;" that we be "merciful as our Father in heaven is merciful," and "perfect as he is perfect," in good will even to the "unthankful and evil." We cannot be infinite as God is, and are not required to be. We cannot operate on his vast scale, nor precisely in the same manner that he does; because we are finite. But we can be inspired by his Spirit, we can act from the same pure motives, we can seek the same blessed results, we can be in holy unison with him and his model Son, Jesus Christ. This is imperatively required of us, and the promise is given that his "strength shall be made perfect in our weakness," and "his grace sufficient for us," to enable us to do our duty. But the idea that we are to love any one whom God hates, or be concerned for any one to whose welfare God is indifferent, or forgive any one to whom God is unforgiving, or seek any one's final holiness and happiness, who in his purposes is an incorrigible reprobate, or that we are to pray for any better results in this world or the next than he has willed and predestined, — is as utterly absurd as it is groundless. God's will must be our will, his purpose our purpose, his motives our motives, his righteousness our righteousness, and his moral character our moral character; that is, in the degree to which finite children can possibly be like their infinite Father. This is the very life of pure and undefiled religion, to which all faith, preaching, and practice, should strictly conform. Thus our inevitable conclusion is, that the final destiny of mankind indicates the real moral character of God; that the real moral character of God determines the absolute standard of righteousness for all moral agents; and that the standard of righteousness decides, in the last resort, what is right or wrong in human conduct, whether pietistically toward God, or morally toward ourselves and fellow-creatures. Therefore let us remember that the question of the final destiny of mankind is not only one of vast theological importance in respect to our hopes and fears, but of still vaster importance in determining what our practical righteousness ought to be, and must be.

Now, then, which of the three distinctive conceptions of man's final destiny, before stated, is in accordance with the pure primitive Christian doctrine, — holiness and happiness, sinfulness and misery, or the annihilation of personal consciousness? We have a diversity of answers. Many will answer, with the utmost confidence, that the righteous are destined to endless holiness, perfection, and happiness; and the wicked to endless sinfulness and misery. Others will answer, with equal assurance, that the righteous are destined to immortality and endless happiness; and the wicked to utter unconsciousness of personal identity, or annihilation. The advocates of these doctrines, solemnly contend that their respective conclusions are authoritatively declared in "the word of God," and that this is their sufficient reason for holding them. The two doctrines themselves are held by different classes of believers in a variety of speculative forms, from those of the most repulsive Calvinism to those of the most refined Arminianism, and are defended with every possible degree of intellectual ingenuity. But both these doctrines, in all their forms and phases, are inherently anti-Christian, demoralizing, and justly deserving to be characterized as corruptions. I should, indeed, have a decided preference between the two general beliefs, and between the very different phases in which they are presented; but it would be only a sad choice between evils all more or less abhorrent. I turn from them, with profound pleasure, to what I firmly believe to be the pure primitive Christian doctrine, — namely, that all mankind are destined to ultimate holiness and happiness. This is the only conception of man's final destiny, which, in my judgment, gives God a perfect moral character, presents a perfect standard of righteousness, sustains a religion of perfect love to God and man, and takes away all justification of caste, pride, bigotry, selfishness, revenge, persecution, and cruelty among human beings. If this is the true primitive doctrine, taught by Christ and his apostles, then the Fatherhood of God and the brotherhood of man are true doctrines in the highest and most complete sense. If not, all assertion and laudation of these doctrines is vain and impracticable rhetoric. Again; if such is the final destiny of the whole human race, then all those sublimely stringent precepts and examples of Christ, which require us to be humble and harmless as little children, to devote all that we have and are to the good of humanity, — to "love our enemies, do good to those who hate us, and bless them that curse us," — are absolutely true, and, with divine help, practicable. Otherwise, they are worthless and impracticable, — sheer impositions, entitled to as little respect and obedience as our popular Christianity pays them. And if I must come to such a lame and impotent conclusion, then, alas! I should be at utter loss to show wherein Christianity excelled Judaism, or the other religions and philosophies of the world. But in my next discourse I will endeavor to demonstrate that I have declared the pure primitive Christian doctrine on this subject, and thus to justify the poet's hopeful vision : —

> "All crimes shall cease, and ancient fraud shall fail;
> Returning justice lift aloft her scale;
> Peace o'er the world her olive wand extend,
> And white-robed innocence from heaven descend."
>
> POPE.

ARTICLE VII.

THE FINAL DESTINY OF MANKIND.

DISCOURSE XXVI.

THE PURE PRIMITIVE CHRISTIAN DOCTRINE OF HUMAN DESTINY VERIFIED.

"Who hath known the mind of the Lord? or who hath been his counsellor? Or who hath first given to him, and it shall be recompensed unto him again? For of him, and through him, and to him, are all things: to whom be glory forever, Amen."— Rom. xi. 34-36.

In my last I endeavored to show that the question of man's final destiny was one of vast importance, not merely in speculative theology, but morally, as vitally affecting the absolute standard of personal righteousness throughout the universe of moral agents. I know that I cannot over-estimate this moral importance of the question. And yet it is painful to witness the low appreciation commonly accorded to it. Multitudes of people seem to be almost entirely indifferent to this great finality: whether heaven, hell, or non-entity be their own doom, or that of their fellow-creatures. They are wholly occupied with the buzz of their little *now*. Many quite sensible and well-disposed minds contrive to imagine that the subject is one of mere theoretical speculation, and of very little practical concern. And among intelligent religionists we have a considerable class who persuade themselves that wisdom forbids them to attempt a definite settlement of the question. "Oh," say they, "God has not revealed the final destiny of mankind. It is a question which it is presumptuous for human reason or faith to dogmatize upon. The result of existence will be right, whatever it be; but whether it will be heaven, hell, or annihilation we cannot tell. We ought to be reverent, humble, and modest enough to leave final issues with God, and confine ourselves to plain duties, and to rewards and punishments plainly revealed." All this may be honestly thought and speciously said, but it is a poor dodge of the inevitable and vital question, — the pivotal question, — that is, For what did the Infinite God give man existence? It never did and never can satisfy a free and unsophisticated mind. Above all other articles of faith in religion, next after the existence of a God, let us understand definitely what sort of a God we have, and what his real moral character is, in relation to the souls he has created. Now this depends decisively on the ultimate use and condition for which he created them. Call him not good, unless he is; nor Father, unless he is; nor love, unless he is. Tell me not to love, trust, and obey him implicitly, with all my heart, all my understanding, and all my powers, unless he is absolutely worthy, absolutely perfect, absolutely incapable of being any less than the adorable friend of every moral agent in the universe. Charm me not with brilliant sentimentalism about the Fatherhood of God, the brotherhood of man, the golden rule, and the blessed philanthropies, unless you can guarantee me a faultless Supreme Mind, faultless destinies for all his rational offspring, and faultless obligations for man to be perfect, as his heavenly Father is, in the exercise of that love which finally overcometh all evil with good. I will honor no moral character in God or man, which can complacently rest in a finality of misery or death for any moral nature.

But I proposed to prove that the final holiness and happiness of all mankind is the pure primitive Christian doctrine on this subject. Can I do it? Yes. How? Not by plunging into the mid-ocean of God's dispensations of penal law, obligation, and retribution, and there floundering about as if there were no continent beyond, — imagining his means to be ends, and his discipline of souls to be their final condition. Thousands do just this. They confine their contemplations to what divine revelation says about God's law, its penalty, man's duty, sinfulness, salvation, damnation, and retribution, — the rewards of the righteous and the punishments of the wicked. And there they stop, as if they had reached the ultimates of human destiny. We ask them, Is there nothing beyond all this divine judgment and retribution? Will they answer, Nothing more important that we can see? What! no grand use of this retribution? "No," say they; "this is the finality. The scenes of man's drama are, to be on temporary probation, to be privileged a little while with gracious opportunities, then to be solemnly judged, and then to be decisively fixed in a good or evil state through a never-ending eternity! There is no end in God's purposes beyond this. There he rests. There close all man's fears and hopes." Of this they are confident.

But I protest against such short-sighted views, such purblind conclusions. These are dispensations of means, not ends; of processes, not ultimate results; of disciplinary stages, not final destinies. All probations, gracious privileges, judgments, rewards, and punishments have their place and use in the divine moral system; but they are not finalities. Ultimate destinies of condition stretch away beyond them into the boundless expanse of futurity. How, then, do I find in God's revelations the testimonies which certify to my faith the absolute final destiny of all human beings; and that it will be a condition of holiness and happiness? I will show you.

1. Divine revelation teaches us the nature of moral goodness, in God, Christ, angels, and men; that it is pure love and wisdom, which seek and work out only the highest good of the beloved. Do you ask me to prove this from the Bible? Ask me to prove that the sun radiates light and heat. Who can doubt it?

2. Divine revelation teaches us that God is good to all his human creation, unchangeably, impartially, and perfectly good, even to the unthankful and evil; that his very nature is love. Who asks me to prove this? It is too obviously declared to need proof. Who will presume to assert the contrary?

3. Divine revelation teaches us that God created mankind in his own image, and pronounced their primal nature good; that he is the sole Creator of the human race, wherefore we are his offspring; and that

for his own glory and pleasure all are and were created. Who questions this? What is the pleasure, and what the glory, of such a Creator?

4. Divine revelation teaches us that it is the will of God that all mankind should come to repentance, and be saved from their sins. Is there any need of proving this? No; it is too plainly and repeatedly declared.

5. Divine revelation teaches us that God foreordained, raised up, and sent forth his Son Jesus Christ, to put away the sin of our world, — to be the Saviour of the world from sin and death. Is there any doubt of this? None, to readers of the sacred volume.

6. Divine revelation teaches us that Christ came, taught divine truth, exemplified a perfect righteousness, and died the self-sacrificing death of the cross, for all mankind, to deliver them from the power of sin and death. This is too plain to require any citation of proofs. It is conspicuous on the record.

7. Divine revelation teaches us that Christ descended into Hades, and preached to the spirits in prison; that he arose from the realm of the dead, ascended into the heavens, became invested with plenary judicial authority over the quick and dead, to judge and discipline all mankind according to their works, and to reign as mediatorial King and Judge till all things shall be subdued unto him. This needs no formal proof. It stands out in bold relief on the sacred pages.

8. Divine revelation teaches us that Christ will actually continue to reign until every knee in the universe shall bow to him, and every tongue confess him

Lord to the glory of God the Father, until death, the very last enemy, shall be destroyed, until all things shall be made new, and until God shall "be all in all." No texts need be cited to prove this. The diligent student of Scripture knows them by heart.

9. Divine revelation teaches us to pray that the kingdom of God may prevail universally, and his will be done in earth as in heaven; to preach the gospel to every creature; to will and work for universal righteousness in the love of God and of Christ; and that we thus pray, preach, will, and work, with all self-sacrifice, confidence, and perseverance, in full assurance of hope. This needs no proof. Who has forgotten these imperative and blessed precepts?

10. Divine revelation teaches us that, in order to be the true disciples of Christ, we must cherish his spirit, have his mind in us, follow his example, seek the same end he sought, and put on his moral character; also, that to be the true children of the Highest, we must love our enemies, bless them that curse us, do good to them that hate us, and overcome evil with good; that is, love as he loves, be merciful as he is merciful, and be perfect as he is perfect. Testimonies of this kind are too plain and memorable to require quotation. Allusion to them is sufficient.

11. Divine revelation teaches us that God's rewards and punishments are not infinite, but meted out according to men's deeds and characters; that in punishment he will not contend forever, nor be always wroth, nor retain his anger forever, nor cast off for-

ever, but will have compassion because he delighteth in mercy, lest the suffering spirits fail before him, and the souls he has made. This significant class of passages needs only to be suggested. They are numerous, plain, and positive.

12. Finally, divine revelation presents, in both Testaments, a grand series of prophetic declarations, all pointing to a distant future of final universal holiness, harmony, and bliss for the human race, which, if ever fulfilled, either in their letter or spirit, accord perfectly with the eleven preceding positions, and cannot be reconciled with the doctrine of endless misery, or that of annihilation. These prophetic declarations are too strong, numerous, and easily remembered to require present repetition. There is a glorious host of them.

Now, what is to be done with these twelve classes of divine testimony? Can they all be overborne and neutralized by quoting as finalities a few highly intensive texts, which treat of judgments, rewards, and punishments, — matters far this side of final destinies? No; yet these same texts are the main reliance and *dernier resort* of believers in the doctrines of endless misery and of final annihilation. They think they have conclusively gained their point when they have quoted such texts as the following: "These shall go away into everlasting punishment;" "Who shall be punished with everlasting destruction," etc. Such expressions do not touch the above twelve solid ramparts of the doctrine I am advocating. Let them bring up some battering-ram that will shake one of these firm bastions. Let them try to prove from the plain testimonies of divine revelation the contrary of all or any of these twelve sublime fundamentals. Yes, let them try to prove that it is *not* the nature of moral goodness, in God, Christ, angels, and men, to love and bless and seek the highest good of its beloved objects. Can they do it? Let them try to prove that God is *not* good, unchangeably, impartially, and perfectly good, even to the unthankful and evil; or that his very nature is *not* love. Can they do it? Let them try to prove that there are any human beings whom God did *not* create in his own image, in their essential inmost nature good; that some human beings are *not* his offspring, and were *not* created for his unselfish glory and pleasure. Can they do it? Let them try to prove that it is *not* the will of God that all mankind should come to repentance and be saved from their sins. Can they do it? Let them try to prove that God did not foreordain, raise us, and send forth his Son Jesus Christ, to take away the sin of the world, to be the Saviour of the world, the whole world. Can they do it? Let them try to prove that Christ did not come, and do, and suffer, and die for all mankind (not a select part), to deliver them from sin and death. Can they do it? Let them try to prove that Christ did *not* descend into the world of the dead for the benefit of the departed, rise thence, and ascend into the heavens for the purpose of subduing all beings to himself. Can they do it? Let them try to prove that Christ will not continue to reign till every knee bows, till every tongue confesses him Lord, till the last enemy, death, is destroyed, till all things be made new, and till God is "all in all." Can they do it?

Let them try to prove that we are not to pray, in sincerity and faith, that the kingdom of God may universally prevail; that his will may be done in earth as in heaven; or that we are not to will and work for universal righteousness, with all self-sacrifice, perseverance, and assurance of hope. Can they do it? Let them try to prove that we can be true disciples of Christ without cherishing his spirit, without having in us his mind, without putting on his moral character, and without seeking the same final results that he sought; or that we can be true children of the Highest, without loving our enemies and seeking their good, as he does, and without being merciful and perfect in spirit, as he is. Can they do it? Let them try to prove that God's rewards and punishments are infinite, measured by his own infinity, not by the finite deserts of his creatures; that in his punishments he will contend forever, retain his anger forever, and cast off forever, regardless of the souls he has made; and that it is *not* the ultimate of his punitive dispensations to have compassion because he delighteth in mercy. Can they do it? Let them try to prove that the law is against the promises of God; and that all those magnificent prophecies which announce the final universal triumph of right over wrong, good over evil, and happiness over misery, are reconcilable with the horrible notion that the masses of mankind are foredoomed to a cursed eternity, or to the more tolerable, yet still dreadful, one of being consigned to dreamless, lifeless, endless oblivion. Can they do it? Let them try to nullify, or explain away, all these divine testimonies, which shine like twelve constellations in the spiritual heavens, and radiate their beams far into that eternity that lies beyond the epoch when God shall accept the mediatorial kingdom of Christ as completed, and be "all in all." And as they try, and try, and try, to prove that a vast majority of the human race will be hopelessly lost, let them pray for that baleful result, if they can. And if they can pray thus, let them consider well what manner of spirit moves them, — whether it be the Holy Spirit of the Father and the Son, or the spirit that rejoices in vengeance and death.

But I refrain. "Great is truth, and it will prevail." Universal holiness and happiness must be the final destiny of mankind. It is the pure primitive Christian doctrine, substantially spoken through God's most pre-eminent Son, and "by the mouth of all his holy prophets since the world began." Oh, do not treat it, my dear friends, as a dry, husky dogma of speculative theology, or a fanciful conjecture, but as the grand coronal truth of pure and undefiled Christianity, joyfully glorious to holy faith and reason, and practically stimulative to all true Christ-likeness in spirit, conduct, and moral character.

> Hark, hear the countless voices
>   From being's endless chain,
> As varied life rejoices,
>   Declare in choral strain
> The love of their Creator, —
>   That boundless, perfect love
> Which blesses sentient nature
>   Below, around, above.

Mark how the revelations
　From ancient times bequeathed,
By heavenly inspirations
　Through seers and prophets breathed,
Proclaim in strains diviner
　This perfect love to man,
As Christ, the All-Refiner,
　Unfolds redemption's plan.

Profoundest adorations
　Let men and angels pay,
With ceaseless acclamations,
　Harmonic night and day,
To Him whose love transcendeth
　Their highest powers of praise,
And endlessly attendeth
　Their souls through all their ways.

ARTICLE VII.

THE FINAL DESTINY OF MANKIND.

DISCOURSE XXVII.

CORRUPTIONS OF THE PURE PRIMITIVE CHRISTIAN DOCTRINE.

"Who is he that saith, and it cometh to pass, when the Lord commandeth it not? Out of the mouth of the Most High proceedeth not evil and good." — LAM. iii. 37, 38.

"I am God, and there is none like me, declaring the end from the beginning, and from ancient times the things that are not yet done, saying. My counsel shall stand, and I will do all my pleasure." — Is. xlvi. 9, 10.

WHEN Jesus announced his mission as the promised Christ, the Son of God, and Saviour of the world, suppose some bold scribe had addressed him in such language as the following: "Master, whether thou art the promised Messiah or not, the Son of God or not, the Saviour of men or not, one thing is certain, the whole world of mankind will never be saved; only a comparative few of the human race will ever believe in thee, obey thy teachings, or embrace thy religion; the vast majority will be utterly lost, — either in endless sinfulness and misery, or in annihilation. Thou sayest that God so loved the world as to send thee to save it. Whatever be God's love to man, he knew from the beginning that only a small number of souls would choose to become righteous during their only day of probation, and that the vast majority would certainly persist in sin to their hopeless ruin. He expects no other result. He cannot have sent thee to accomplish anything more than this for mankind. Thou art teaching men to pray in faith for the universal triumph of God's kingdom in the world. No such thing can ever be. There is no ground to pray for it in faith. It is against the destiny of man, as God foresaw, expected, and arranged his government before the foundation of the world. Thou art commanding thy disciples to love their enemies, to bless those who curse them, to do good to those who hate them, and to overcome evil with good, that they may be godlike, — may be true children of their Father in heaven, — loving, kind, merciful, and perfect as he is. Now this is impossible for them, as human nature is constituted. They could not do it if they would, and would not if they could. Moreover, if they should actually do it, they would transcend the goodness of God. God is just, as well as merciful. He has established his holy laws with the penalty of eternal misery or death for all sins not repented of in the present life. He must execute that penalty, or abdicate the throne of the universe. He will execute it without mercy. He is now kind and merciful to sinners, even to his wicked and thankless enemies; but it is only for a probationary moment in comparison with eternity. On the great whole, he loves those who love him, abhors those who hate him, and will curse all who curse him with the blackness of black despair forever. Hast not thou thyself declared that his enemies shall be doomed to 'everlasting fire,' and will go away into 'everlasting punishment?' Master, do I understand thee correctly? And must we not all give these qualifications to thy claims and testimonies?"

What answer may we imagine Jesus would have returned to such a scribe? Would he have replied: "Thou hast spoken the truth. Such is really the final destiny of mankind. I am indeed the promised Christ, the Son of God, sent by his love to be the Saviour of the world, — that is, of the few who in this life believe in and obey me. I have come to seek and save the lost, and I shall lay down my life a ransom for mankind; but nothing that I profess, or shall do, or suffer, must be understood as intended or expected to eventuate in their universal holiness and happiness. The finally saved will be but a handful compared with the lost. But I shall be as much glorified in the damnation of the lost as in the salvation of the saved. For I shall have the honor of sitting in final judgment on the righteous and wicked, and of pronouncing the sentence of their eternal doom. My Father, too, will be as much glorified in the hopeless perdition of the wicked as he could possibly be in their regeneration; for his holy law will be maintained inviolate by the awful sanction of its justly inflicted penalty; whilst the saved and the lost, standing forth in perpetual contrast, will exhibit to the whole universe the most salutary illustration both of divine mercy and justice. So when I enjoin prayer that God's kingdom may come, and his will be done in earth as in heaven, let it be understood that his kingdom is one of penal justice as well as saving grace. And if I teach my disciples to be loving, merciful, and perfect, as their heavenly Father is, even toward enemies, haters, and evil-doers, let it be understood always that neither God nor his saints are to be, or ought to be, thus loving and kind to the wicked, except incidentally and momentarily in ordinary cases; for the severities of penal, vindictive, and destructive justice are absolutely indispensable in the great moral system. Therefore, when I speak of love, mercy, and goodness toward wicked offenders, whether in God toward his enemies, or the saints toward theirs, let me be understood in a very qualified sense, as meaning that love and mercy are proper incidental, temporary exceptions, yet that stern and inexorable penal justice is the rule. But on the contrary, when I speak of the judgments and punishments of God against the wicked, let me always be understood in the severest and extremest sense of my language; for the great law of retributive order must be upheld and magnified, though the sinful universe should groan in spiteful anguish and its countless millions be confirmed in blasphemous rebellion forever! Thus far do I claim to be the Saviour of the world — no farther!" Can we conceive of a more hideous caricature of the gospel than is thus imagined?

But let us follow it up by supposing the same bold scribe to interrogate the Apostles John and Paul, and to be answered by them: "Beloved disciple of Jesus, what meanest thou in saying, that Christ 'is the propitiation for our sins; and not for ours only, but also for the sins of the whole world.' 'God is love.' 'In this was manifested the love of God toward us, because that God sent his only-begotten Son into the world, that we might live through him. Herein is love, not that we loved God, but that he loved us, and sent his Son to be the propitiation for our sins.' 'We have seen and do testify that the Father sent the Son to be the Saviour of world.' 'And I heard a great voice out of heaven, saying, Behold, the tabernacle of God is with men, and he will dwell with them, and they shall be his people, and God himself shall be with them, and be their God. And God shall wipe away all tears from their eyes; and there shall be no more death, neither sorrow, nor crying, neither shall there be any more pain; for the former things are passed away. And he that sat upon the throne said, Behold, I make all things new. And he said unto me, Write; for these words are true and faithful.' Now, most worthy apostle, such language is very sweeping, and liable to be construed too benevolently against God's solemn threatenings. Surely thou canst not mean to imply that it is the final destiny of mankind that all should ever be rendered regenerate, holy, and happy, or that God is love in any sense inconsistent with his inflicting endless punishment, or, at least, everlasting destruction, on all who die out of Christ."

Suppose John to respond: "Surely not, O scribe! Whatever I may *seem* to mean, the final utter wretchedness and ruin of that vast majority of mankind who shall not be regenerated through faith in Christ and true repentance before death, is certain. God clearly foresaw that result before he created man, and orders all things accordingly. I hold to no love or purpose of God, to no mission or propitiation of Christ, and to no regeneration of all things, which interferes with the execution of inexorable vengeance on the vast masses of this wicked world. It is only the few that die in Christ who will be saved. And all my glorious declarations, which thou hast cited, refer to that few exclusively." What a mockery would such a response be!

But suppose our scribe finally addresses Paul: "Most learned of the apostles, thou hast said some things hard to be understood, which the unlearned are likely to pervert. Thou hast written thus: 'Moreover the law entered that the offence might abound. But where sin abounded grace did much more abound; that as sin hath reigned unto death, even so might grace reign through righteousness unto eternal life, by Jesus Christ our Lord.' 'Blindness in part is happened to Israel, until the fulness of the Gentiles be come in; and so all Israel shall be saved.' 'For God hath concluded them all in unbelief, that he might have mercy upon all.' 'For as in Adam all die, even so in Christ shall all be made alive.' 'For he must reign till he hath put all enemies under his feet.' 'And when all things shall be subdued unto him, then shall the Son also himself be subject unto him that put all things under him, that God may be all in all.' 'Having made known unto us the mystery of his will, according to his good pleasure, which he hath purposed in himself: that in the dispensation of the fulness of times he might gather together in one all things in Christ, both which are in heaven, and which are in earth, even in him.' 'That at the name of Jesus every knee should bow, of things in heaven, and things in earth, and things under the earth, and that every tongue should confess that Jesus Christ is Lord, to the glory of God the Father.' 'For it pleased the Father that in him should all fulness dwell, and having made peace through the blood of his cross, by him to reconcile all things unto himself; by him, whether things in earth or things in heaven.' Therefore pray for all men; 'for this is good and acceptable in the sight of God our Saviour; who will have all men to be saved, and to come unto the knowledge of the truth. For there is one God, and one mediator between God and men, the man Christ Jesus; who gave himself a ransom for all, to be testified in due time.' Now, O Paul, does not such very strong and seemingly unqualified language, as these specimens from thy pen exhibit, afford ground for over-hopeful minds to infer that universal regeneration, holiness, and happiness is the final destiny of the human race? What sayest thou?" Dare we imagine an answer like the following?

"The ardor of my faith, hope, and charity may have transported me beyond the cold and solemn truth in which I am firmly established; to wit, that Christ will actually be the Saviour of those only who shall have believed on him and become true Christians in this probationary life. All the rest must certainly be forever lost. There is no hope for them. My words may seem to favor the idea of some better finality; but I do not mean it. I must refer you to the ninth chapter of my epistle to the Romans, wherein I have taught plainly the doctrine of election, and to various passages in my other writings in which I treat of God's indignation, wrath, and vengeance toward the wicked, and particularly to that passage in 2d Thessalonians, in which I say, 'The Lord Jesus shall be revealed from heaven in flaming fire, taking vengeance on them that know not God, and that obey not the gospel of his Son, Jesus Christ: who shall be punished with everlasting destruction from the presence of the Lord, and from the glory of his power.' This testimony is conclusive. I meant it should be understood in its most literal and extreme sense, and not with the qualifying limitations proper for the texts you have quoted. Understand that I am perfectly sound on the final destiny of mankind, namely, that Christ will save the few, and devote the many to hopeless punishment. This is the gospel which I preach, and let no man construe my language otherwise." Again I exclaim, What a mockery! Let us never imagine Paul capable of such paradoxes.

Who can doubt that these supposed interlocutions between the scribe, Christ, John, and Paul make Christ, John, and Paul grossly falsify their real fundamental principles, — the true gospel? Yet these same supposed falsifications are virtually and substantially the very corruptions which the vast majority of professing Christians have fastened on the pure primitive Christian doctrine of man's final destiny. A small but noble minority, headed by the celebrated Clemens of Alexandria, near the close of the second and beginning of the third century, followed by the no less celebrated Origen, his pupil, by the merciful Doctors of the succeeding centuries, by a scattering few down through the dark ages to the Reformation, and latterly by a comparative host, have reaffirmed the original doctrine. The future gives auspicious signs that the pure primitive conception of the final universal triumph of good over evil in the universe, through Christ, will not only be regained, but become the mainspring of a moral progress such as our world has never seen, and as only the highest divine inspirees contemplated in prophetic vision.

If we ask how it happened that the pure primitive Christian doctrine of man's glorious final destiny became obscured by these gross corruptions, the answer readily suggests itself. It is not necessary to impute insincerity or any monstrous evil motives to the corruptionists. The true doctrine, though at once simple and sublime, and though fundamentally inherent in the very conception of a successful Christ (so that we can have only a dwarfed Christ and Christianity without it), is not a mere rudimental article of faith, like most others taught in the Scriptures. It is the one comprehensive and climacteric doctrine in which all others logically end, and without which no other is perfect. It is certainly taught in both Testaments, not as one of the A B C's of revealed religion, but as its grand resultant, coronal truth, without which revealed religion would be a sickly, solemn farce, or a tremendous and ever lamentable tragedy. That Christ foresaw with undoubting assurance his final universal triumph over the powers of sin, death, and evil, it would be impiously absurd to doubt. That his chief apostles looked confidently into the unfolding future for that blessed consummation is scarcely less certain. But it is highly probable that thousands of the primitive Christians, while eminently animated by the benignant spirit of this doctrine, held it vaguely, and lacked the intellectual development necessary to its clear comprehension. Only the wisest and best would be likely to grasp it rationally and firmly, — as must have been the case in respect to several other cardinal truths less complex, far-reaching, and comprehensive. Meantime more narrow, mechanical, and angular minds, at once conscientious, zealous, and contracted, would very naturally dwell on smaller points of faith and practice, and stop at the judgments and retributions of Christianity as finalities. These once fossilized into solemn traditions were sure of a long and general perpetuity among such converts from barbarism as replenished the nominal church from the third to the seventeenth century. The evils which attended and have resulted from these corruptions will be considered in my next discourse, which will close this theological department.

>Great principle of Truth,
>That guidest age and youth
> In Wisdom's ways,
>Thy welcome light we greet,
>With heavenly grace replete,
>To save our plodding feet
> From error's maze.
>
>Thyself, a Spirit, dwell,
>An ever-living well,
> Within our breasts,

And make it our delight
To view all things aright,
With vision clear and bright,
   As Truth attests.

Whate'er we learn, or tell,
Of heaven, or earth, or hell,
   Be Truth our aim;
And falsehood justly deemed,
Though plausibly enschemed,
And high by man esteemed,
   Consigned to shame.

ARTICLE VII.

THE FINAL DESTINY OF MANKIND.

DISCOURSE XXVIII.

THE EVILS OCCASIONED BY CORRUPTING THE PURE PRIMITIVE DOCTRINE.

"Doth a fountain send forth at the same place sweet water and bitter?"—James iii. 11.

"God is not the God of confusion."—1 Cor. xiv. 33.

"Our word toward you was not yea and nay. For the Son of God, Jesus Christ, who was preached among you by us, . . . was not yea and nay, but in him was yea. For all the promises of God in him are yea, and in him Amen, unto the glory of God by us."—2 Cor. i. 18–20.

This discourse concludes my exposition of Primitive Christianity and its Corruptions in the Department of Theological Doctrines. Two other departments will be considered in their order; namely, Personal Righteousness, and Ecclesiastical Polity. But these await my future convenience. I am now to notice some of the principal evils which have resulted from the corruptions treated of in my last discourse. I contended that universal regeneration, holiness, and happiness was the pure primitive Christian doctrine concerning the final destiny of mankind; and that the doctrine of endless sinfulness and misery for the larger portion of the human race, as their final destiny, together with the less dreadful doctrine of their annihilation, are gross corruptions. I did not question the sincerity, or impugn the motives, of the corruptionists, but insisted on the fact that their errors, however honestly imbibed or maintained, are fundamental and pernicious. What, then, are some of the prominent evils resulting from those corruptions?

1. The very fountain-head of religion is poisoned. The character of God is debased. It is assumed that he *will* not or *cannot* render all his rational offspring finally holy and happy, — only a few of them, — and that he forces into existence the vast majority of them, knowing that their final destiny must be an accursed one. If he *can* but *will* not be equally and impartially their friend, he is the Almighty Enemy of countless millions. Yet we must worship, love, and serve him with all the powers of our nature. Yea, we must be godlike to the extent of our ability, and be actuated by his Spirit. If he wills to be equally and impartially the friend of all, and ensure to all a blessed final destiny, but *cannot*, then he is a weak God, unable to actualize his own good will, and liable to be utterly thwarted in his best desires. Yet we are commanded to pray to him, trust in him, and rely upon him implicitly, as the Almighty, for whom nothing is "too hard," with whom "all things are possible," "who doeth his will in the armies of heaven and among the inhabitants of the earth." Can mankind worship a God of partiality and malevolence without being inspired with the spirit of their God, or without at least being confirmed in their own predisposi-

tions to partiality and malevolence? Are worshippers expected to be better than their God? Can mankind habitually pray to, trust in, and place their dependence on, a weak God, whose will is liable to be thwarted in its noblest longings, whose very best aims may be utterly impossible of accomplishment, without weakness, vacillation, and instability of mind and moral character? Can they hope for more than God? Can they expect better results than their God? Can they work for triumphs of truth, righteousness, and joy, where their God foresees only failure and defeat? Or, if so blind and stupid as thus to hope, expect, and work for impossible success, what will all their religious devotion be but noise, bustle, and empty confusion? Here is a great evil. The world is full of it. The character of God is debased, and so religion is debased. The fountain is poisoned, and the drinkers therefrom are poisoned.

2. Jesus Christ is dwarfed, degraded, and inverted by these corrupt assumptions. He and his gospel are resolved into "yea and nay." In words he is proclaimed to be the Saviour of the world; yet it is at the same moment assumed as certain that he will be the damnator of the world in general, and merely the Saviour of a few.. His atonement is beglorified as "a propitiation for the sins of the whole world," "a ransom for all," "death tasted for every man," and his lordship as waxing in grandeur till all things shall be subdued unto him in heaven, earth, and the underworld; nevertheless, what is the assumed certain result? That a choice handful of mankind will be taken into heaven with him as the fruit of all his

travail and mediatorial operations, whilst multitudinous masses shall lie down in sinful anguish forever, or be doomed to utter annihilation. They are to be treated as incorrigible enemies, rebels, and reprobates; and his triumph over them is to be celebrated in making them the hopeless victims of his wrath! To contradict this monstrous assumption of corruption is to ensure the anathema of nearly all the nominal church — Roman, Greek, and Protestant — for a most damnable heresy. Can any one imagine how such a state of ecclesiastical public opinion has become enthroned in Christendom? Yet this abomination stands unabashed in its holy places. And what is the result? Jesus Christ is dwarfed, degraded, inverted, — resolved into a contradiction. The gospel of glad tidings to all people is turned into the gospel of salvation for a fraction of the human race, and a proclamation of irrevocable vengeance for all the rest. Christianity itself is resolved into a system of tremendous retributions, with a mere sprinkling of partial grace. I call this a dismal evil.

3. Christ, primitively the Prince of love, forgiveness, and peace, — the grand exemplar, model, and pattern of his professed disciples, — is metamorphosed into the Prince of vindictive justice, inexorable vengeance to the wicked, and destructive war for righteousness' sake. He is made to sanction hatred and persecution of heretics, deadly conflict with carnal weapons, and all sorts of punitive coercion, till Christians are proud to move on a moral, social, political, military, and penal plane as low as the world's semi-barbarous civilization will tolerate. Their Chris-

tianity is graduated, not to the standard of the New Testament, but to that of mere worldly civilization. Moreover, they presume to contend that Christ himself demands nothing essentially higher of them. He only requires them to be Christian warriors, Christian speculators, Christian politicians, Christian penalists; in fine, Christian worldlings. And if these doctrines which I denounce as corruptions are not such, our Christian worldlings are right. The streams of their morality rise as high as the fountain-head. But I insist that they are under a wretched delusion. They have a metamorphosed Christ, — metamorphosed mainly by these very corruptions. He is not the original, humble, meek, lowly, self-sacrificing Lamb of God, that taketh away the sin of the world. They have made him practically too near akin to that warlike religious conqueror, whose holy city is Mecca. This is another deplorable evil which darkens the atmosphere of Christianity. The savor of the salt has been spoiled.

4. These corruptions have generated and nourished bigotry, unholy zeal, and a self-righteous vindictiveness toward all who were deemed enemies of the church, of Christ, and of God, — whose destiny is assumed to be eternal perdition. I cannot give a better illustration of this than by quoting an extract from Tertullian, who lived in the third century, one of the first of this bitter school, which during the succeeding ages has multiplied into millions. In his *Spectaculis*, chapter thirty, he says, addressing himself to the pagans: —

"You are fond of your spectacles; there are other

spectacles: that day disbelieved, derided, by the nations, that last and eternal day of judgment, when all ages shall be swallowed up in one conflagration,—what a variety of spectacles shall then appear! How shall I admire, how laugh, how rejoice, how exult, when I behold so many kings, worshipped as gods in heaven, together with Jove himself, groaning in the lowest abyss of darkness! So many magistrates who persecuted the name of the Lord, liquefying in fiercer flames than they ever kindled against Christians; so many sage philosophers blushing in raging fire, with their scholars whom they persuaded to despise God, and to disbelieve the resurrection; and so many poets shuddering before the tribunal, not of Rhadamanthus, not of Minos, but of the disbelieved Christ! Then shall we hear the tragedians more tuneful under their own sufferings; then shall we see the players far more sprightly amidst the flames; the charioteer all red-hot in his burning car; and the wrestlers hurled, not upon the accustomed list, but on a plain of fire."

How delicious to contemplate! For other and kindred illustrations I refer you to the sermons of such celebrated Doctors of modern times as Edwards, Saurin, etc., etc. What a charming Christianity is this to those who have been baptized into its spirit of vindictive wrath and vengeance! To me how absolutely repulsive and horrible! Is it any wonder that such a poisoned and perverted Christianity bred morose fanatics and persecuting priests? That it married itself to civil and military government at its first opportunity? That it propagated itself by pious frauds, fire, and sword? That it established the cruel and abominable Inquisition? That even now, in the most enlightened countries, it hires out its chaplains to pray on both sides for the success of hostile armies and navies in every war; and that it draggles as the tail of politics, and aspires to govern worldly affairs "peaceably if it can, forcibly if it must"? Away with these corruptions, and the evils they nourish! Let us have the pure primitive Christianity of self-sacrifice, love, mercy, and peace, with more holy martyrdom, and less brute force.

5. These corruptions have occasioned and confirmed another great evil in the nominal church. It is the magnification of all Scripture threatenings, so-called, and the belittlement of the promises. Every threatening or descriptive representation of the punishment of the wicked, however limited by the nature of the case, or by its intensely figurative language, or by the dictates of great first principles, is strained to its utmost capacity. It is made to loom up like a peak of the Alps or the Andes. It is a divine volcano of vindictive justice, wrath, and retributive vengeance, out of which boils the torment, or the destruction, of the finally impenitent. All such texts are held up as par excellence "the word of God." "Hear," say their magnifiers, "this is the irrevocable word of God; beware how you trifle with it; presume not to diminish its awful import by explanation or rationalization; it is strictly the terrible word of the terrible God"! But if we quote a passage from that sublime and magnificent chain of texts, extending through both grand continents of Scripture, in which the love, goodness, mercy, and gracious designs of God declaratively

transcend all the threatenings of punishment, and point to a glorious BEYOND where sin and misery and death shall have utterly passed away, what then? Why, their magnifying glass is instantly reversed, and all these lofty mountains are resolved into molehills. There is no more solemn reiteration about the strict word of God, which must not be limited, modified, or explained away. Doubtless they are the word of God; but then they are not to be understood in their literal sweeping sense, like the wrathful threatenings. There is infinite peril in making God too universally loving and merciful, but none at all in making him too vindictive and merciless to his enemies! All the promises and predictions of final bliss are to be confined to God's friends. If they seem to say anything else, they mean nothing else. But all the threatenings are for God's enemies, — the reprobate and finally impenitent. When it is said, through David, "All the ends of the world shall remember and turn unto the LORD; and all the kindreds of the nations shall worship before thee" (Psal. xxii. 27), it means, of course, only the few believers and saints. But when it is said, "The wicked shall be turned into hell, and all the nations that forget God" (Psal. ix. 17), it means endless punishment, or at the least utter annihilation, to the vast masses indicated. When it is said, "The LORD is good to all; and his tender mercies are over all his works" (Psal. cxlv. 9), "we must be careful not to make it mean too much." But when it is said, "God is angry with the wicked every day" (Psal. vii. 11); "Consider this, ye that forget God, lest I tear you in pieces, and there be none to deliver" (Psal. l. 22), we must be exceedingly careful to understand it literally. When it is said, "I will not contend forever, neither will I be always wroth, — for the spirit should fail before me, and the souls I have made" (Is. lvii. 16); and again, "The Lord God will wipe away tears from off all faces" (Is. xxv. 8), it refers only to the chastisements of God's saints and chosen friends. But when it is said, "I will meet them as a bear bereaved, and will rend the caul of their heart, and there will I devour them like a lion" (Hos. xiii. 8); "There shall be wailing and gnashing of teeth" (Matt. xiii. 42); "These shall go away into everlasting punishment" (Ibid. xxv. 46); "And the smoke of their torment ascendeth up forever and ever" (Rev. xiv. 11),—why, then, we get the plain, literal, unmistakable word of God respecting the final destiny of the numberless wicked.

When it is said "God is love," we have an obscure text of little meaning; but when we read that "God is a consuming fire," we have a plain and terrible truth, — literally the word of God, at which sinners should tremble. So it goes with these miseducated millions of professing Christians. What is the matter with them? Simply they have learned to take for granted that the final destiny of all but a few human beings is sin, misery, and hopeless ruin. These corruptions have done this. They have foreclosed the case, and thus theologically superinduced this violent subversion of the threatenings and promises of the Bible. Away with such mischief and its causes! Else how are the Bible and Christianity to be decently understood?

6. Finally, these corruptions have superinduced, among their numerous progeny of evils, the following: They have obliged a considerable class of minds, who are sufficiently advanced, to revolt at the monstrous conclusion of the few finally saved and the many lost, but who yet lack the truthfulness, or the moral courage, to reject the whole notion in toto; to defend it in part, by contending that the finally saved will be the vast majority, and the finally lost a small minority, of the human race, or that, perhaps, the finally lost will prefer to stay lost, and enjoy themselves better in hell than heaven. Such are very pitiful subterfuges, however comfortable to their inventors. Say they, All who die in infancy — one-third of the race — will be saved; all sincere, virtuous heathen — of whom there must be many — will be saved; millions of death-bed penitents will be saved; those generations who are to be born and live during the Millennium — many thousands of millions — will be saved; and it is possible that, even after death, all but the very worst of sinners may repent; or, if they remain voluntary reprobates, that their condition will be comparatively tolerable. What is all such special pleading worth? It is giving up nine hundred and ninety-nine parts of the argument to save the one-thousandth, and that one thousandth still involving the evil principle of the whole assumption. If the smallest few are finally lost, the perfect character of God is lost, evil is thus far triumphant, and we know not what to fear or to hope; final good results are wholly uncertain, very bad ones probable.

But the plea of these thinkers is utterly fallacious.

They claim to be Christians, and to rest their faith on the Bible. Does the Bible anywhere teach that the ultimately punished will have a comfortable hell; that they will choose it of their own free will as preferable to heaven, and that they will consist only of a few extreme sinners? Such a hint cannot be found between its lids. Does the Bible teach that God is so partial to one-third of the human race as to make sure of their eternal salvation by cutting them off before they are old enough to commit sin; that virtuous heathens are good enough to be saved without faith in Christ; that he saves millions of adults on the ground of death-bed repentance; and that he will so exclusively favor those who shall happen to be born during the Millennium as to treat them incomparably better, on the whole, than the earlier generations of mankind? Not a syllable of it. It is a vain imagination. If the Bible does not teach the final regeneration, holiness, and happiness of the whole human race, it teaches that the vast majority will be miserably and hopelessly lost. I am firmly confident of the former, and therefore pronounce the latter, in all its phases, a gross corruption of the pure primitive Christian doctrine, and fraught with manifold evils, from which Christianity must be purged in order to its predicted universal triumph. That it will be purged of all its corruptions, and will finally be accepted as the one pure and undefiled religion, by the entire family of mankind, I cannot doubt. On this solid and broad foundation I will proceed, at my earliest convenience, to set forth the superstructure of a corresponding Personal Righteousness, and the Ecclesiastical Polity of the true Universal Church.

> The mighty archangels their trumpets are sounding,
> As epochs on epochs of progress are rounding,
> Announcing responsive the *final to-morrow*,
> The end of transgression, the close of all sorrow.
>
> Be dumb, ye dark doubters that magnify Evil,
> Who fear it immortal, of Good the dire equal,
> And dream its dominion must be everlasting
> As God's own existence, his creatures still blasting.
>
> Sublime hallelujahs and deep adoration
> Be anthemed forever by ransomed creation.

www.ingramcontent.com/pod-product-compliance
Lightning Source LLC
Chambersburg PA
CBHW021157230426
43667CB00006B/436